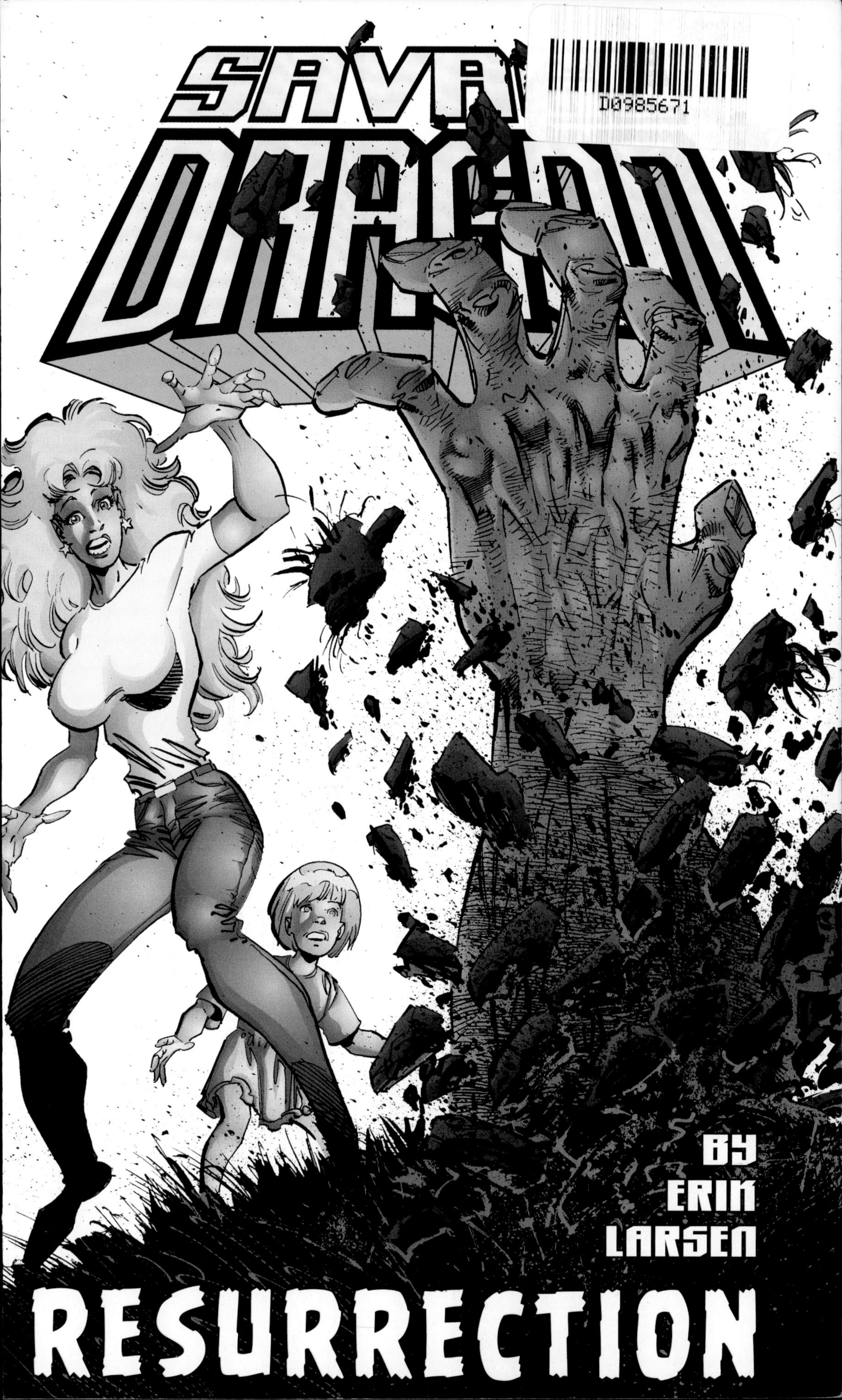
BY
ERIK
LARSEN
RESURRECTION

SAVAGE DRAGON

RESURRECTION

ERIK LARSEN Creator • Writer • Artist

CHRIS ELIOPOULOS Letterer

I.H.O.C. Colors

REUBEN RUDE, ABEL MOUTON, BILL ZINDEL, LEA RUDE

JOSE EICHORN Black panties with an angel's face

IMAGE COMICS

Erik Larsen	Publisher
Todd McFarlane	President
Marc Silvestri	CEO
Jim Valentino	Vice President
Eric Stephenson	Executive Director
Mark Haven Britt	Director of Marketing
Thao Le	Accounts Manager
Traci Hui	Administrative Assistant
Joe Keatinge	Traffic Manager
Allen Hui	Production Manager
Jonathan Chan	Production Artist
Drew Gill	Production Artist
Chris Giarrusso	Production Artist

INTRODUCTION

BY ERIK LARSEN

It's going to be pretty much impossible to write an introduction to this volume without spoiling some major plot point contained in the stories collected therein.

And yeah, I know, that sucks. This is supposed to be an "introduction," after all, not an "after word" but what else can I do? I mean, we pick up with our harried hero having kicked the bucket in the previous book--and this book is called "Savage Dragon: Resurrection"--it pretty much stands to reason that the guy's going to get out of the perilous pickle he was previously placed in. Truth be told (and I'm all about telling it like it is) my whole motivation for penning the tumultuous tale collected in this volume was to pay homage to the Dragon stories I drew as a kid.

"What?" you might say, "You drew Dragon comics as a kid? Where can I get a hold of some of those?"

You can't.

All those comics were destroyed in a house fire. I couldn't collect them if I wanted to. But let it be known (if you didn't know already) that I started writing and drawing the Dragon's adventures when I was nine years old.

Believe it or not, as a kid I spent an ungodly amount of time writing and drawing Dragon comics on 8 1/2 x 11 paper, folded in half and stapled up the center. I'm not sure where the drive to produce these wacky wonders came from but I was obsessed with the Dragon and driven to tell his story. I drew over fifty comics, some as long as 100 pages, featuring the character. And honestly, I don't remember exactly when the Dragon came into existence. It happened when I was so young that I don't remember exactly. I do remember that he was an amalgam of Captain Marvel (the Fawcett version--the one that said "Shazam" to change from Billy Batson into the Big Red Cheese--not the one found elsewhere), Speed Racer and Batman (Dragon had a cape and cowl to begin with and a utility belt filled with handy gadgets--few of which I actually used in any story). But beyond that, I don't remember a whole heck of a lot. I was a kid.

The Dragon evolved as I went along. When I started out he was an alien on a mysterious Red Planet (where everything looked and felt pretty much like Earth, so I don't know why I bothered to set it there), to being the alter ego of Flash Mercury (a racecar driver--like Speed Racer), to being the secret identity of William Jonson (changing into him in "times of stress," much like a certain green goliath from a major comic book company).

That last one is where we'll pause for a few minutes. I was putting together a miniseries called Savage Dragon: Sex & Violence some time back and it was a hellacious experience. Everything that could go wrong did go wrong. The artist I wanted to draw it dropped out (vanished, really) and several replacements tanked out as well. This frustrated me to no end because I was hoping to have this miniseries introduce Jennifer Murphy, a character who would play a major role in upcoming issues of the Dragon's nearly-monthly mag and the longer it took to get it out, the longer I'd have to wait to have her show up in the ongoing book. Eventually, I had a solid artist lined up and a decent inker committed to embellish that solid penciller's pencils into pages that could be printed. That inker was a fellow named Mark Lipka, who turned out to be something of a Savage Dragon fan.

And Mark would ask me from time to time where I was going with this or that or ask various questions pertaining to the Savage Dragon series.

Having heard about the fact that I wrote and drew Dragon comics as a youngster, Mark asked me a question that would, ultimately, get my mind buzzing to the point that I produced the issues collected in this book--

"Have you done any stories that were based on ones that you did as a kid?"

The answer was, at the time, no.

While many characters in the Savage Dragon book were based on those that I created years ago, there weren't any actual issues or even plot points that sprang from those stories.

I had a sort of "master plan" when I started the Savage Dragon series. There were a couple of stories that saw print as fanzines in 1982 and my idea was to work it out so that this book would incorporate those stories at some point. My thought was to start this book in a different place but to eventually work my way to where I'd left off as a kid. Those fanzines marked the end of the old era--they were the last two stories following my unpublished yarns--and I thought it would be nifty to have my new book get to that same point and then pick things up from there.

Mark's question had me thinking about other ideas that I might incorporate.

In the series I did as a kid, the Dragon I settled with was one that changed from William Jonson to the Dragon. I thought to myself--why not do THAT? And that lead to me "killing" the Dragon in Savage Dragon #50 and temporarily re-titling the book "Savage She-Dragon" while, in actuality, Dragon's consciousness (and accompanying superpowers) merged with William Jonson.

William Jonson was part of the cast of Savage Dragon from the beginning (or nearly the beginning). He was a plainclothes detective who worked for the Chicago police department.

I can't remember what his job was when I was a kid--or if he even had a job. As a kid, I wasn't as concerned with such things. Certainly when I'd started decades ago, William and the Dragon shared the same personality. William changed into the Dragon but there really wasn't anything lost there. It wasn't as though he was missing out on pieces of his life because of time spent under the cape and cowl. But as the series progressed I got bored with the regular secret identity nonsense and I got tired of having to draw all of the parts of the Dragon outfit with its belt and shoes and cape and cowl and so I wanted to ease William out of the picture. I started by simply having him be Dragon all the time but that wasn't an acceptable solution—it sidestepped the problem instead of solving it. But separating the two proved to be a little more complicated than I had anticipated.

Dragon's romantic entanglements and his other relationships complicated things. William was introduced with a girlfriend already in tow. And the William version of Dragon had a partner, Star, who fought alongside with him. Star had his own girlfriend and the two girls were fast friends. I ditched Star after a while and as William spent more and more time as Dragon my interests wandered. When Dragon got into a big brawl with the villainous Bloop and his sinister siblings I started considering other options.

Bloop was a liquid-like being that could stretch and bend and reform. His brother was a monstrous hulk that could do much the same and his sister had same powers as well. This sister, it turned out, became something more. She eventually became Dragon's girlfriend. And that meant trouble because, like I said, William had a girlfriend.

As it turned out (and again, we're still talking about the comics I drew as a kid--not the ongoing Savage Dragon series) the Dragon had developed a slightly different personality and William Jonson had been submerged. Eventually, The Dragon and William Jonson were split from each other to become two separate entities. In that way, William could go back to his old girlfriend and Dragon could pursue Bloop's sister. Bloop's sister, incidentally, was a certain Susan Wilson, who was renamed when she was introduced in the Savage Dragon title. Susan Wilson became Jennifer Murphy.

Now--none of the comics I drew as a kid are considered canon. All of those stories were ditched or reworked. Some elements have worked themselves into the series--others are long gone. The old stories were written and drawn by a child, after all, and they had much of the naiveté that goes along with that. My world-view was alarmingly limited and the stories that I came up with were based on knowledge gleaned from grammar school and other comic books.

Regardless, with this yarn I was able to pay homage to my old comics. William Jonson was turning into the Dragon, William's brother Ralph was being a prick--Bloop and his over-sized brother were there and Jennifer and Fon~Ti as well as a few other goodies here and there.

Ralph Jonson had been Dragon's Lex Luthor for years--a persistent pest with a hard on to do harm. When I started up the ongoing Savage Dragon book, I hadn't even considered having Ralph rear his ugly head. He was too tied to the William Jonson character and as a normal man, he really wasn't the formidable threat that the Dragon needed. But for this yarn, in this story, Ralph was a natural.

I stuck in as many of the characters that I'd introduced as a kid in this particular run (even if they weren't directly involved with William and Dragon's part of the story). Dragon, William and Ralph Jonson were there of course, as well as Jennifer Murphy and Angel, but so were the Deadly Duo (Kill-Cat and the Kid Avenger), Zeek, Rock, Powerhouse, Exroe-5, Overlord (who was a revised-version of an old foe named the Bronze Man), Horridus, SuperPatriot, Simon Kane, Mace, Sgt. Marvel, Bloop, Animal and the wizard Fon~Ti. All these characters graced my unpublished comics in one form or another (and Star even shows up…kind of. Chris Robinson was the guy under Star's mask in both my old and new comics).

But these issues aren't just a trip down memory lane. The characters in Brute Force were recent creations, having been introduced (for a panel at least) in Savage Dragon #27. These heroes sprang from an idea that I'd kicked around with writer/inker "amiable" Al Gordon. At that time it seemed as though every super-team in comics had one big brute of a guy. My thought was to make this team comprised entirely of big brutes. Al and I had talked about it and it was Al, who suggested killing suggested killing off all of them and then having the replacement members be less-than-suitable replacements. We'd actually talked about telling their tale in a miniseries or one shot but that never quite came together (for whatever reason) so I snuck them into this book.

Abner Cadaver was another new addition. It seems like every time I talk to my Dad he'll rattle off some atrocious gag name and suggest I turn that into a character for my comics. Most often they're real groaners and frankly, "Abner Cadaver" falls into that category as well (it's a play on "abracadabra" in case you couldn't figure it out) but I thought it would be a good name for my magical dead guy. I like goofy names as well as the next guy and my Dad's suggestions are always appreciated even if I've only used one of them to date.

So, there you go: a bit of insight into the issues compiled in this bombastic book. If you have half the fun reading them as I did creating them you'll have a blast--and if you don't, well, there's always the next volume…

-Erik Larsen

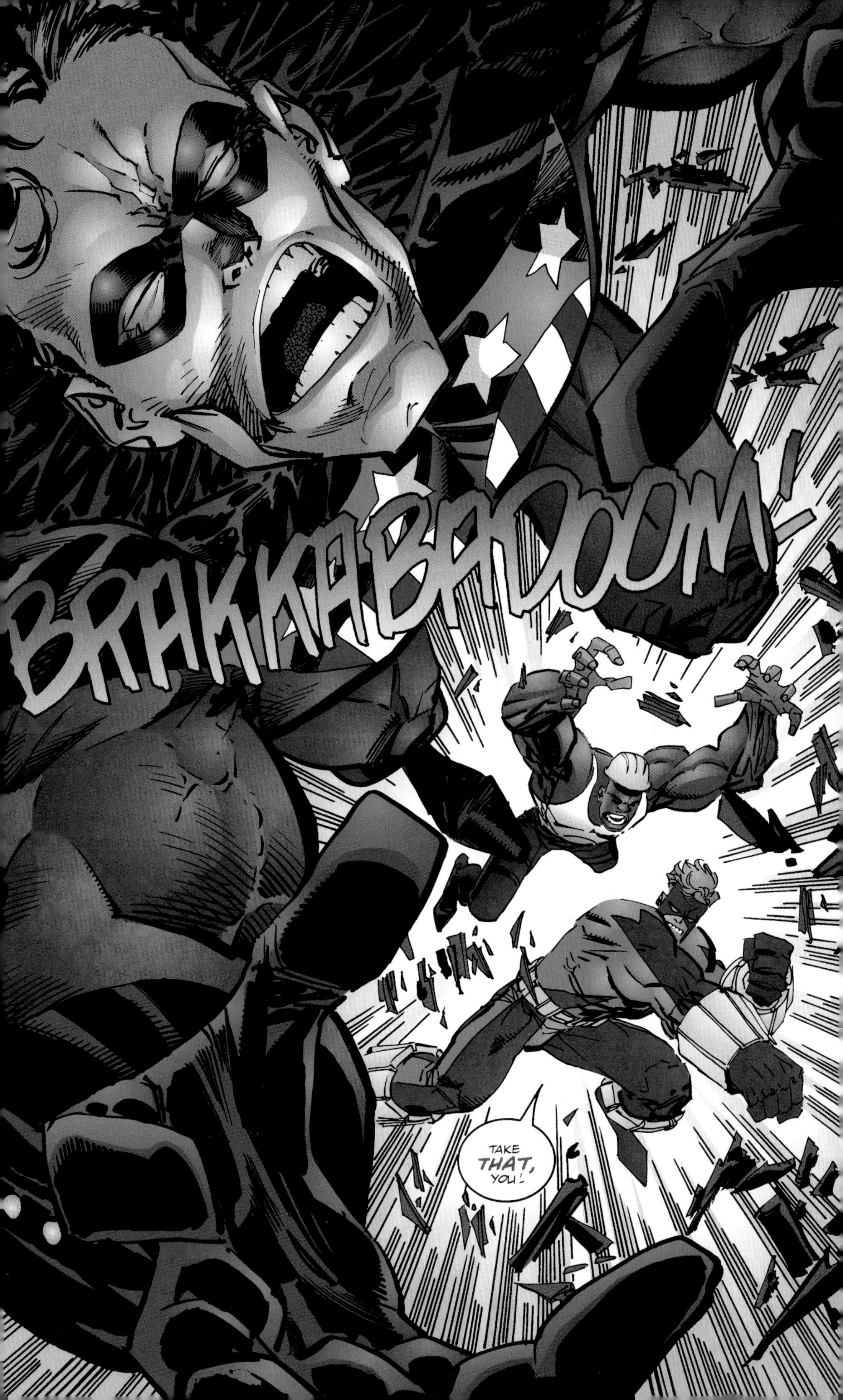
BRAKKABROOOM!
TAKE THAT, YOU!

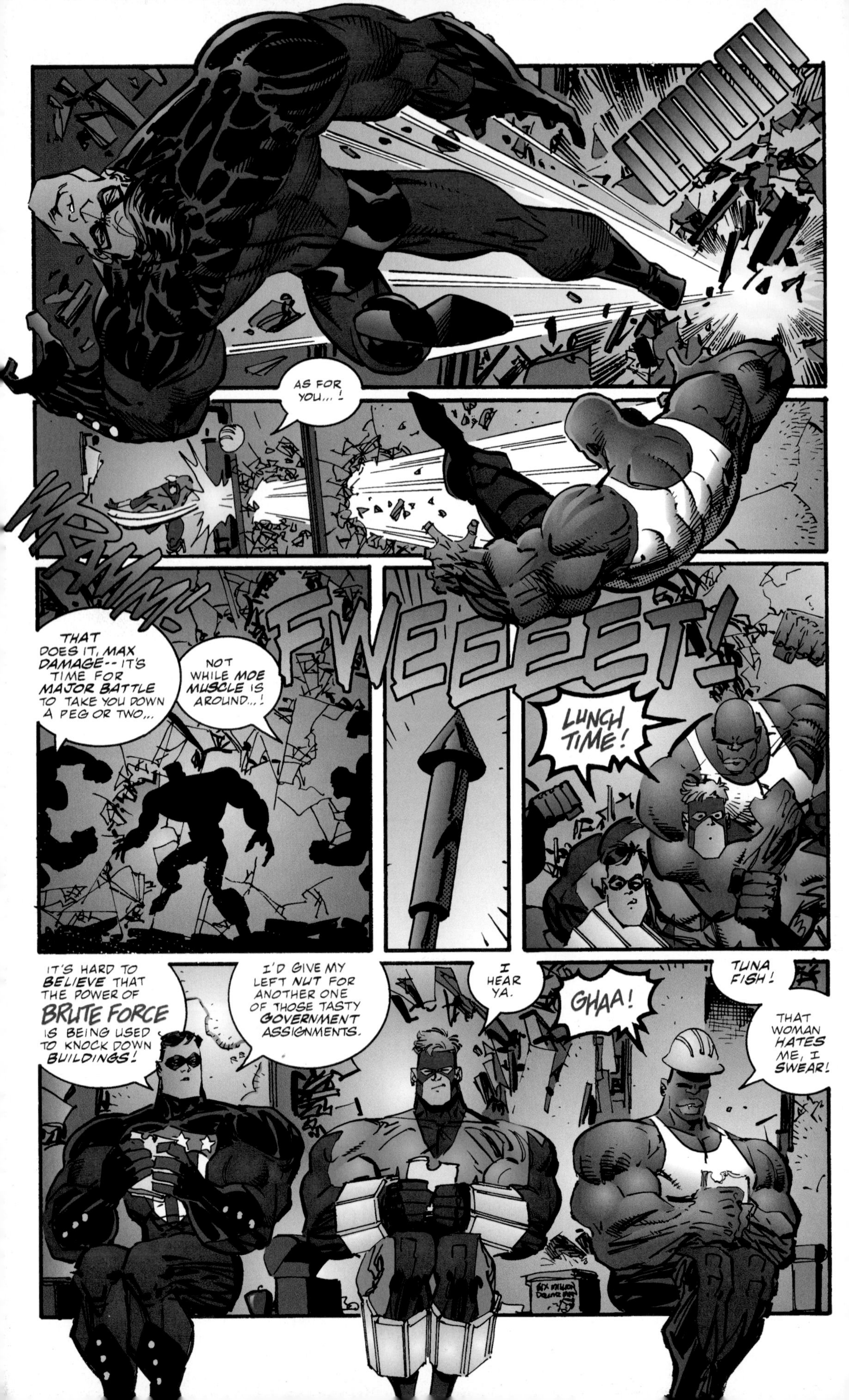
VROOOM!
AS FOR YOU...!
WHAMM!
THAT DOES IT, MAX DAMAGE-- IT'S TIME FOR MAJOR BATTLE TO TAKE YOU DOWN A PEG OR TWO...
NOT WHILE MOE MUSCLE IS AROUND...!
FWEEEET!
LUNCH TIME!
IT'S HARD TO BELIEVE THAT THE POWER OF BRUTE FORCE IS BEING USED TO KNOCK DOWN BUILDINGS!
I'D GIVE MY LEFT NUT FOR ANOTHER ONE OF THOSE TASTY GOVERNMENT ASSIGNMENTS.
I HEAR YA.
GHAA!
TUNA FISH!
THAT WOMAN HATES ME, I SWEAR!

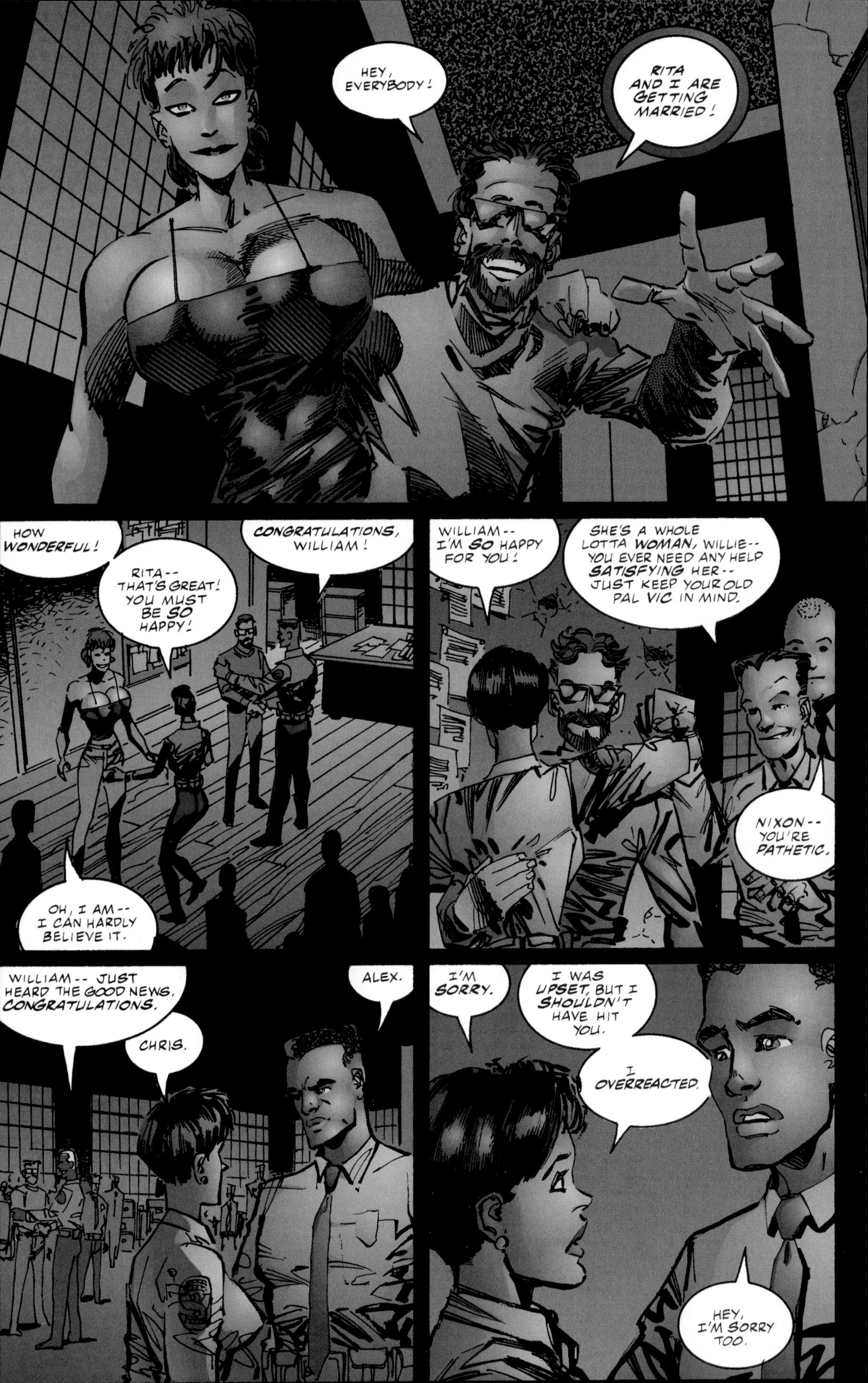
HEY, EVERYBODY!
RITA AND I ARE GETTING MARRIED!
HOW WONDERFUL!
RITA-- THAT'S GREAT! YOU MUST BE SO HAPPY!
CONGRATULATIONS, WILLIAM!
OH, I AM-- I CAN HARDLY BELIEVE IT.
WILLIAM-- I'M SO HAPPY FOR YOU!
SHE'S A WHOLE LOTTA WOMAN, WILLIE-- YOU EVER NEED ANY HELP SATISFYING HER-- JUST KEEP YOUR OLD PAL VIC IN MIND.
NIXON-- YOU'RE PATHETIC.
WILLIAM-- JUST HEARD THE GOOD NEWS. CONGRATULATIONS.
CHRIS.
ALEX.
I'M SORRY.
I WAS UPSET, BUT I SHOULDN'T HAVE HIT YOU.
I OVERREACTED.
HEY, I'M SORRY TOO.

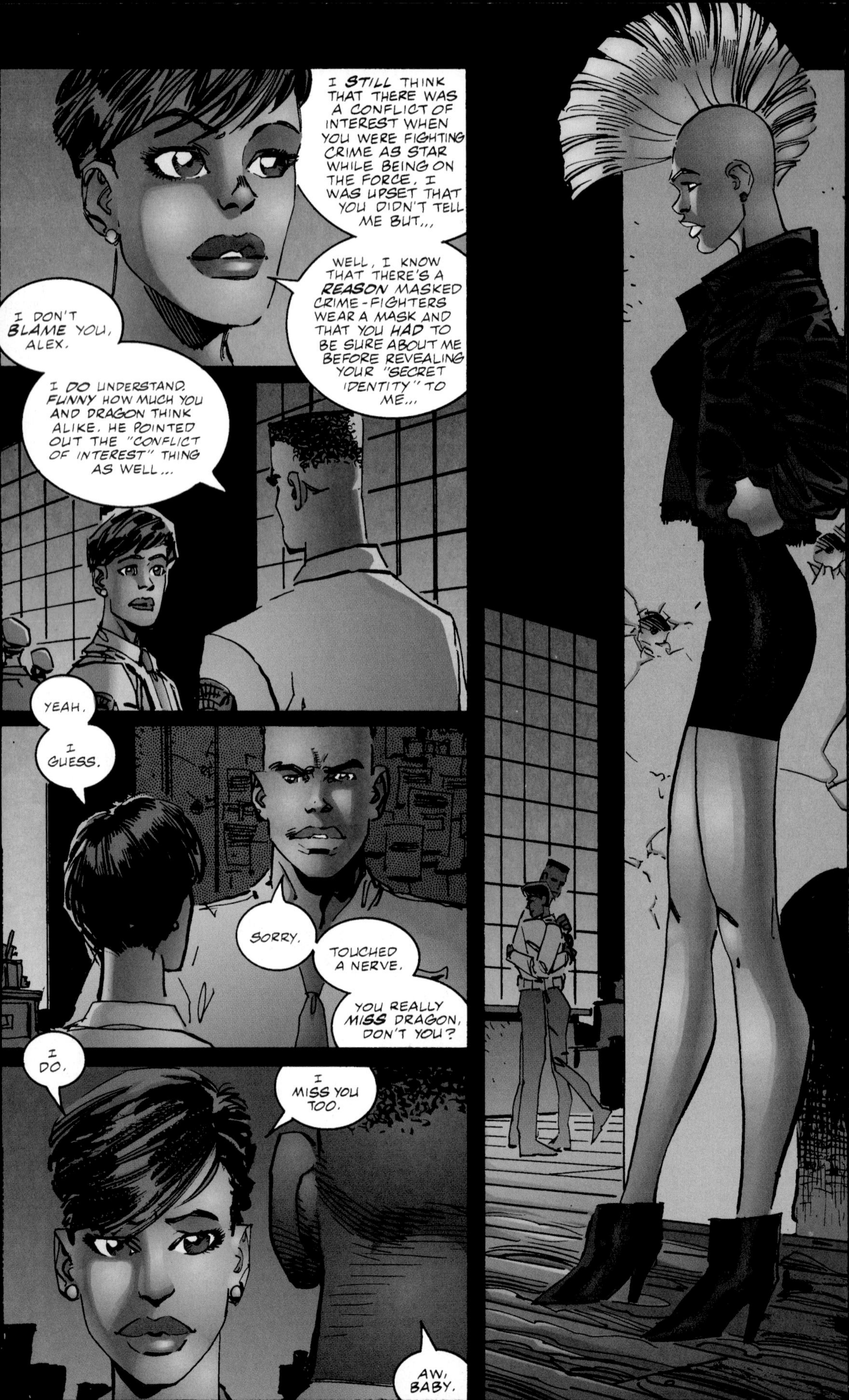
I STILL THINK THAT THERE WAS A CONFLICT OF INTEREST WHEN YOU WERE FIGHTING CRIME AS STAR WHILE BEING ON THE FORCE. I WAS UPSET THAT YOU DIDN'T TELL ME BUT...
WELL, I KNOW THAT THERE'S A REASON MASKED CRIME-FIGHTERS WEAR A MASK AND THAT YOU HAD TO BE SURE ABOUT ME BEFORE REVEALING YOUR "SECRET IDENTITY" TO ME...
I DON'T BLAME YOU, ALEX.
I DO UNDERSTAND. FUNNY HOW MUCH YOU AND DRAGON THINK ALIKE. HE POINTED OUT THE "CONFLICT OF INTEREST" THING AS WELL...
YEAH.
I GUESS.
SORRY.
TOUCHED A NERVE.
YOU REALLY MISS DRAGON, DON'T YOU?
I DO.
I MISS YOU TOO.
AW, BABY.

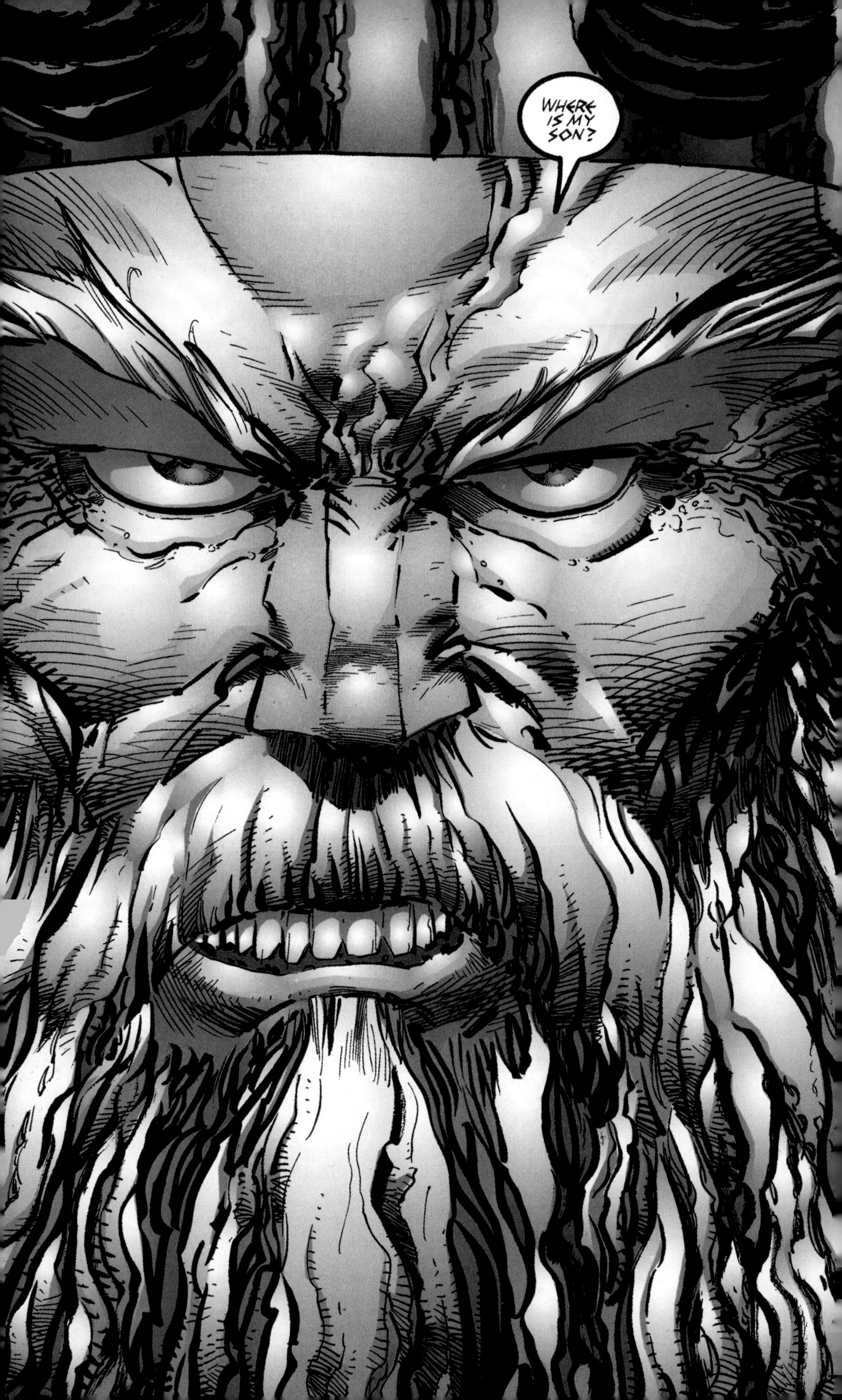
WHERE IS MY SON?

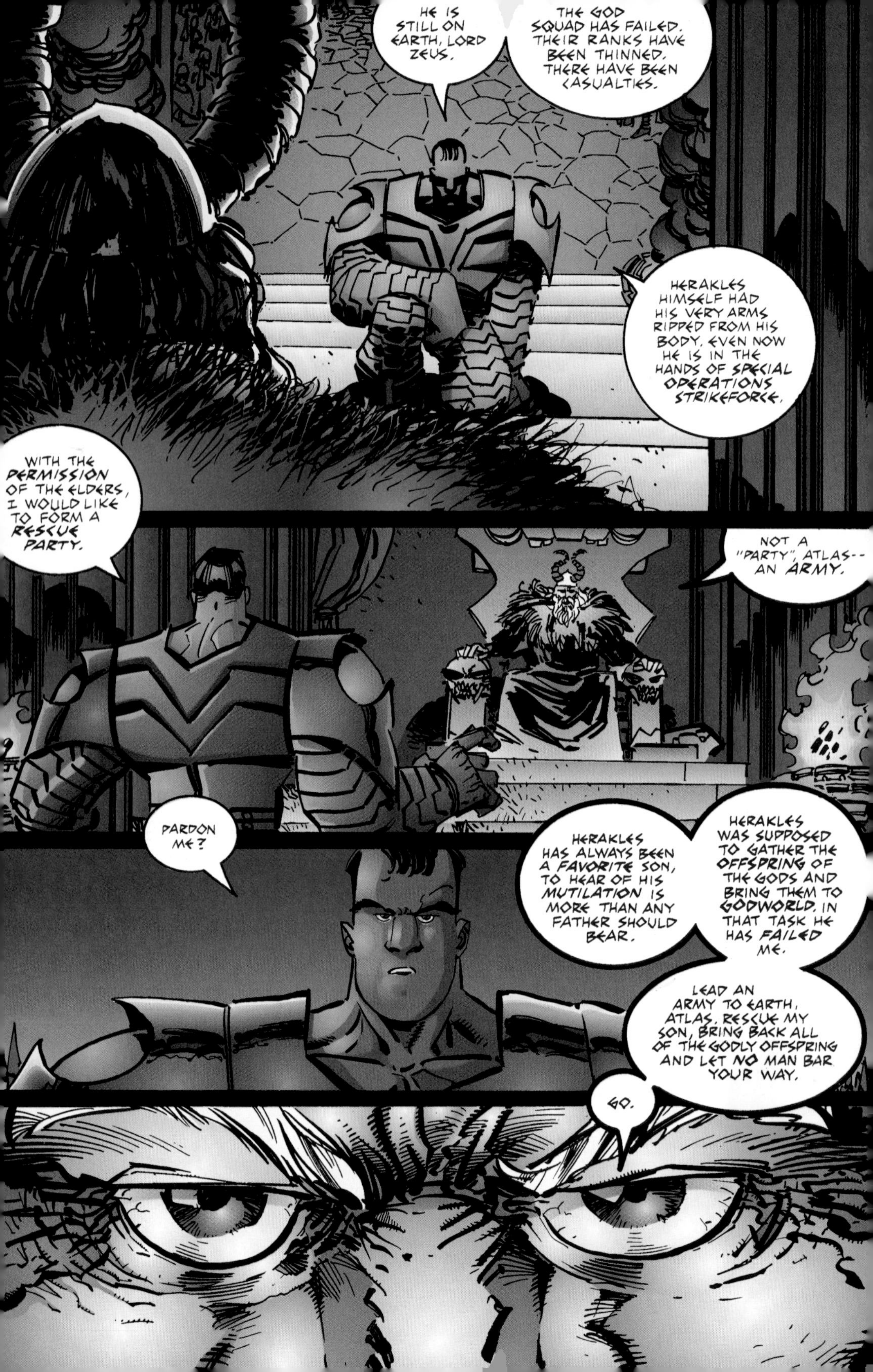
HE IS STILL ON EARTH, LORD ZEUS.
THE GOD SQUAD HAS FAILED. THEIR RANKS HAVE BEEN THINNED. THERE HAVE BEEN CASUALTIES.
HERAKLES HIMSELF HAD HIS VERY ARMS RIPPED FROM HIS BODY. EVEN NOW HE IS IN THE HANDS OF SPECIAL OPERATIONS STRIKEFORCE.
WITH THE PERMISSION OF THE ELDERS, I WOULD LIKE TO FORM A RESCUE PARTY.
NOT A "PARTY", ATLAS-- AN ARMY.
PARDON ME?
HERAKLES HAS ALWAYS BEEN A FAVORITE SON, TO HEAR OF HIS MUTILATION IS MORE THAN ANY FATHER SHOULD BEAR.
HERAKLES WAS SUPPOSED TO GATHER THE OFFSPRING OF THE GODS AND BRING THEM TO GODWORLD. IN THAT TASK HE HAS FAILED ME.
LEAD AN ARMY TO EARTH, ATLAS. RESCUE MY SON, BRING BACK ALL OF THE GODLY OFFSPRING AND LET NO MAN BAR YOUR WAY.
GO.

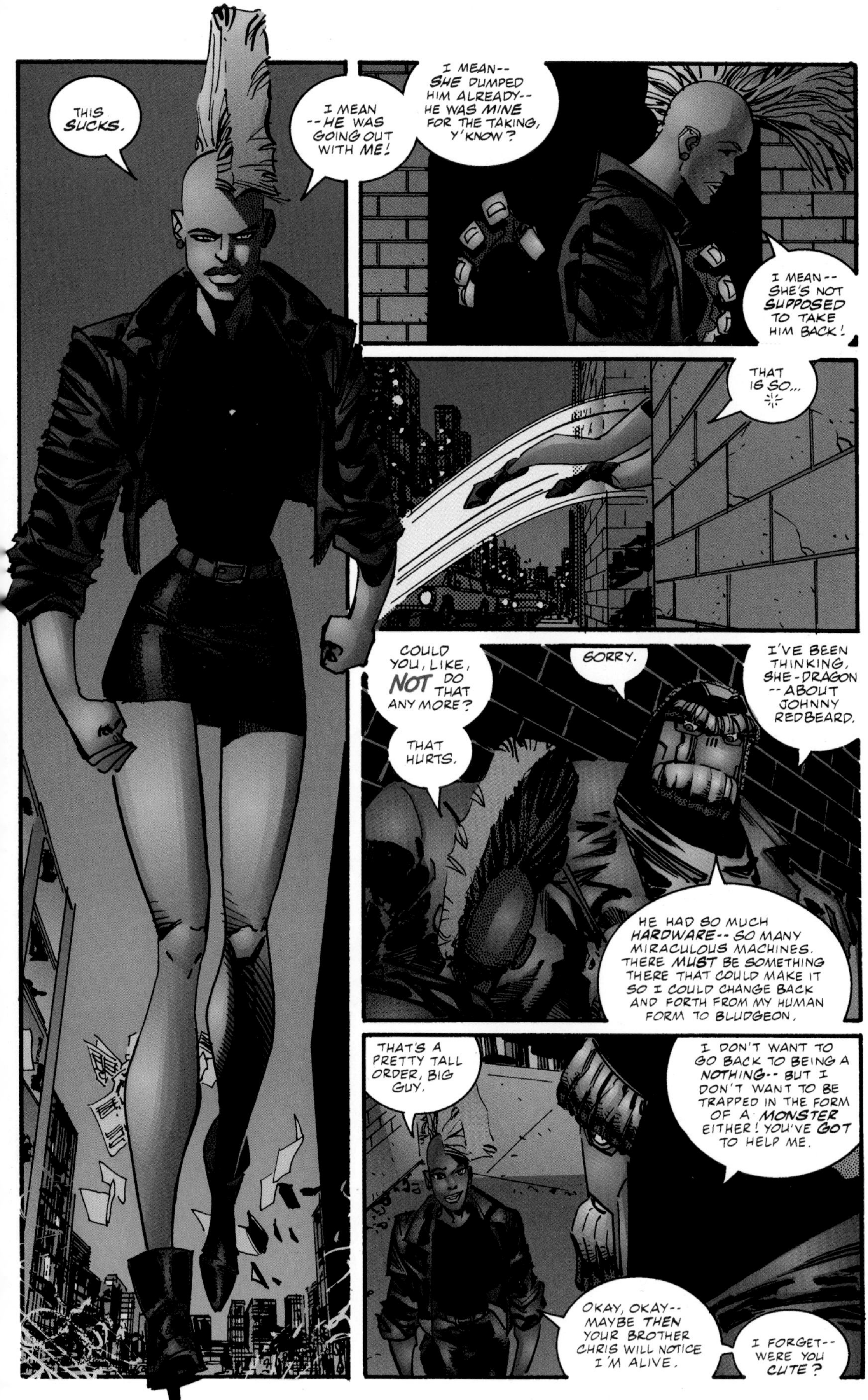
THIS SUCKS.
I MEAN --HE WAS GOING OUT WITH ME!
I MEAN-- SHE DUMPED HIM ALREADY-- HE WAS MINE FOR THE TAKING, Y'KNOW?
I MEAN-- SHE'S NOT SUPPOSED TO TAKE HIM BACK!
THAT IS SO...
COULD YOU, LIKE, NOT DO THAT ANY MORE?
THAT HURTS.
SORRY.
I'VE BEEN THINKING, SHE-DRAGON --ABOUT JOHNNY REDBEARD.
HE HAD SO MUCH HARDWARE-- SO MANY MIRACULOUS MACHINES. THERE MUST BE SOMETHING THERE THAT COULD MAKE IT SO I COULD CHANGE BACK AND FORTH FROM MY HUMAN FORM TO BLUDGEON.
THAT'S A PRETTY TALL ORDER, BIG GUY.
I DON'T WANT TO GO BACK TO BEING A NOTHING-- BUT I DON'T WANT TO BE TRAPPED IN THE FORM OF A MONSTER EITHER! YOU'VE GOT TO HELP ME.
OKAY, OKAY-- MAYBE THEN YOUR BROTHER CHRIS WILL NOTICE I'M ALIVE.
I FORGET-- WERE YOU CUTE?

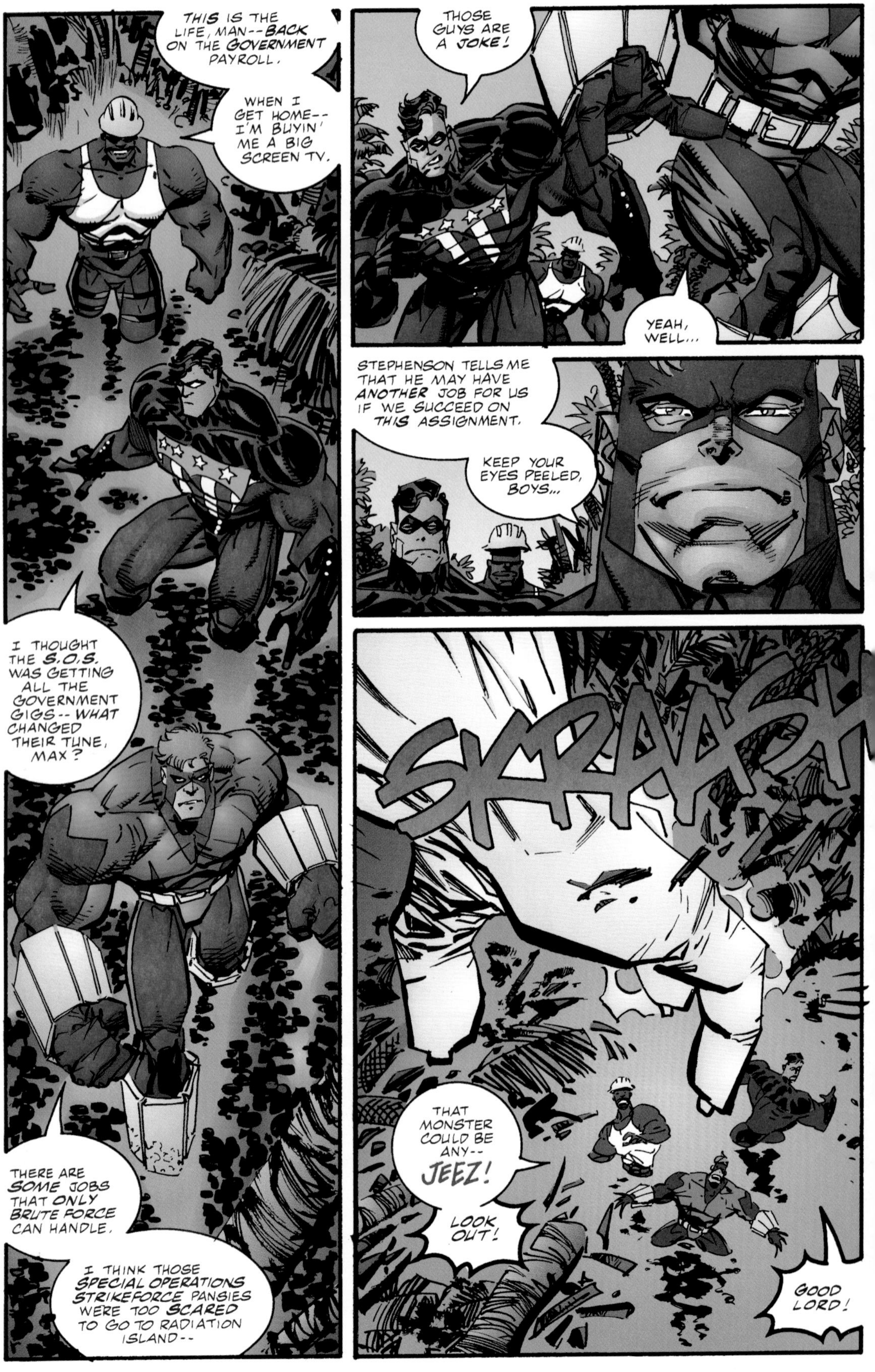
THIS IS THE LIFE, MAN--BACK ON THE GOVERNMENT PAYROLL.
WHEN I GET HOME--I'M BUYIN' ME A BIG SCREEN TV.
I THOUGHT THE S.O.S. WAS GETTING ALL THE GOVERNMENT GIGS--WHAT CHANGED THEIR TUNE, MAX?
THERE ARE SOME JOBS THAT ONLY BRUTE FORCE CAN HANDLE.
I THINK THOSE SPECIAL OPERATIONS STRIKEFORCE PANSIES WERE TOO SCARED TO GO TO RADIATION ISLAND--
THOSE GUYS ARE A JOKE!
YEAH, WELL...
STEPHENSON TELLS ME THAT HE MAY HAVE ANOTHER JOB FOR US IF WE SUCCEED ON THIS ASSIGNMENT.
KEEP YOUR EYES PEELED, BOYS...
SKRAASH
THAT MONSTER COULD BE ANY--
JEEZ!
LOOK OUT!
GOOD LORD!

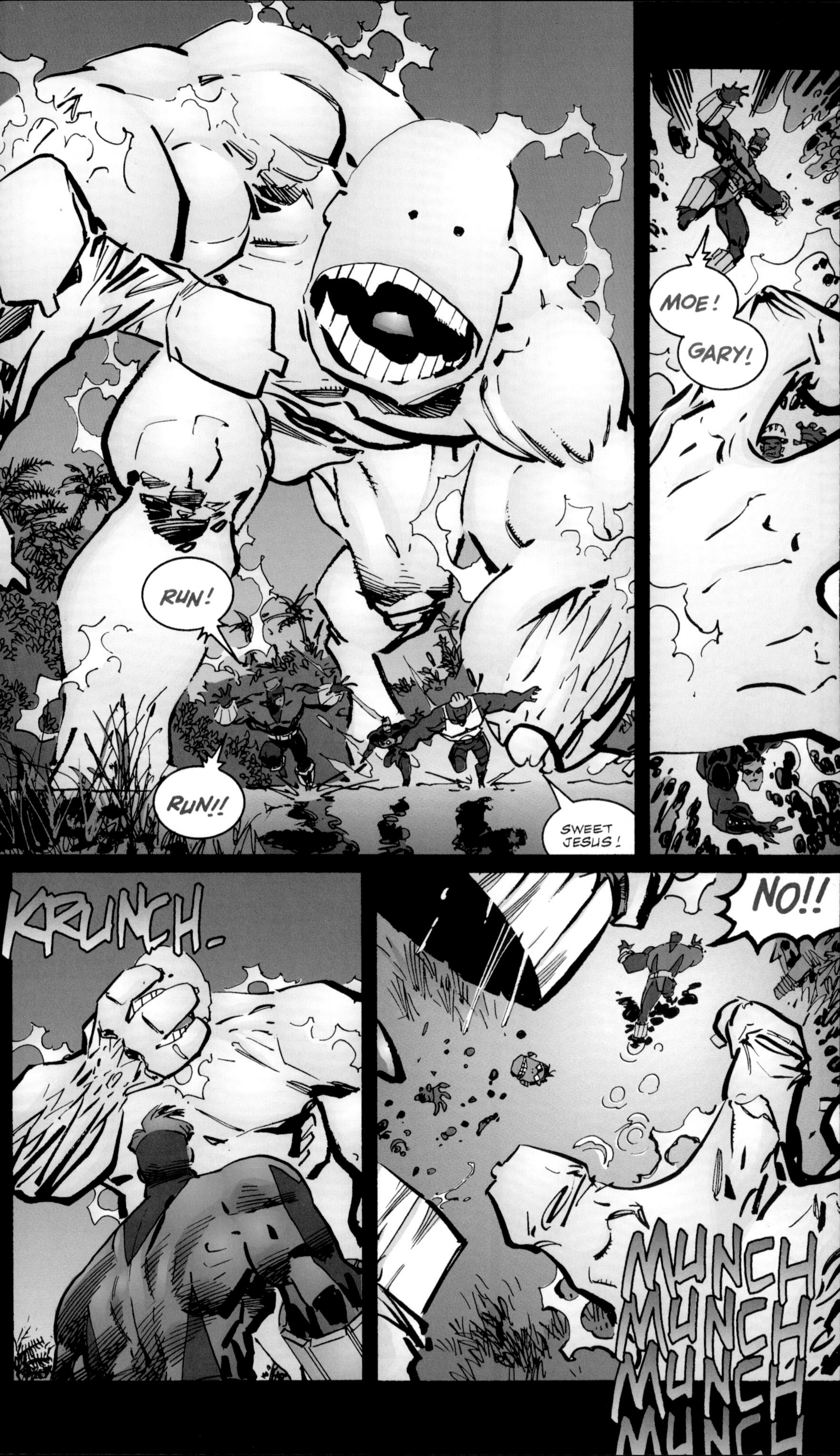

RUN!
RUN!!
SWEET JESUS!
MOE!
GARY!
KRUNCH.
NO!!
MUNCH
MUNCH
MUNCH
MUNCH

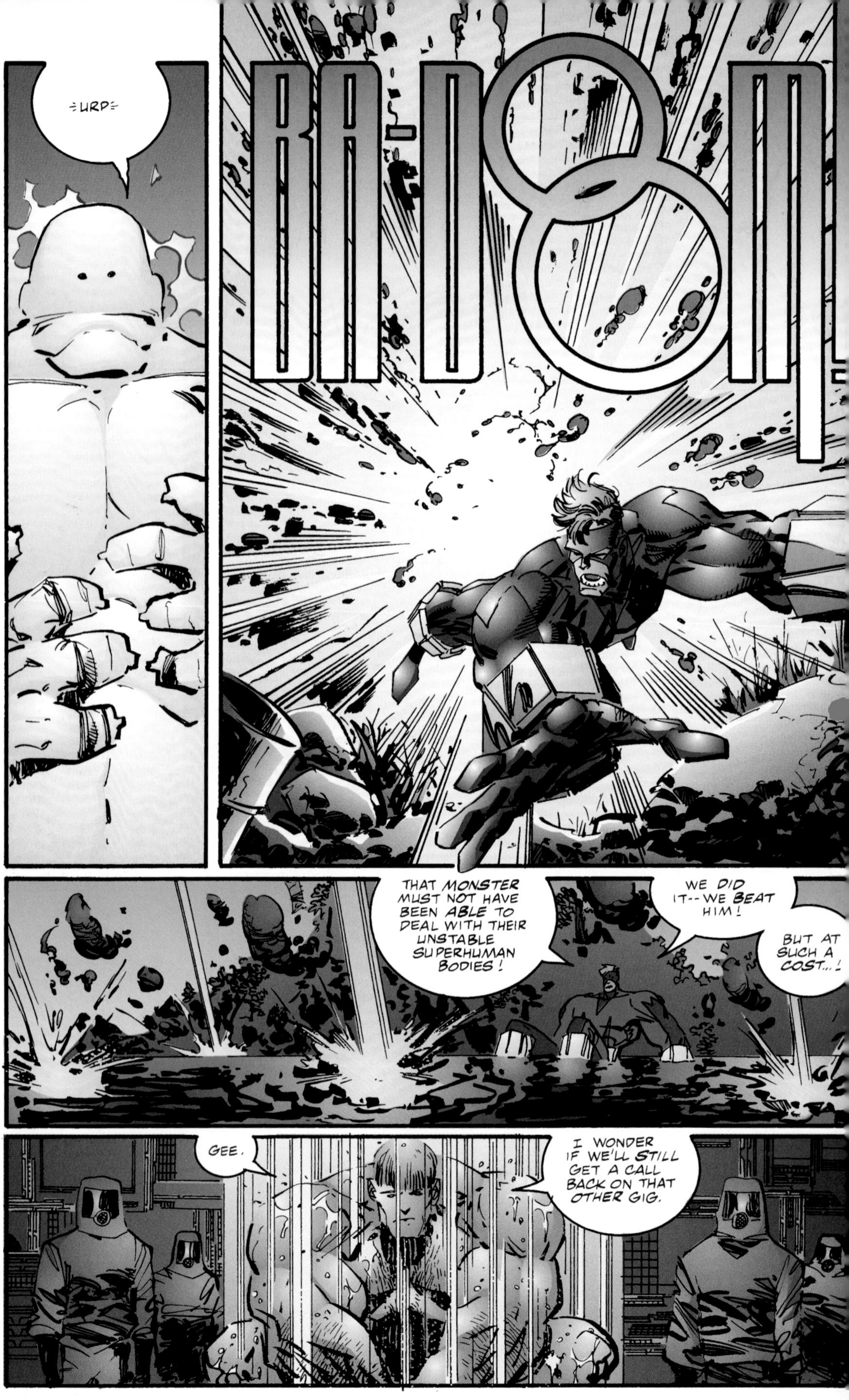
URP
BA-DOOM
THAT MONSTER MUST NOT HAVE BEEN ABLE TO DEAL WITH THEIR UNSTABLE SUPERHUMAN BODIES!
WE DID IT-- WE BEAT HIM!
BUT AT SUCH A COST...!
GEE.
I WONDER IF WE'LL STILL GET A CALL BACK ON THAT OTHER GIG.

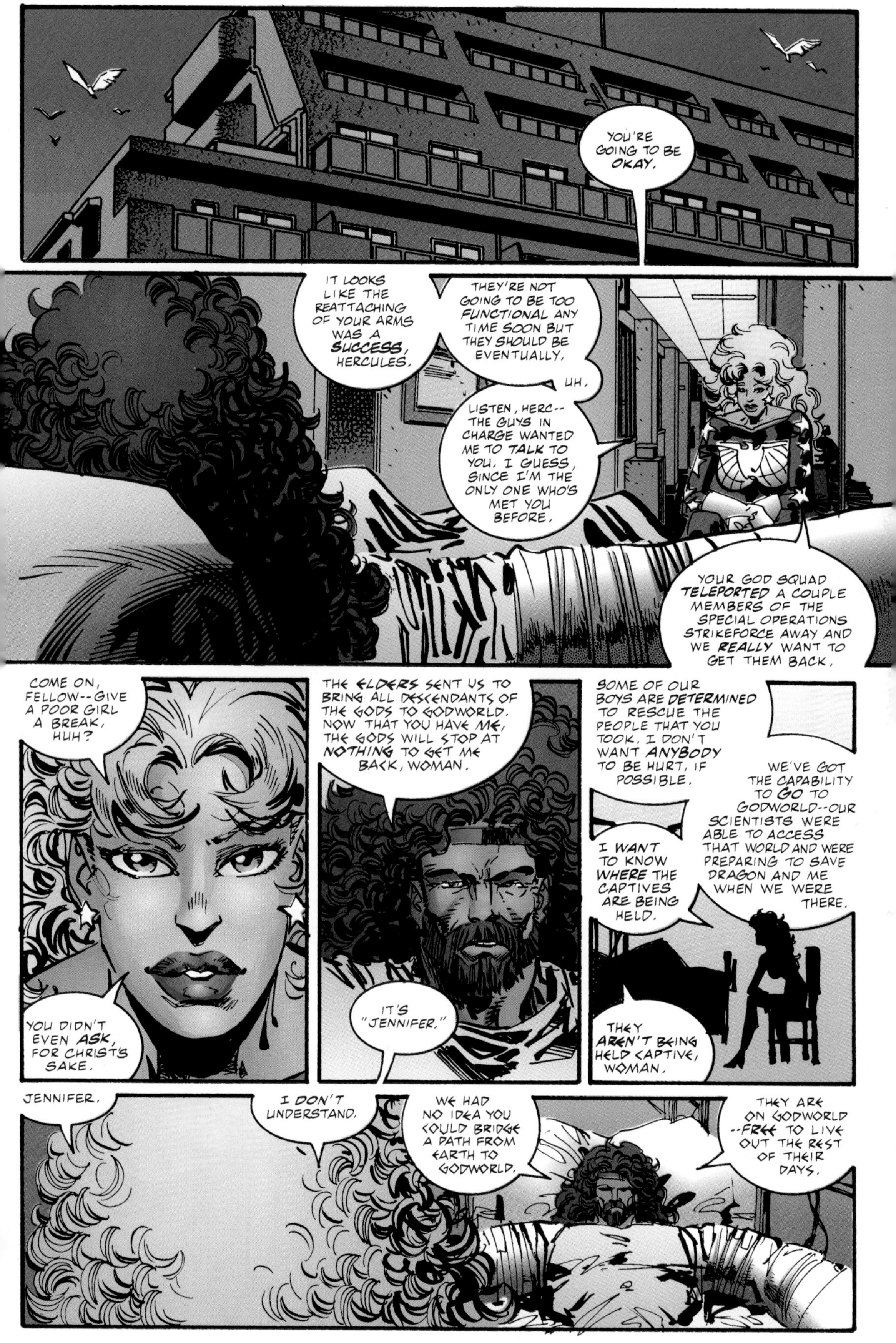
YOU'RE GOING TO BE OKAY.
IT LOOKS LIKE THE REATTACHING OF YOUR ARMS WAS A SUCCESS, HERCULES.
THEY'RE NOT GOING TO BE TOO FUNCTIONAL ANY TIME SOON BUT THEY SHOULD BE EVENTUALLY.
UH,
LISTEN, HERC-- THE GUYS IN CHARGE WANTED ME TO TALK TO YOU, I GUESS, SINCE I'M THE ONLY ONE WHO'S MET YOU BEFORE.
YOUR GOD SQUAD TELEPORTED A COUPLE MEMBERS OF THE SPECIAL OPERATIONS STRIKEFORCE AWAY AND WE REALLY WANT TO GET THEM BACK.
COME ON, FELLOW--GIVE A POOR GIRL A BREAK, HUH?
YOU DIDN'T EVEN ASK, FOR CHRIST'S SAKE.
THE ELDERS SENT US TO BRING ALL DESCENDANTS OF THE GODS TO GODWORLD. NOW THAT YOU HAVE ME, THE GODS WILL STOP AT NOTHING TO GET ME BACK, WOMAN.
IT'S "JENNIFER."
SOME OF OUR BOYS ARE DETERMINED TO RESCUE THE PEOPLE THAT YOU TOOK. I DON'T WANT ANYBODY TO BE HURT, IF POSSIBLE.
WE'VE GOT THE CAPABILITY TO GO TO GODWORLD--OUR SCIENTISTS WERE ABLE TO ACCESS THAT WORLD AND WERE PREPARING TO SAVE DRAGON AND ME WHEN WE WERE THERE.
I WANT TO KNOW WHERE THE CAPTIVES ARE BEING HELD.
THEY AREN'T BEING HELD CAPTIVE, WOMAN.
JENNIFER.
I DON'T UNDERSTAND.
WE HAD NO IDEA YOU COULD BRIDGE A PATH FROM EARTH TO GODWORLD.
THEY ARE ON GODWORLD --FREE TO LIVE OUT THE REST OF THEIR DAYS.

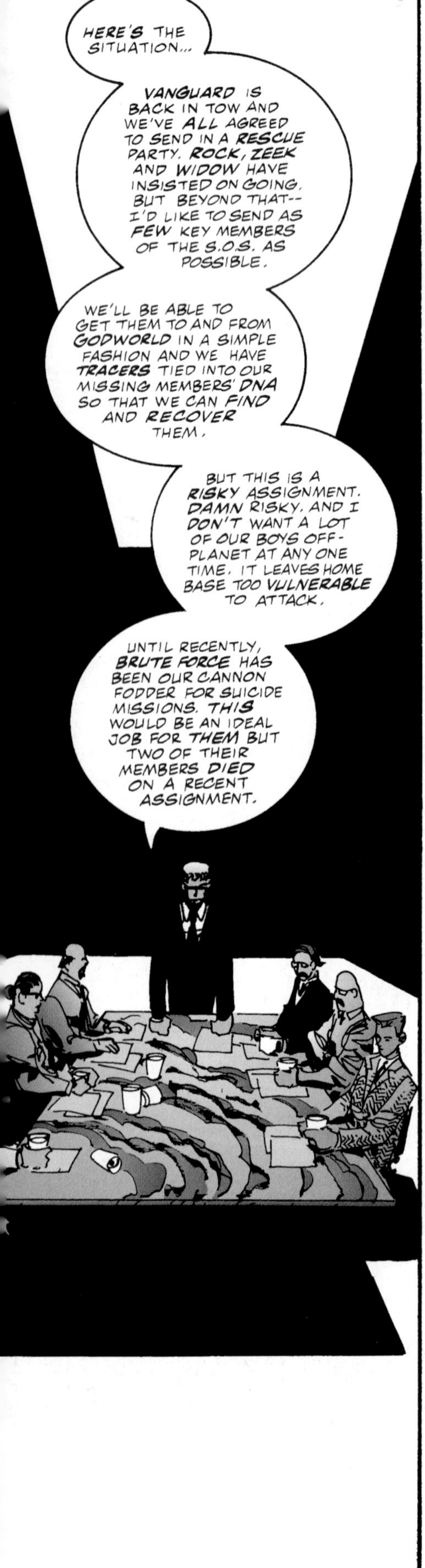
HERE'S THE SITUATION...
VANGUARD IS BACK IN TOW AND WE'VE ALL AGREED TO SEND IN A RESCUE PARTY. ROCK, ZEEK AND WIDOW HAVE INSISTED ON GOING. BUT BEYOND THAT-- I'D LIKE TO SEND AS FEW KEY MEMBERS OF THE S.O.S. AS POSSIBLE.
WE'LL BE ABLE TO GET THEM TO AND FROM GODWORLD IN A SIMPLE FASHION AND WE HAVE TRACERS TIED INTO OUR MISSING MEMBERS' DNA SO THAT WE CAN FIND AND RECOVER THEM.
BUT THIS IS A RISKY ASSIGNMENT. DAMN RISKY. AND I DON'T WANT A LOT OF OUR BOYS OFF-PLANET AT ANY ONE TIME. IT LEAVES HOME BASE TOO VULNERABLE TO ATTACK.
UNTIL RECENTLY, BRUTE FORCE HAS BEEN OUR CANNON FODDER FOR SUICIDE MISSIONS. THIS WOULD BE AN IDEAL JOB FOR THEM BUT TWO OF THEIR MEMBERS DIED ON A RECENT ASSIGNMENT.

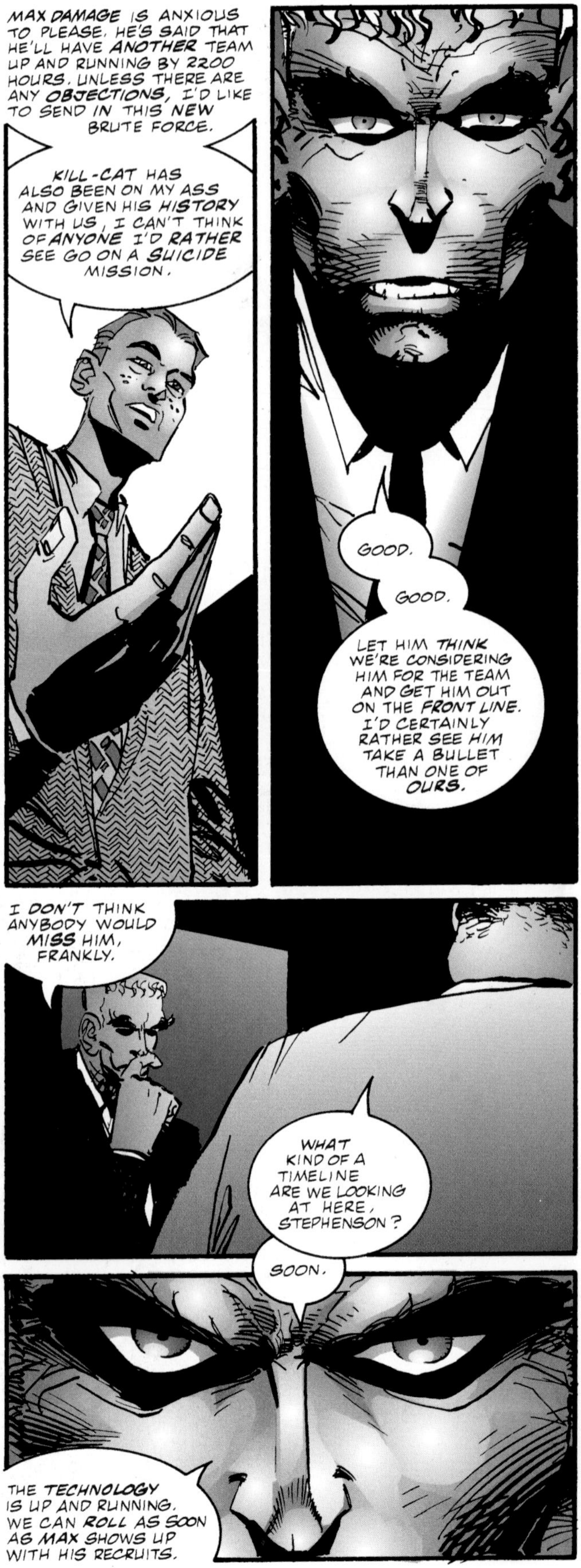
MAX DAMAGE IS ANXIOUS TO PLEASE. HE'S SAID THAT HE'LL HAVE ANOTHER TEAM UP AND RUNNING BY 2200 HOURS. UNLESS THERE ARE ANY OBJECTIONS, I'D LIKE TO SEND IN THIS NEW BRUTE FORCE.
KILL-CAT HAS ALSO BEEN ON MY ASS AND GIVEN HIS HISTORY WITH US, I CAN'T THINK OF ANYONE I'D RATHER SEE GO ON A SUICIDE MISSION.
GOOD.
GOOD.
LET HIM THINK WE'RE CONSIDERING HIM FOR THE TEAM AND GET HIM OUT ON THE FRONT LINE. I'D CERTAINLY RATHER SEE HIM TAKE A BULLET THAN ONE OF OURS.
I DON'T THINK ANYBODY WOULD MISS HIM, FRANKLY.
WHAT KIND OF A TIMELINE ARE WE LOOKING AT HERE, STEPHENSON?
SOON.
THE TECHNOLOGY IS UP AND RUNNING. WE CAN ROLL AS SOON AS MAX SHOWS UP WITH HIS RECRUITS.

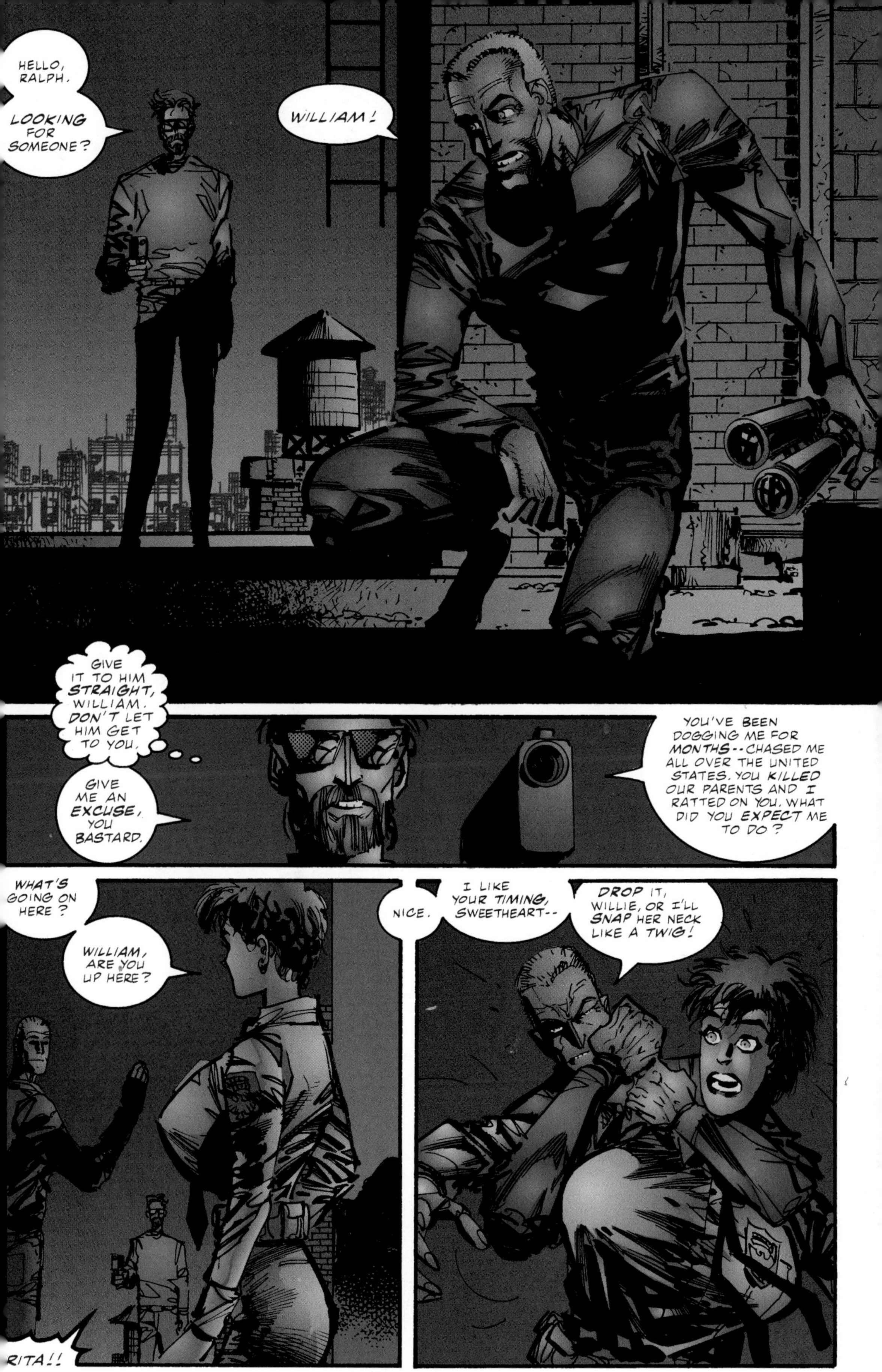
HELLO, RALPH.
LOOKING FOR SOMEONE?
WILLIAM!
GIVE IT TO HIM STRAIGHT, WILLIAM. DON'T LET HIM GET TO YOU.
GIVE ME AN EXCUSE, YOU BASTARD.
YOU'VE BEEN DOGGING ME FOR MONTHS--CHASED ME ALL OVER THE UNITED STATES. YOU KILLED OUR PARENTS AND I RATTED ON YOU. WHAT DID YOU EXPECT ME TO DO?
WHAT'S GOING ON HERE?
WILLIAM, ARE YOU UP HERE?
RITA!!
NICE.
I LIKE YOUR TIMING, SWEETHEART--
DROP IT, WILLIE, OR I'LL SNAP HER NECK LIKE A TWIG!

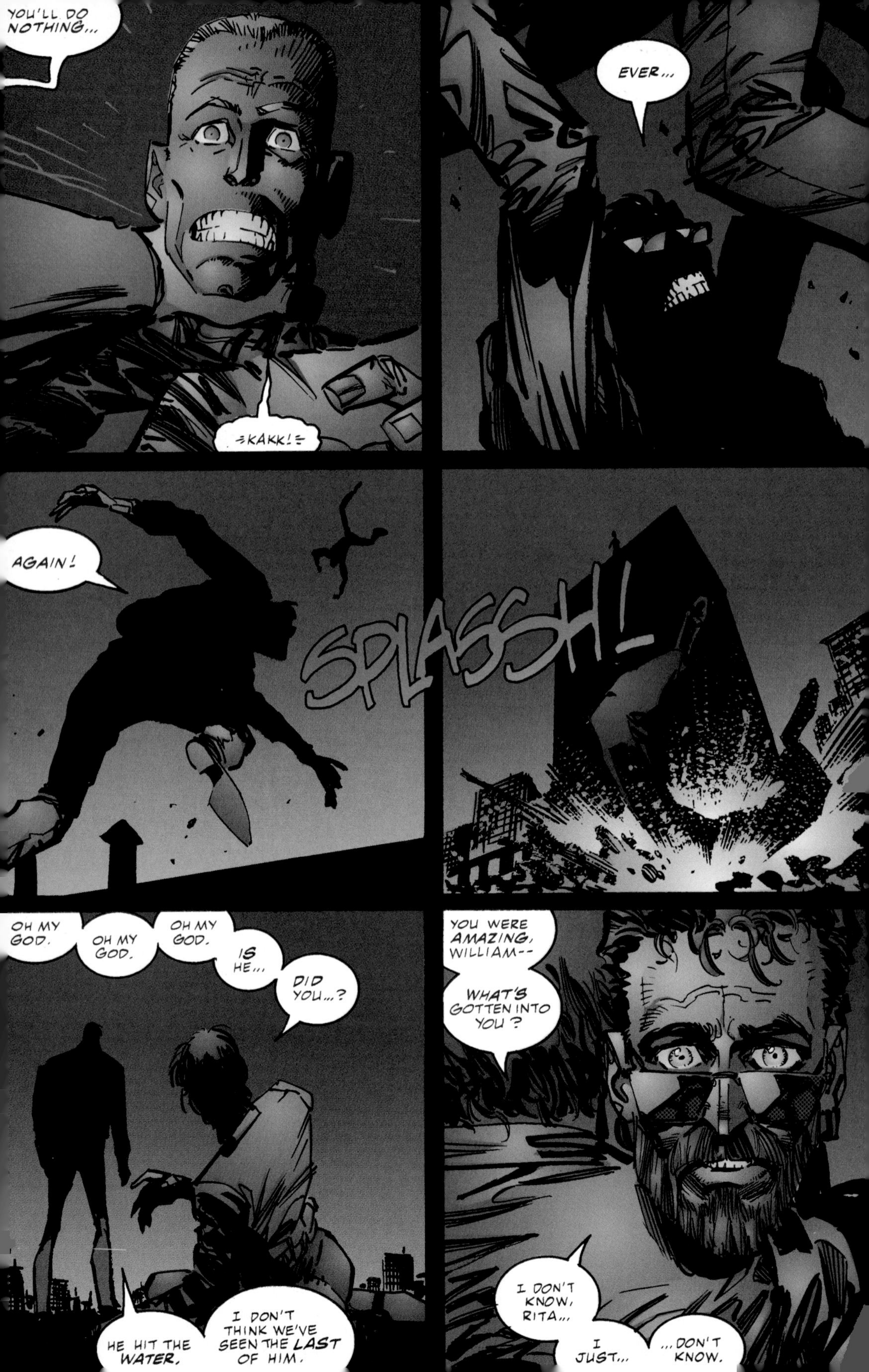
YOU'LL DO NOTHING...
KAKK!
EVER...
AGAIN!
SPLASSH!
OH MY GOD.
OH MY GOD.
OH MY GOD.
IS HE...
DID YOU...?
HE HIT THE WATER.
I DON'T THINK WE'VE SEEN THE LAST OF HIM.
YOU WERE AMAZING, WILLIAM--
WHAT'S GOTTEN INTO YOU?
I DON'T KNOW, RITA...
I JUST...
...DON'T KNOW.

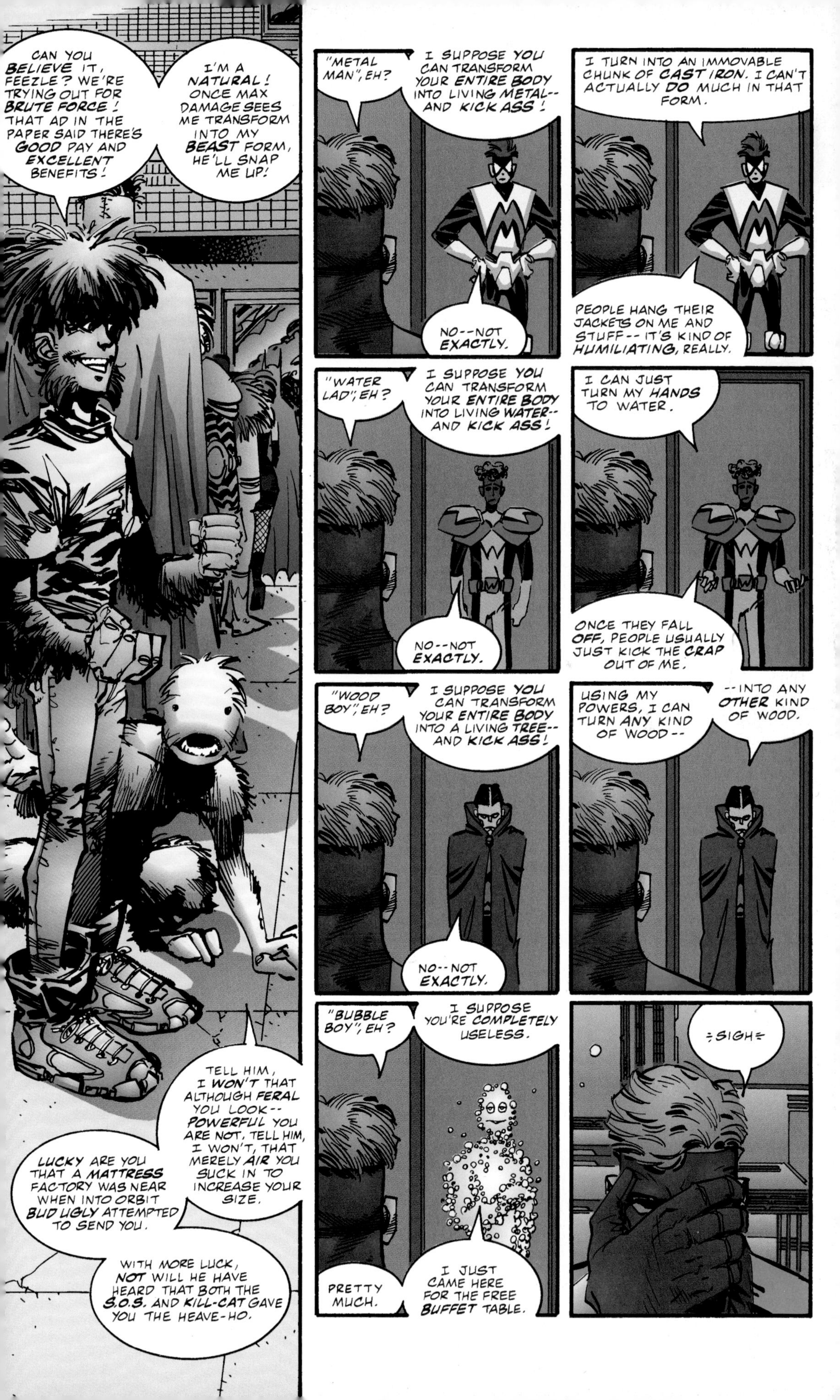

CAN YOU BELIEVE IT, FEEZLE? WE'RE TRYING OUT FOR BRUTE FORCE! THAT AD IN THE PAPER SAID THERE'S GOOD PAY AND EXCELLENT BENEFITS!
I'M A NATURAL! ONCE MAX DAMAGE SEES ME TRANSFORM INTO MY BEAST FORM, HE'LL SNAP ME UP!
TELL HIM, I WON'T THAT ALTHOUGH FERAL YOU LOOK-- POWERFUL YOU ARE NOT. TELL HIM, I WON'T, THAT MERELY AIR YOU SUCK IN TO INCREASE YOUR SIZE.
LUCKY ARE YOU THAT A MATTRESS FACTORY WAS NEAR WHEN INTO ORBIT BUD UGLY ATTEMPTED TO SEND YOU.
WITH MORE LUCK, NOT WILL HE HAVE HEARD THAT BOTH THE S.O.S. AND KILL-CAT GAVE YOU THE HEAVE-HO.
"METAL MAN", EH?
I SUPPOSE YOU CAN TRANSFORM YOUR ENTIRE BODY INTO LIVING METAL-- AND KICK ASS!
NO--NOT EXACTLY.
I TURN INTO AN IMMOVABLE CHUNK OF CAST IRON. I CAN'T ACTUALLY DO MUCH IN THAT FORM.
PEOPLE HANG THEIR JACKETS ON ME AND STUFF-- IT'S KIND OF HUMILIATING, REALLY.
"WATER LAD", EH?
I SUPPOSE YOU CAN TRANSFORM YOUR ENTIRE BODY INTO LIVING WATER-- AND KICK ASS!
NO--NOT EXACTLY.
I CAN JUST TURN MY HANDS TO WATER.
ONCE THEY FALL OFF, PEOPLE USUALLY JUST KICK THE CRAP OUT OF ME.
"WOOD BOY", EH?
I SUPPOSE YOU CAN TRANSFORM YOUR ENTIRE BODY INTO A LIVING TREE-- AND KICK ASS!
NO--NOT EXACTLY.
USING MY POWERS, I CAN TURN ANY KIND OF WOOD--
--INTO ANY OTHER KIND OF WOOD.
"BUBBLE BOY", EH?
I SUPPOSE YOU'RE COMPLETELY USELESS.
PRETTY MUCH.
I JUST CAME HERE FOR THE FREE BUFFET TABLE.
=SIGH=

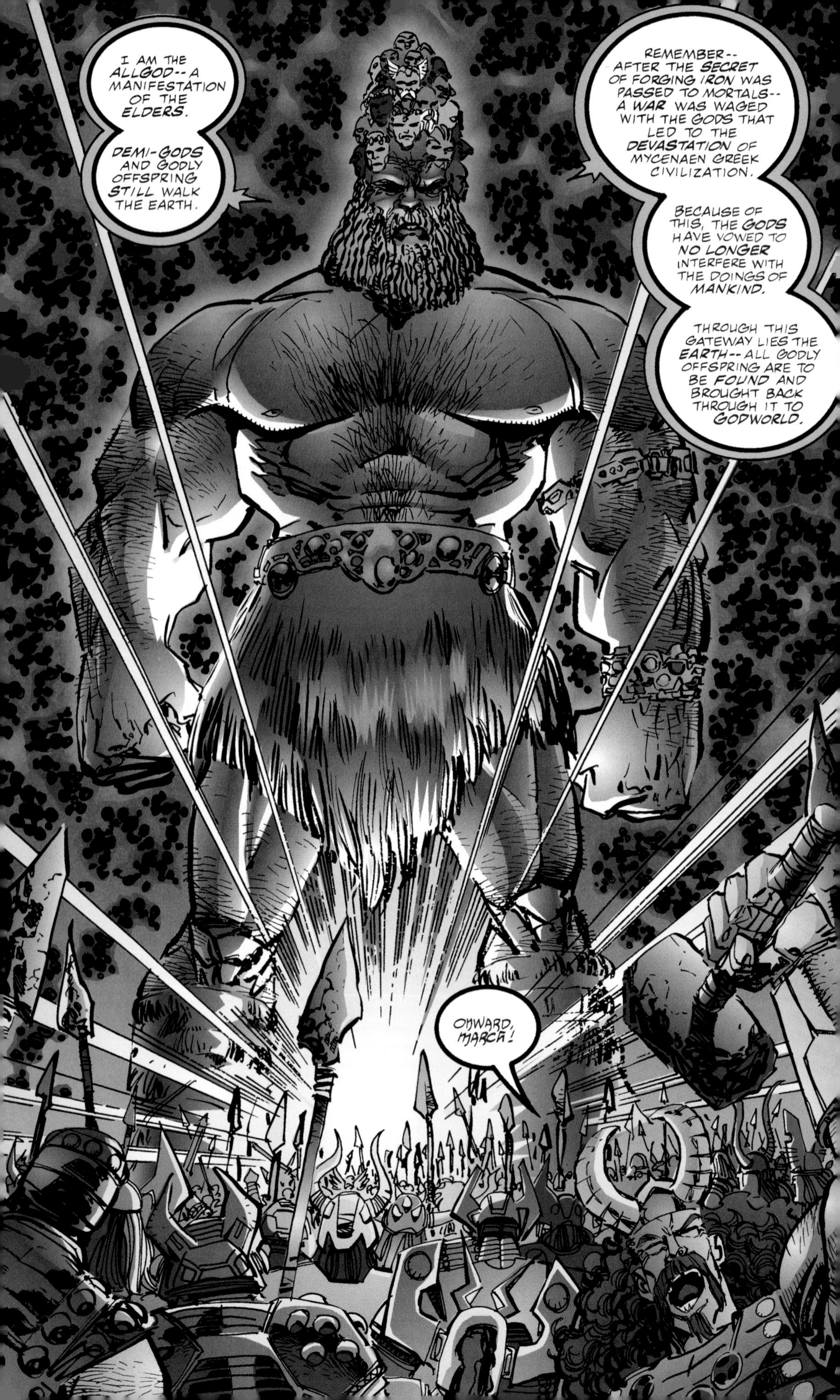

I AM THE ALLGOD-- A MANIFESTATION OF THE ELDERS.
DEMI-GODS AND GODLY OFFSPRING STILL WALK THE EARTH.
REMEMBER-- AFTER THE SECRET OF FORGING IRON WAS PASSED TO MORTALS-- A WAR WAS WAGED WITH THE GODS THAT LED TO THE DEVASTATION OF MYCENAEN GREEK CIVILIZATION.
BECAUSE OF THIS, THE GODS HAVE VOWED TO NO LONGER INTERFERE WITH THE DOINGS OF MANKIND.
THROUGH THIS GATEWAY LIES THE EARTH-- ALL GODLY OFFSPRING ARE TO BE FOUND AND BROUGHT BACK THROUGH IT TO GODWORLD.
ONWARD, MARCH!

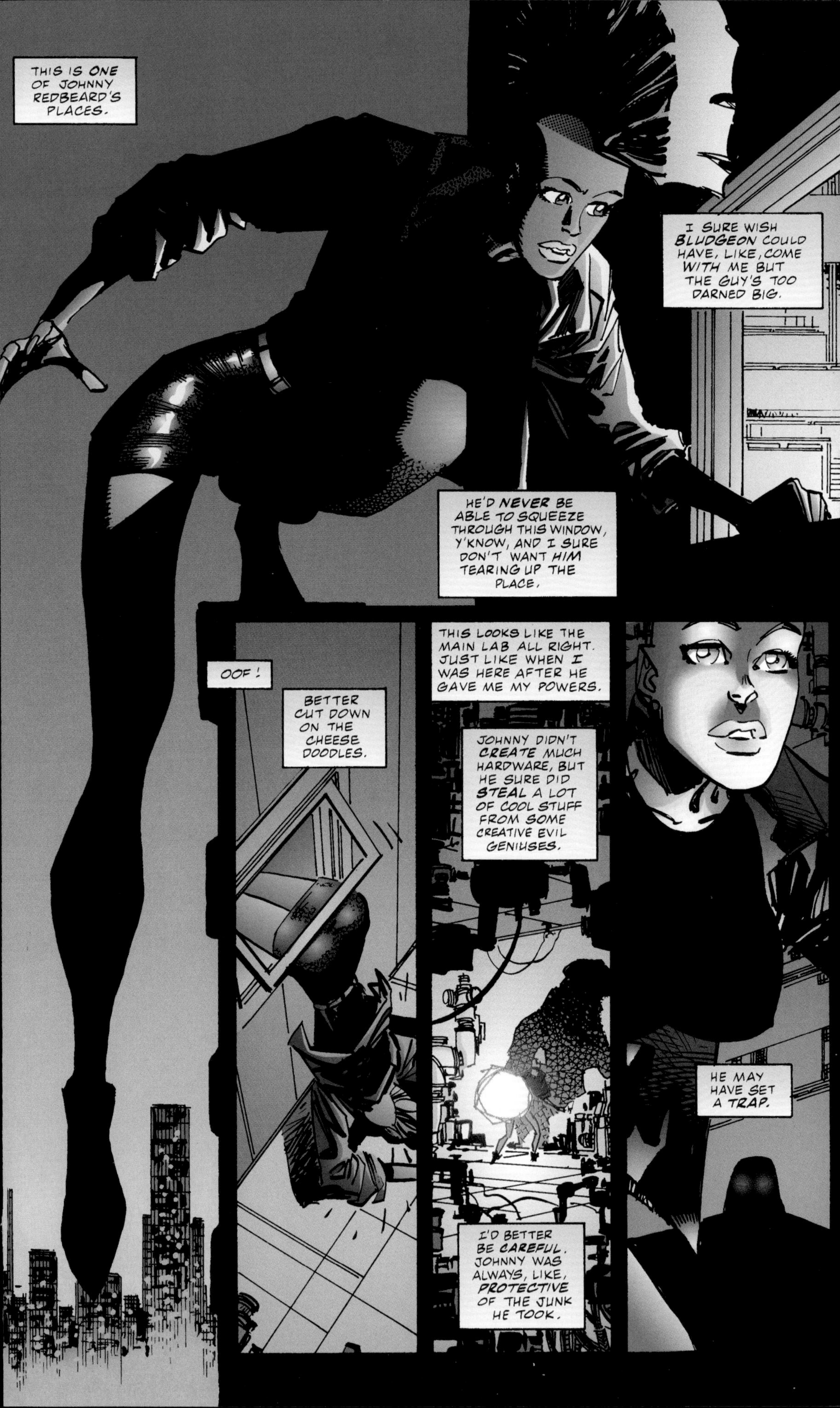
THIS IS ONE OF JOHNNY REDBEARD'S PLACES.
I SURE WISH BLUDGEON COULD HAVE, LIKE, COME WITH ME BUT THE GUY'S TOO DARNED BIG.
HE'D NEVER BE ABLE TO SQUEEZE THROUGH THIS WINDOW, Y'KNOW, AND I SURE DON'T WANT HIM TEARING UP THE PLACE.
OOF!
BETTER CUT DOWN ON THE CHEESE DOODLES.
THIS LOOKS LIKE THE MAIN LAB ALL RIGHT. JUST LIKE WHEN I WAS HERE AFTER HE GAVE ME MY POWERS.
JOHNNY DIDN'T CREATE MUCH HARDWARE, BUT HE SURE DID STEAL A LOT OF COOL STUFF FROM SOME CREATIVE EVIL GENIUSES.
I'D BETTER BE CAREFUL. JOHNNY WAS ALWAYS, LIKE, PROTECTIVE OF THE JUNK HE TOOK.
HE MAY HAVE SET A TRAP.

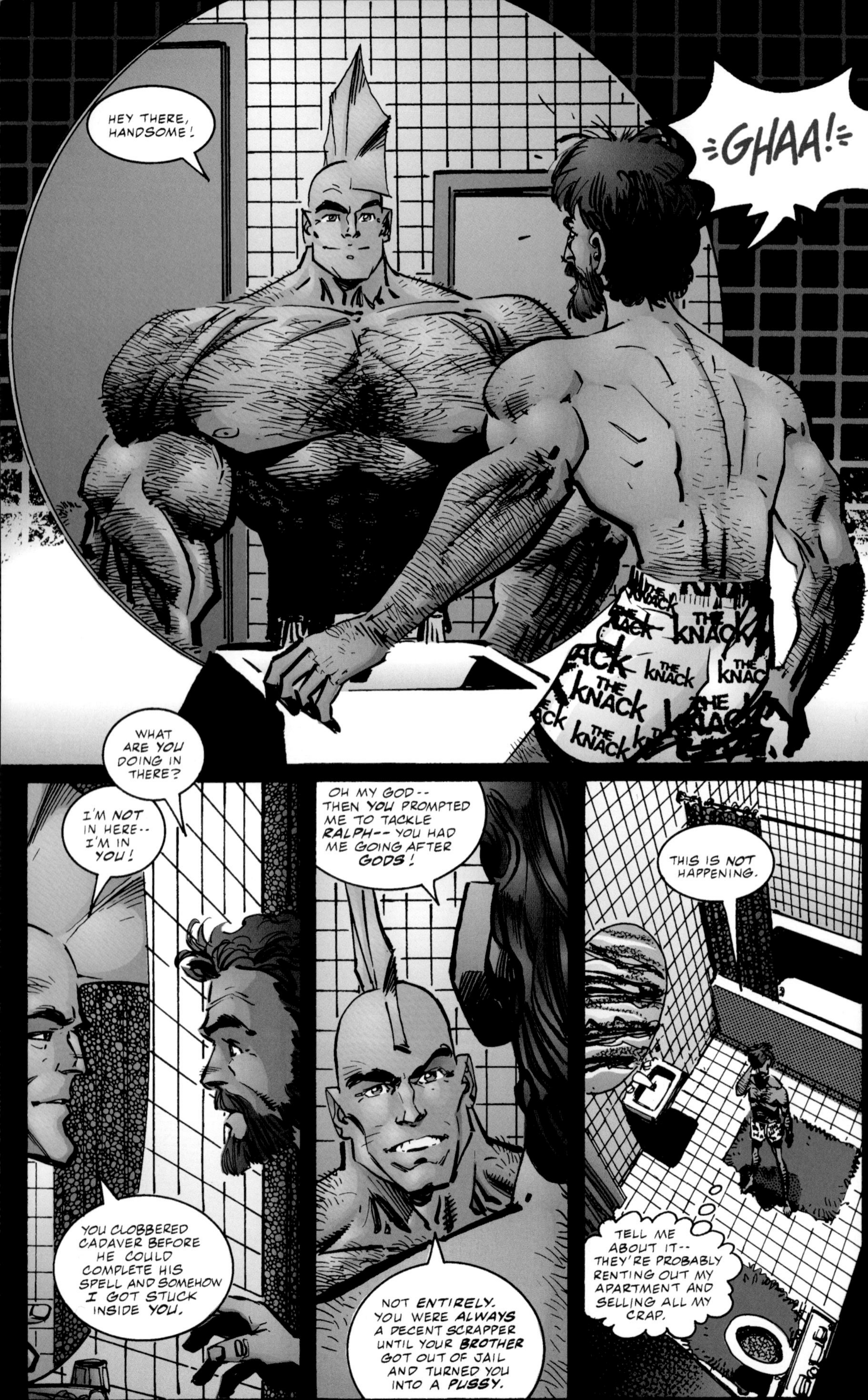
HEY THERE, HANDSOME!
GHAA!
WHAT ARE YOU DOING IN THERE?
I'M NOT IN HERE-- I'M IN YOU!
YOU CLOBBERED CADAVER BEFORE HE COULD COMPLETE HIS SPELL AND SOMEHOW I GOT STUCK INSIDE YOU.
OH MY GOD-- THEN YOU PROMPTED ME TO TACKLE RALPH-- YOU HAD ME GOING AFTER GODS!
NOT ENTIRELY. YOU WERE ALWAYS A DECENT SCRAPPER UNTIL YOUR BROTHER GOT OUT OF JAIL AND TURNED YOU INTO A PUSSY.
THIS IS NOT HAPPENING.
TELL ME ABOUT IT-- THEY'RE PROBABLY RENTING OUT MY APARTMENT AND SELLING ALL MY CRAP.

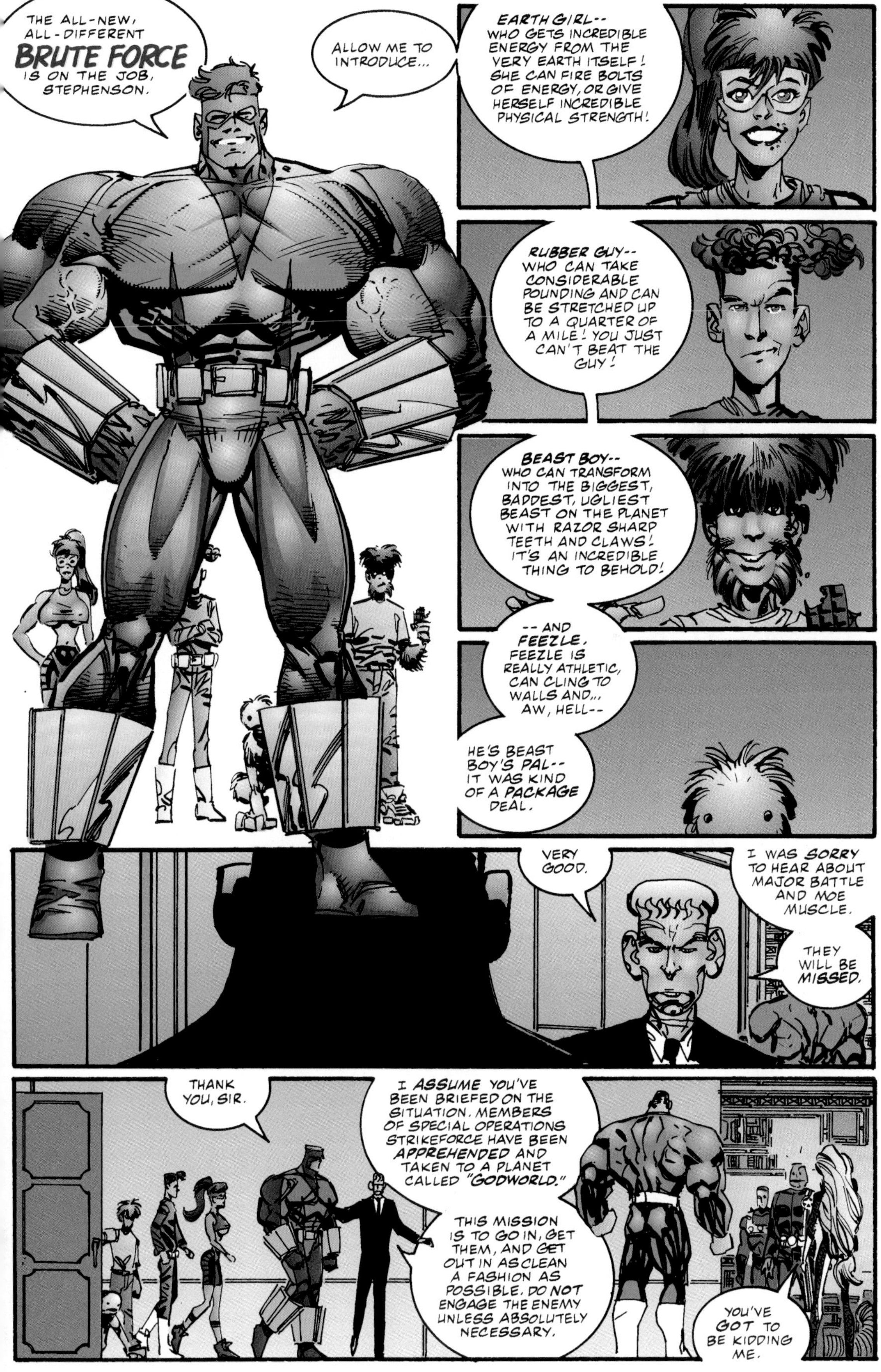
THE ALL-NEW, ALL-DIFFERENT BRUTE FORCE IS ON THE JOB, STEPHENSON.
ALLOW ME TO INTRODUCE...
EARTH GIRL-- WHO GETS INCREDIBLE ENERGY FROM THE VERY EARTH ITSELF! SHE CAN FIRE BOLTS OF ENERGY, OR GIVE HERSELF INCREDIBLE PHYSICAL STRENGTH!
RUBBER GUY-- WHO CAN TAKE CONSIDERABLE POUNDING AND CAN BE STRETCHED UP TO A QUARTER OF A MILE! YOU JUST CAN'T BEAT THE GUY!
BEAST BOY-- WHO CAN TRANSFORM INTO THE BIGGEST, BADDEST, UGLIEST BEAST ON THE PLANET WITH RAZOR SHARP TEETH AND CLAWS! IT'S AN INCREDIBLE THING TO BEHOLD!
-- AND FEEZLE. FEEZLE IS REALLY ATHLETIC, CAN CLING TO WALLS AND... AW, HELL--
HE'S BEAST BOY'S PAL-- IT WAS KIND OF A PACKAGE DEAL.
VERY GOOD.
I WAS SORRY TO HEAR ABOUT MAJOR BATTLE AND MOE MUSCLE.
THEY WILL BE MISSED.
THANK YOU, SIR.
I ASSUME YOU'VE BEEN BRIEFED ON THE SITUATION. MEMBERS OF SPECIAL OPERATIONS STRIKEFORCE HAVE BEEN APPREHENDED AND TAKEN TO A PLANET CALLED "GODWORLD."
THIS MISSION IS TO GO IN, GET THEM, AND GET OUT IN AS CLEAN A FASHION AS POSSIBLE. DO NOT ENGAGE THE ENEMY UNLESS ABSOLUTELY NECESSARY.
YOU'VE GOT TO BE KIDDING ME.

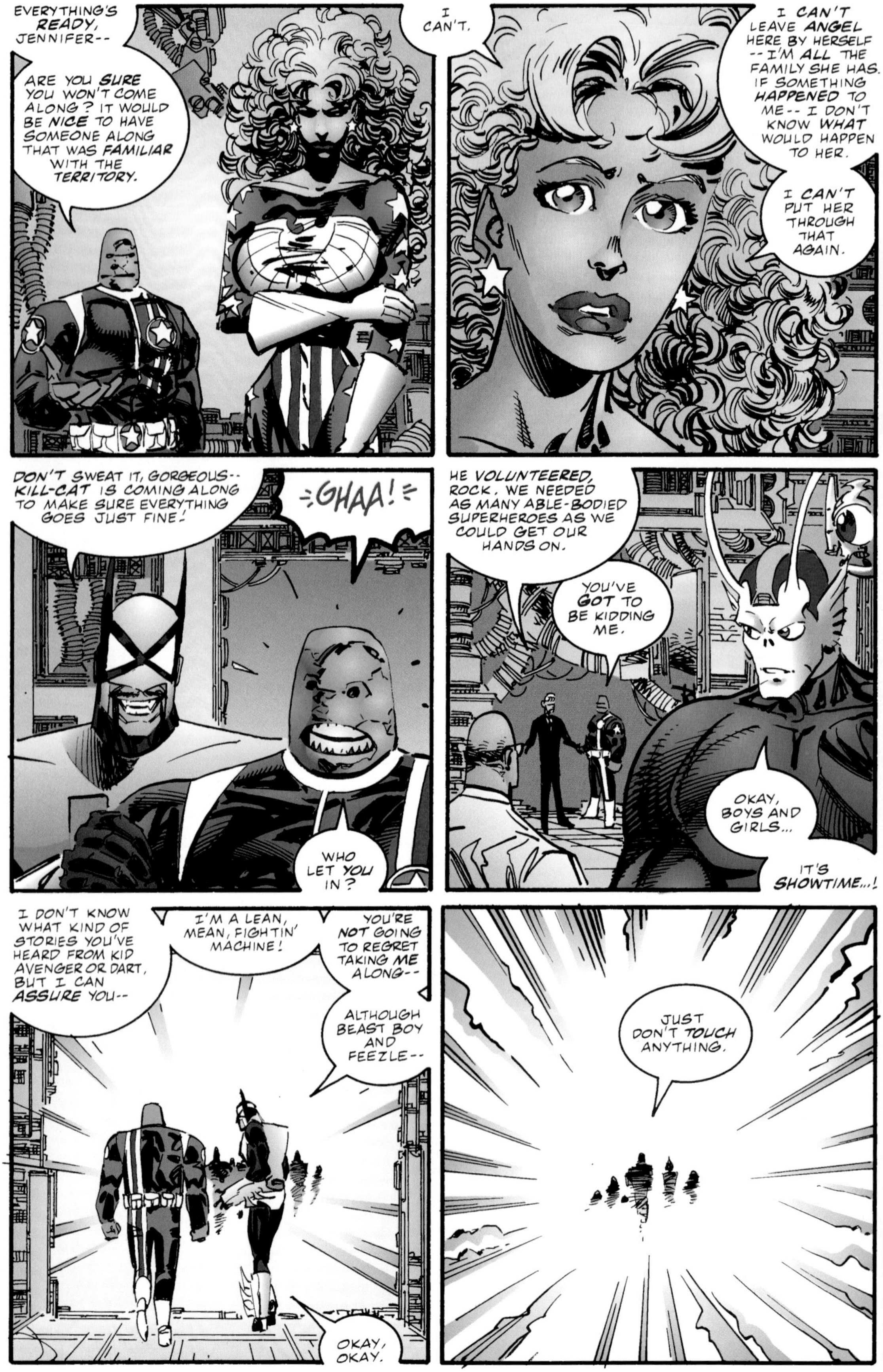

EVERYTHING'S READY, JENNIFER--
ARE YOU SURE YOU WON'T COME ALONG? IT WOULD BE NICE TO HAVE SOMEONE ALONG THAT WAS FAMILIAR WITH THE TERRITORY.
I CAN'T.
I CAN'T LEAVE ANGEL HERE BY HERSELF --I'M ALL THE FAMILY SHE HAS. IF SOMETHING HAPPENED TO ME-- I DON'T KNOW WHAT WOULD HAPPEN TO HER.
I CAN'T PUT HER THROUGH THAT AGAIN.
DON'T SWEAT IT, GORGEOUS-- KILL-CAT IS COMING ALONG TO MAKE SURE EVERYTHING GOES JUST FINE!
GHAA!
WHO LET YOU IN?
HE VOLUNTEERED, ROCK. WE NEEDED AS MANY ABLE-BODIED SUPERHEROES AS WE COULD GET OUR HANDS ON.
YOU'VE GOT TO BE KIDDING ME.
OKAY, BOYS AND GIRLS...
IT'S SHOWTIME...!
I DON'T KNOW WHAT KIND OF STORIES YOU'VE HEARD FROM KID AVENGER OR DART, BUT I CAN ASSURE YOU--
I'M A LEAN, MEAN, FIGHTIN' MACHINE!
YOU'RE NOT GOING TO REGRET TAKING ME ALONG--
ALTHOUGH BEAST BOY AND FEEZLE--
OKAY, OKAY.
JUST DON'T TOUCH ANYTHING.

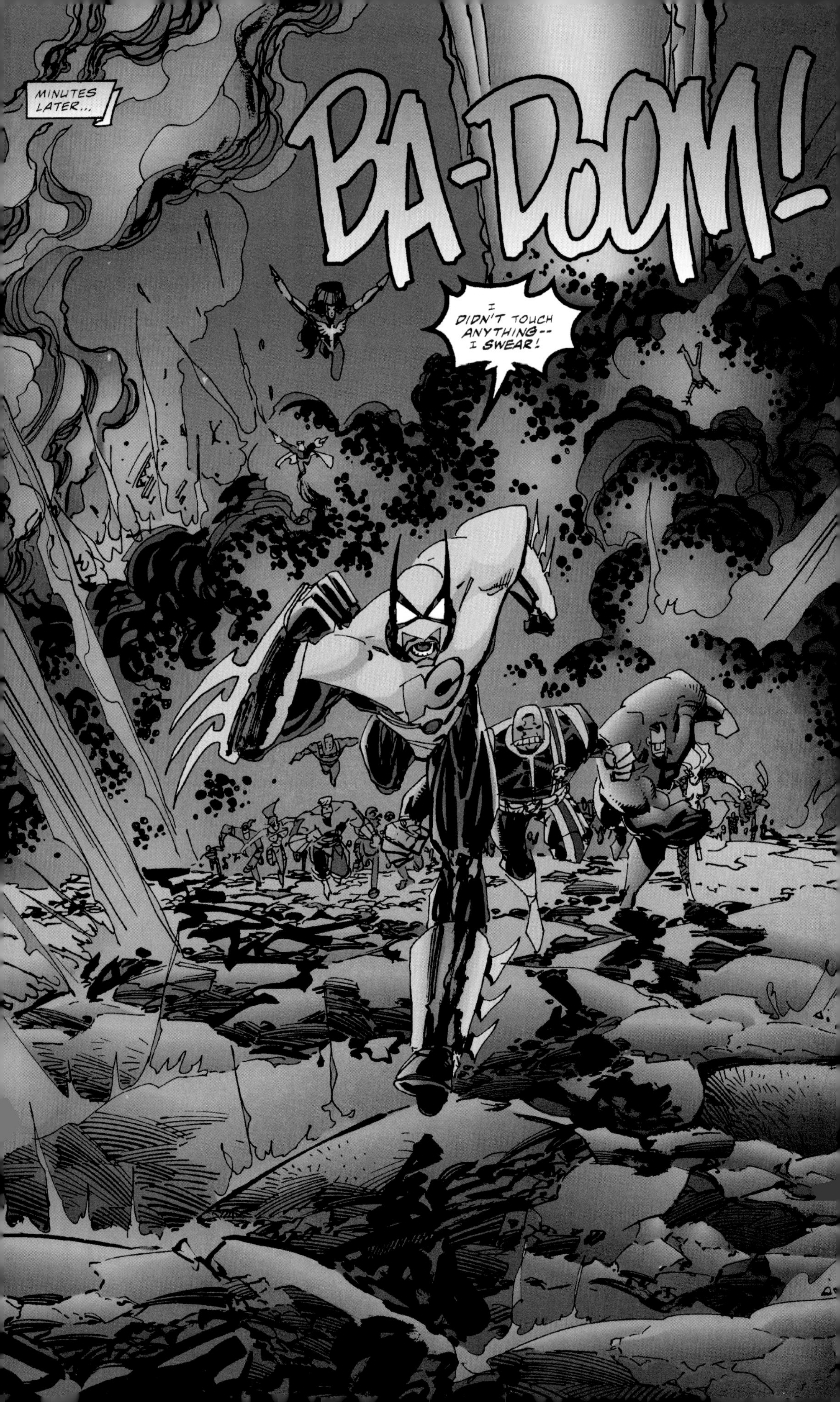

MINUTES LATER...
BA-DOOM!
I DIDN'T TOUCH ANYTHING-- I SWEAR!

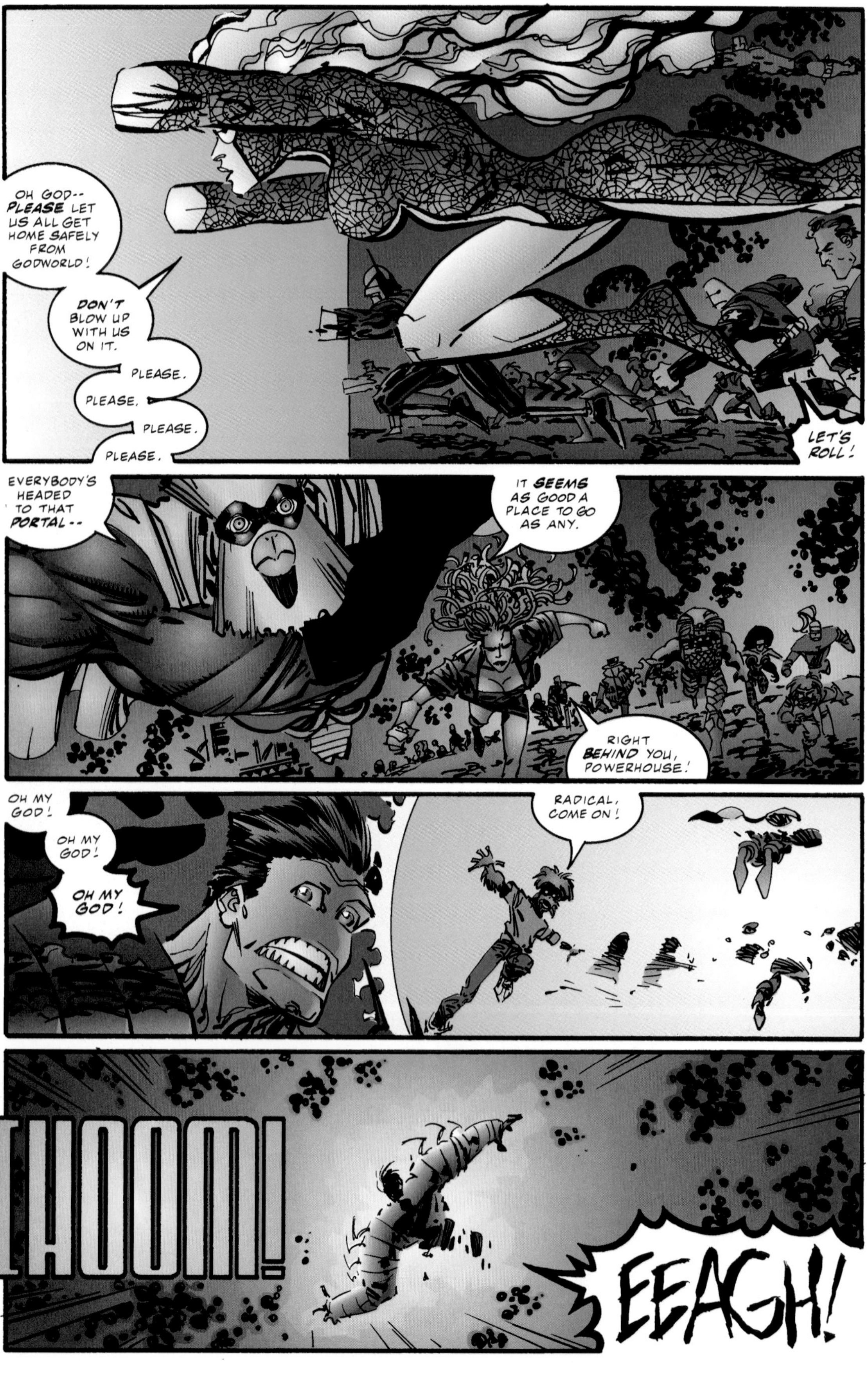

OH GOD-- PLEASE LET US ALL GET HOME SAFELY FROM GODWORLD!
DON'T BLOW UP WITH US ON IT.
PLEASE.
PLEASE.
PLEASE.
PLEASE.
LET'S ROLL!
EVERYBODY'S HEADED TO THAT PORTAL--
IT SEEMS AS GOOD A PLACE TO GO AS ANY.
RIGHT BEHIND YOU, POWERHOUSE!
OH MY GOD!
OH MY GOD!
OH MY GOD!
RADICAL, COME ON!
CHOOM!
EEAGH!

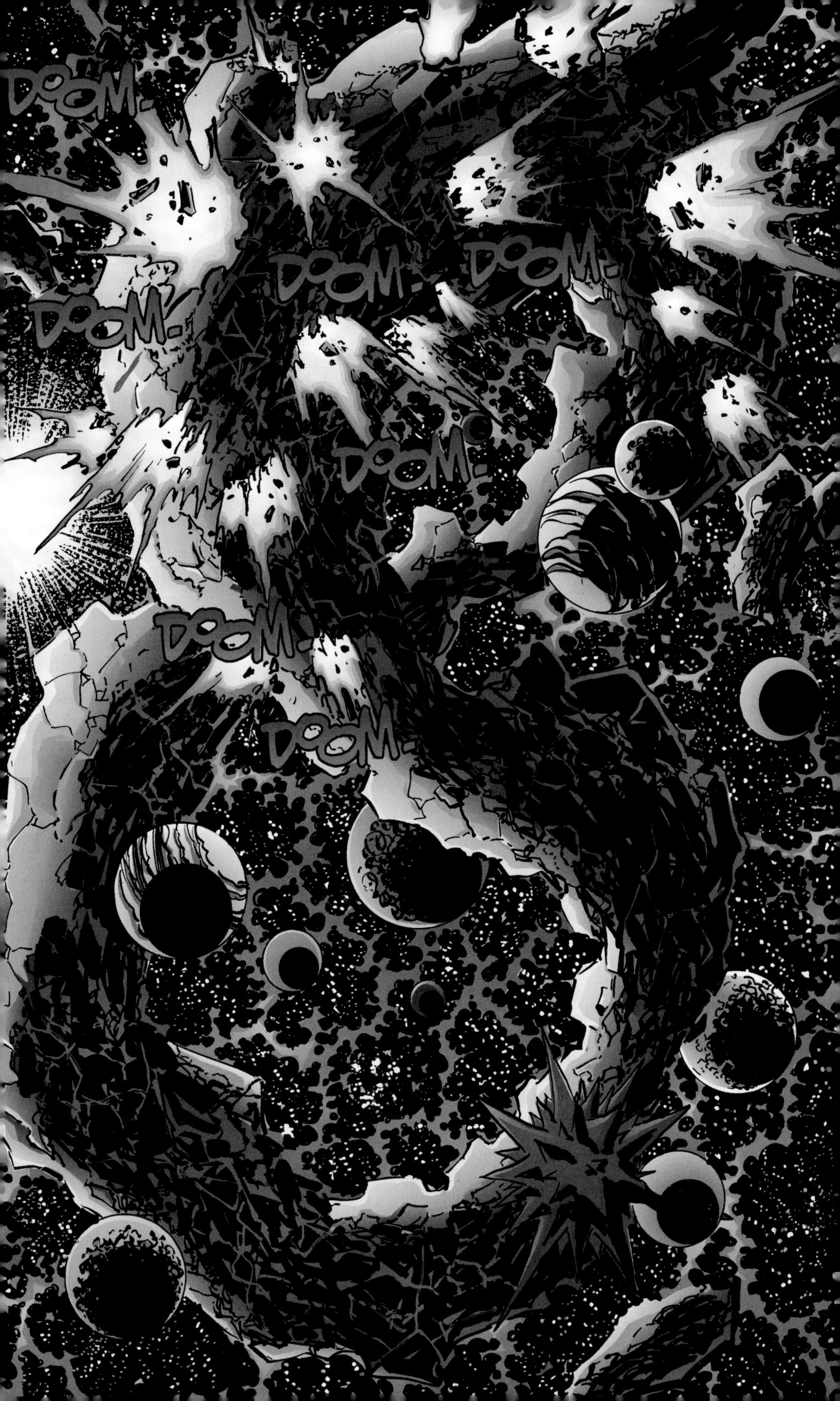
DOOM-
DOOM-
DOOM-
DOOM-
DOOM-
DOOM-
DOOM-
DOOM-

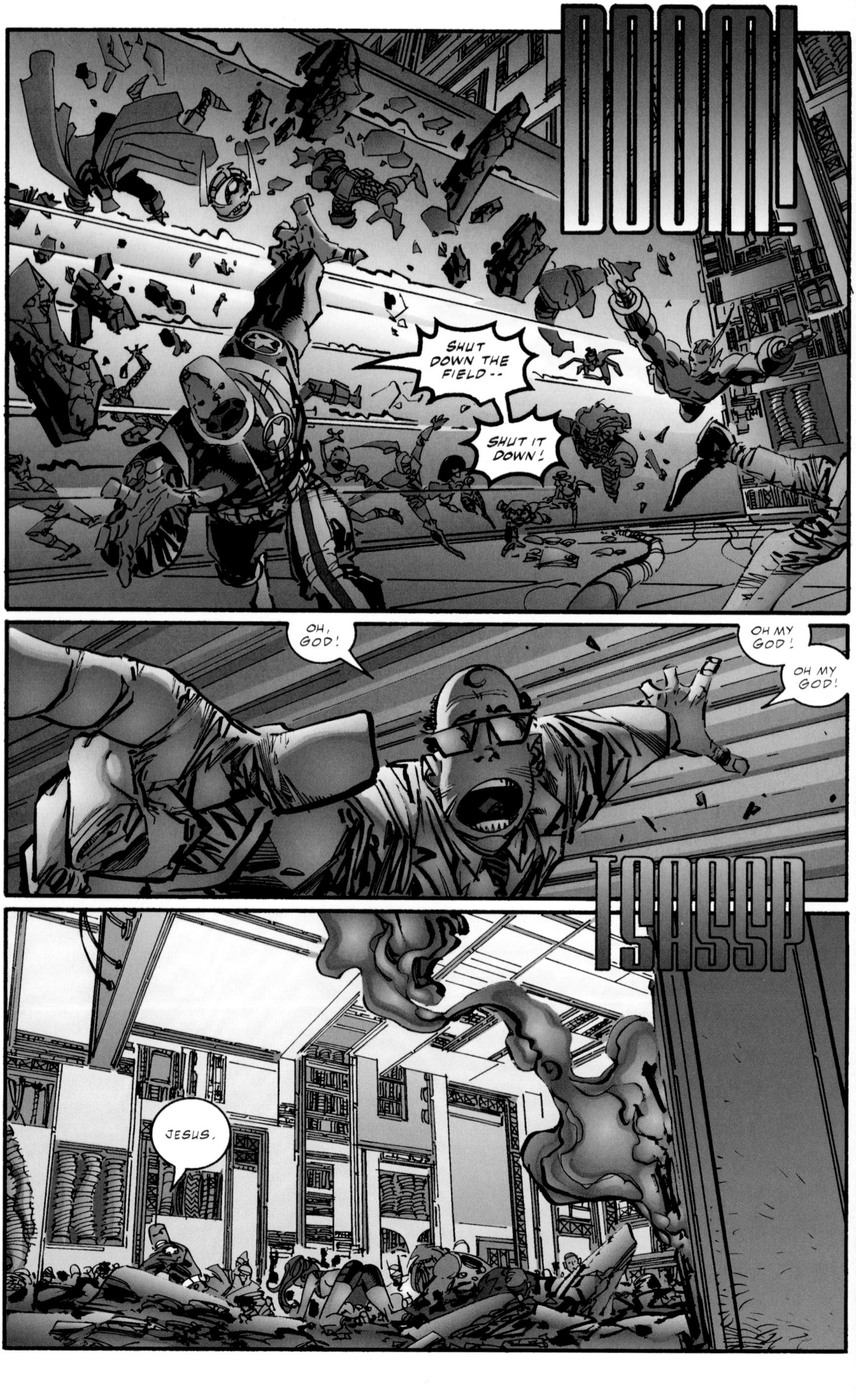
DOOM!
SHUT DOWN THE FIELD --
SHUT IT DOWN!
OH, GOD!
OH MY GOD!
OH MY GOD!
TSASSP
JESUS.

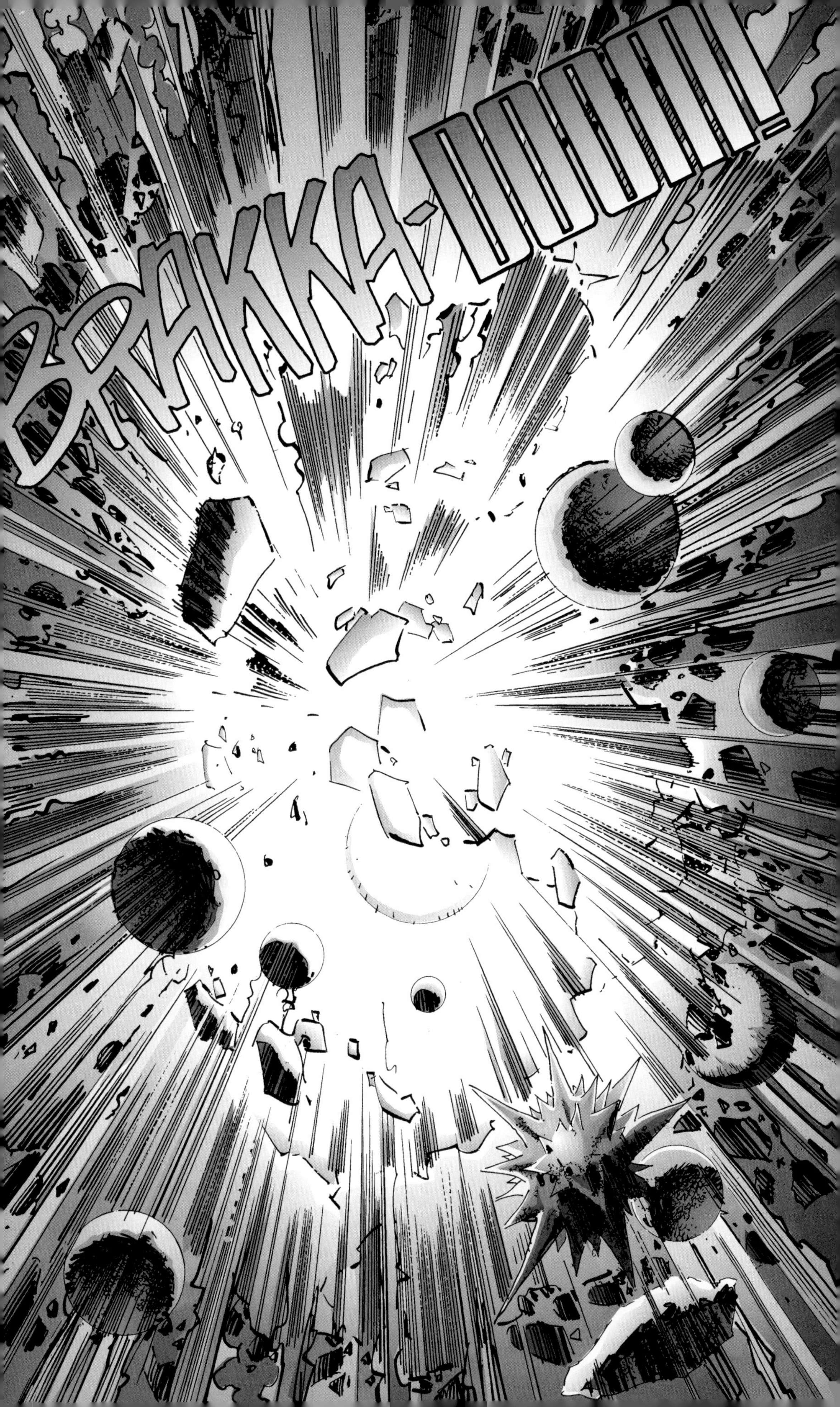
BRAKKA-DOOOM!

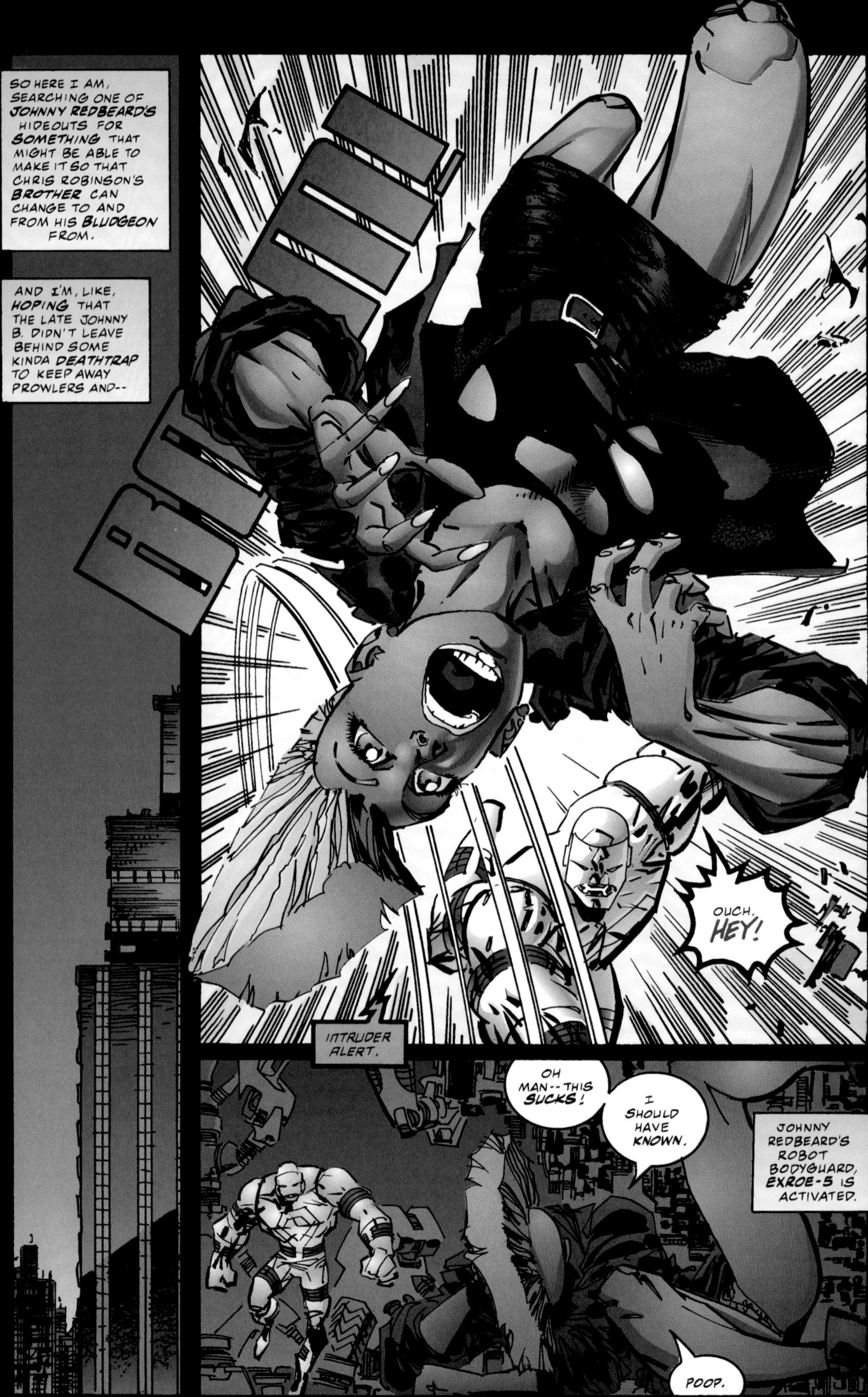

SO HERE I AM, SEARCHING ONE OF JOHNNY REDBEARD'S HIDEOUTS FOR SOMETHING THAT MIGHT BE ABLE TO MAKE IT SO THAT CHRIS ROBINSON'S BROTHER CAN CHANGE TO AND FROM HIS BLUDGEON FROM.
AND I'M, LIKE, HOPING THAT THE LATE JOHNNY B. DIDN'T LEAVE BEHIND SOME KINDA DEATHTRAP TO KEEP AWAY PROWLERS AND--
OUCH. HEY!
INTRUDER ALERT.
OH MAN--THIS SUCKS!
I SHOULD HAVE KNOWN.
JOHNNY REDBEARD'S ROBOT BODYGUARD, EXROE-5 IS ACTIVATED.
POOP.

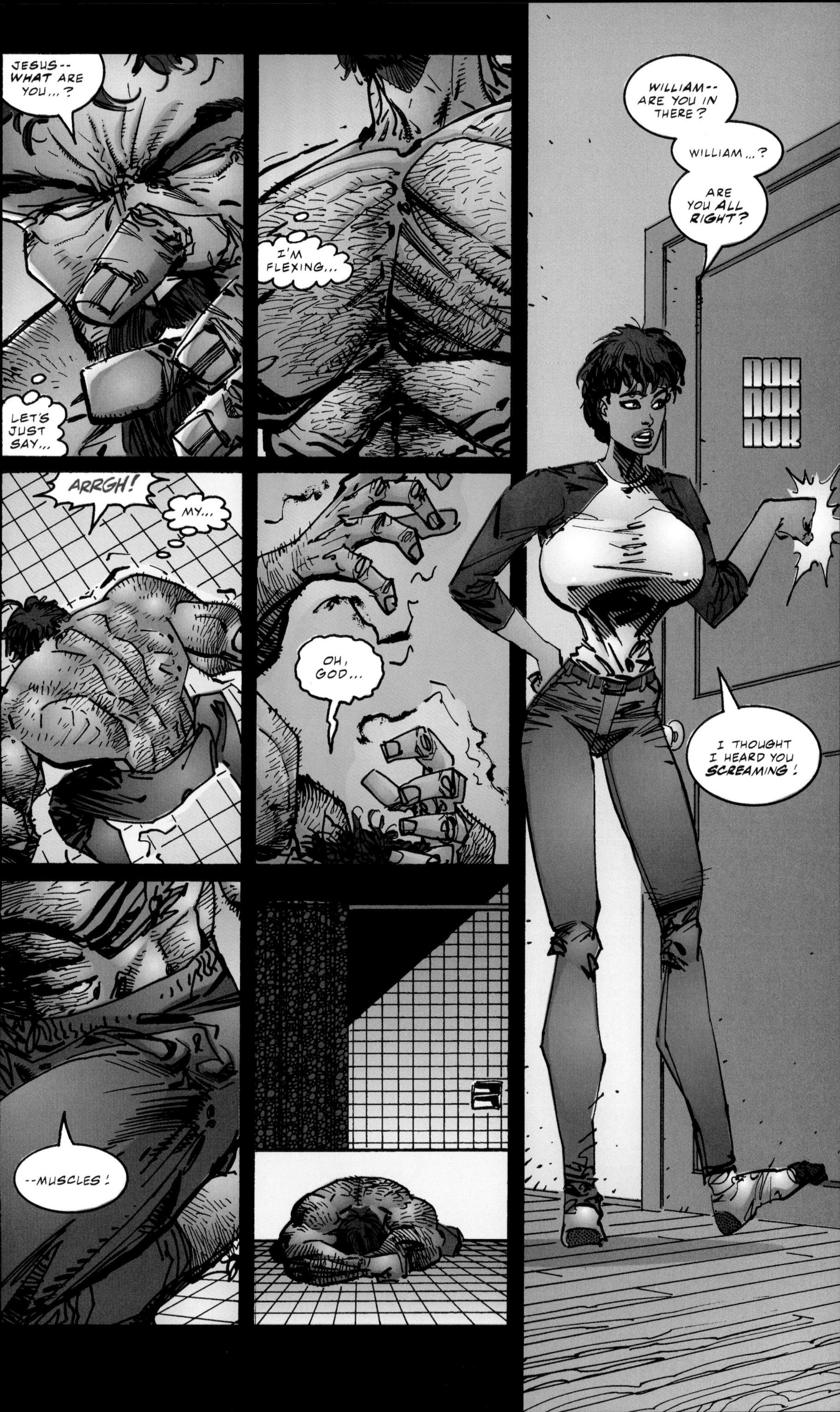
JESUS-- WHAT ARE YOU...?
LET'S JUST SAY...
I'M FLEXING...
WILLIAM-- ARE YOU IN THERE?
WILLIAM...?
ARE YOU ALL RIGHT?
NOK NOK NOK
ARRGH!
MY...
OH, GOD...
I THOUGHT I HEARD YOU SCREAMING!
--MUSCLES!

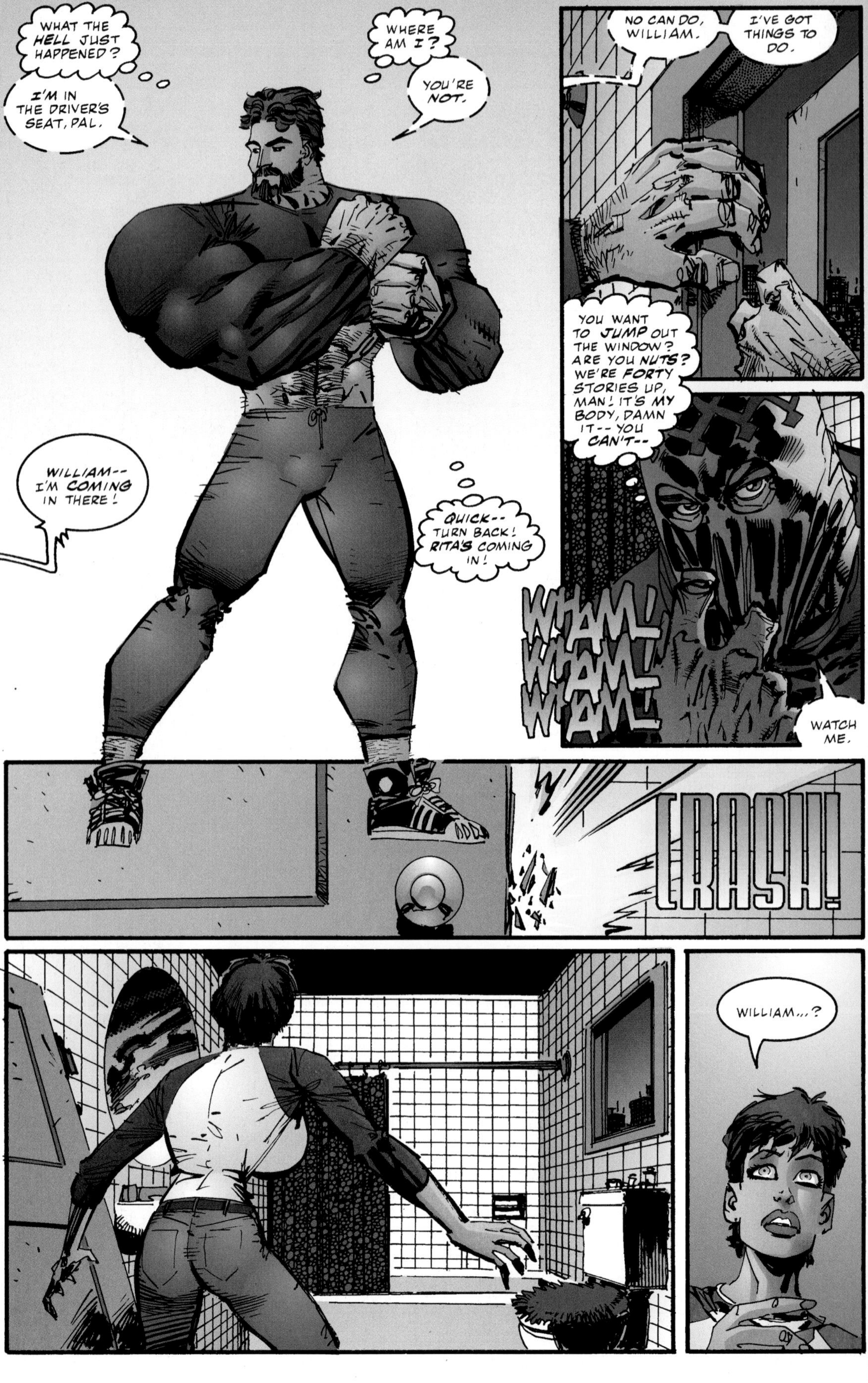
WHAT THE HELL JUST HAPPENED?
I'M IN THE DRIVER'S SEAT, PAL.
WHERE AM I?
YOU'RE NOT.
NO CAN DO, WILLIAM.
I'VE GOT THINGS TO DO.
YOU WANT TO JUMP OUT THE WINDOW? ARE YOU NUTS? WE'RE FORTY STORIES UP, MAN! IT'S MY BODY, DAMN IT-- YOU CAN'T--
WILLIAM-- I'M COMING IN THERE!
QUICK-- TURN BACK! RITA'S COMING IN!
WHAM! WHAM! WHAM!
WATCH ME.
CRASH!
WILLIAM...?

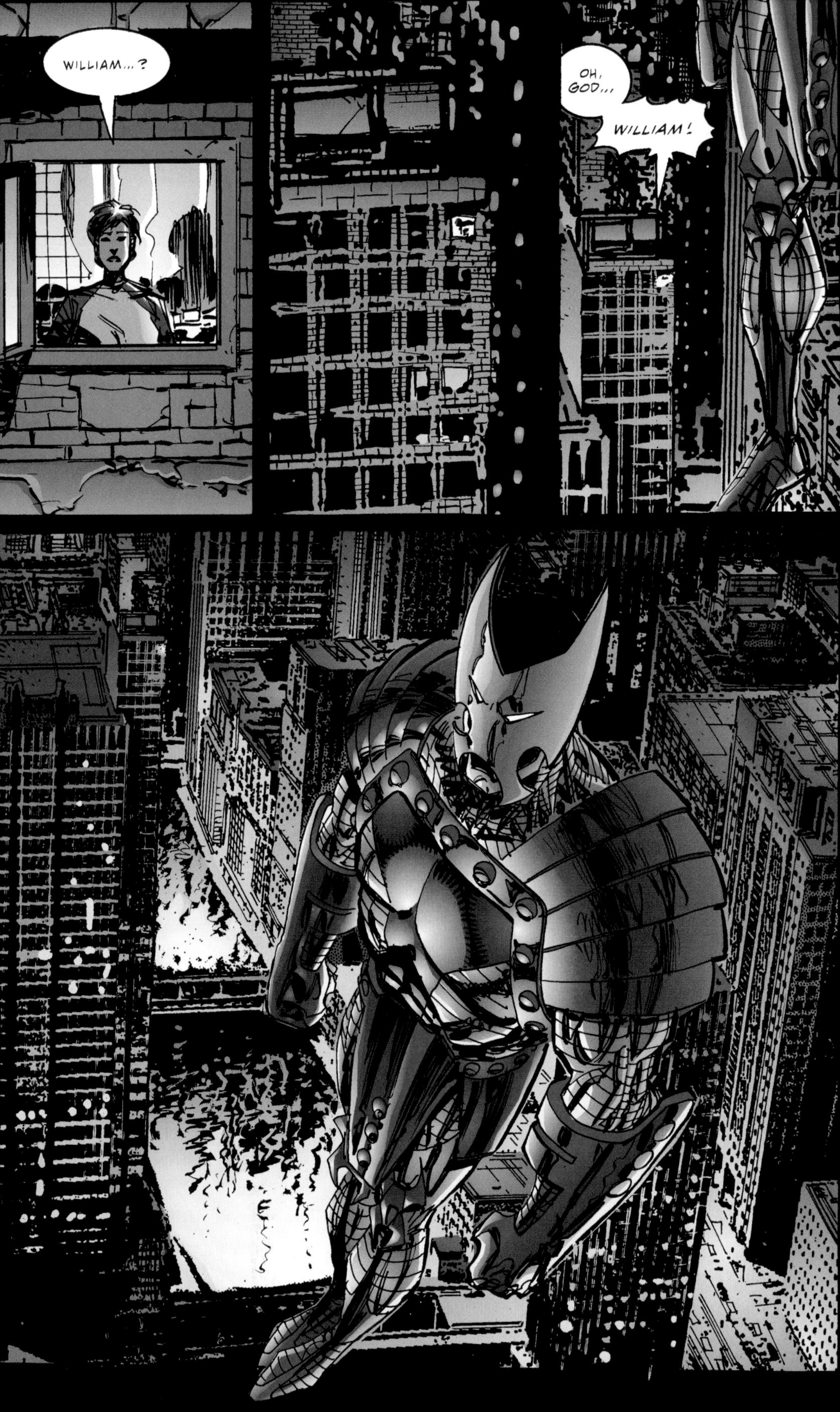
WILLIAM...?
OH, GOD...
WILLIAM!

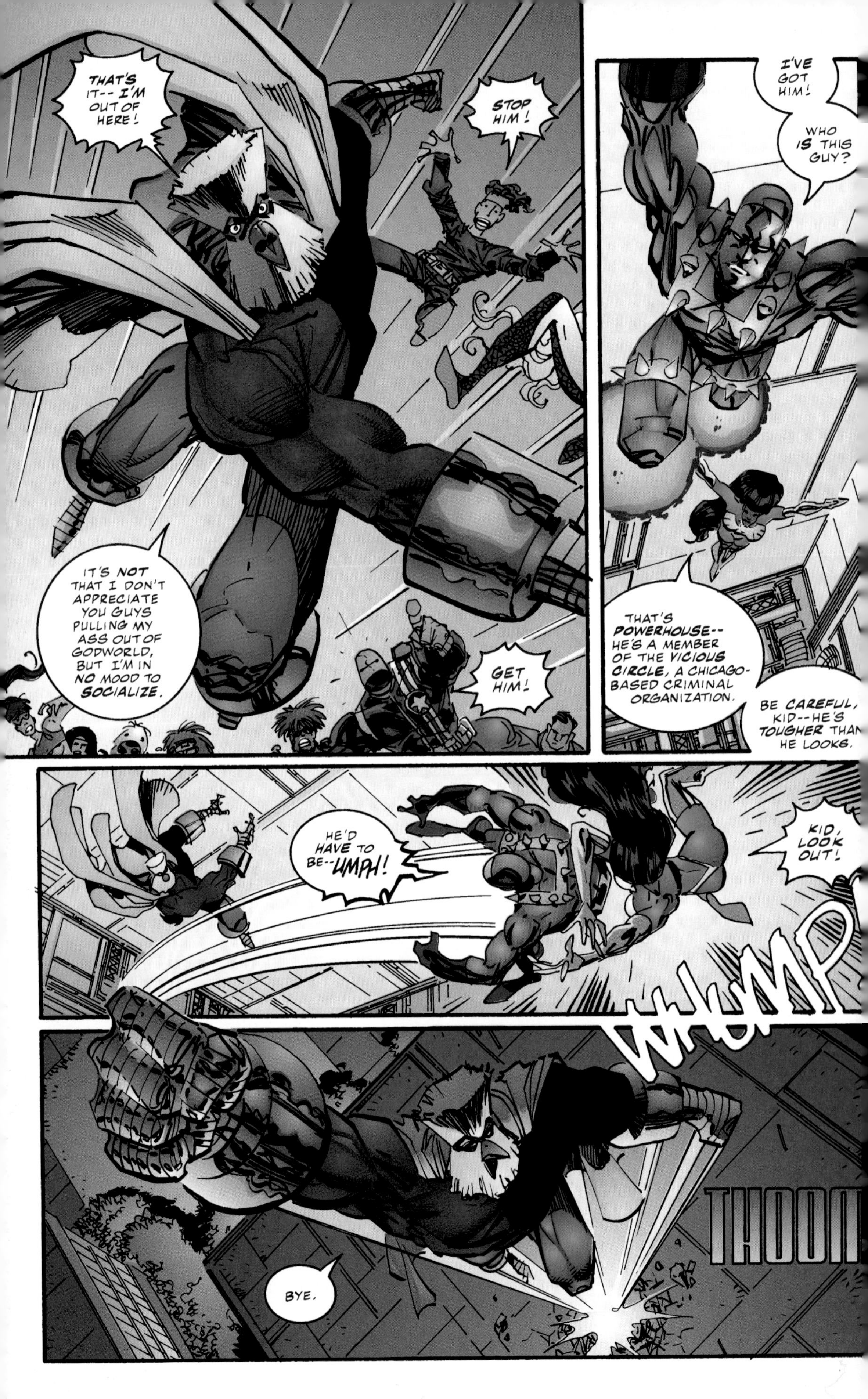
THAT'S IT-- I'M OUT OF HERE!
STOP HIM!
IT'S NOT THAT I DON'T APPRECIATE YOU GUYS PULLING MY ASS OUT OF GODWORLD, BUT I'M IN NO MOOD TO SOCIALIZE.
GET HIM!
I'VE GOT HIM!
WHO IS THIS GUY?
THAT'S POWERHOUSE-- HE'S A MEMBER OF THE VICIOUS CIRCLE, A CHICAGO-BASED CRIMINAL ORGANIZATION.
BE CAREFUL, KID--HE'S TOUGHER THAN HE LOOKS.
HE'D HAVE TO BE--UMPH!
KID, LOOK OUT!
WHUMP
THOOM
BYE.

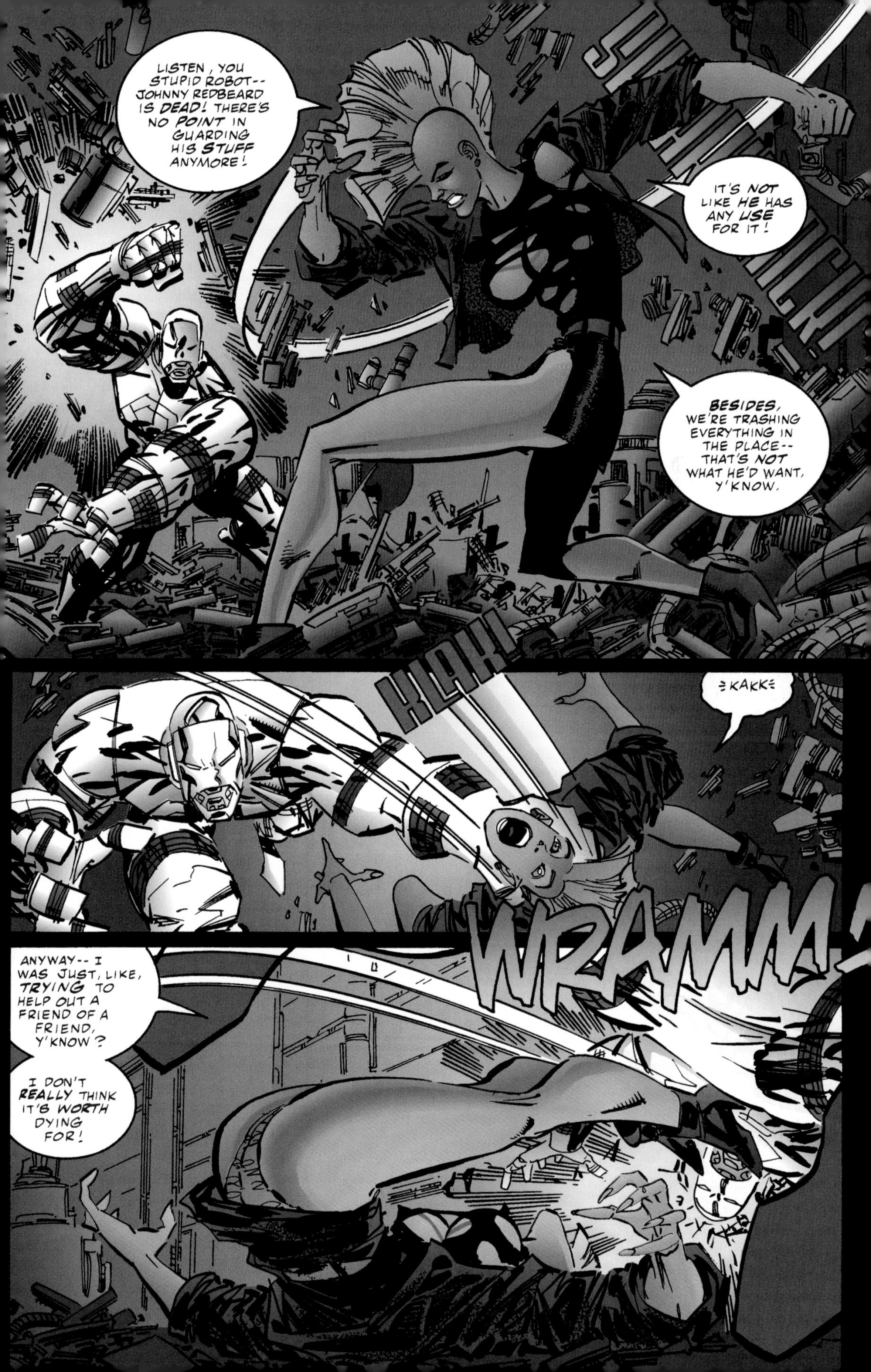
LISTEN, YOU STUPID ROBOT-- JOHNNY REDBEARD IS DEAD! THERE'S NO POINT IN GUARDING HIS STUFF ANYMORE!
IT'S NOT LIKE HE HAS ANY USE FOR IT!
BESIDES, WE'RE TRASHING EVERYTHING IN THE PLACE-- THAT'S NOT WHAT HE'D WANT, Y'KNOW.
KLAK
KAKK
WRAMM
ANYWAY-- I WAS JUST, LIKE, TRYING TO HELP OUT A FRIEND OF A FRIEND, Y'KNOW?
I DON'T REALLY THINK IT'S WORTH DYING FOR!

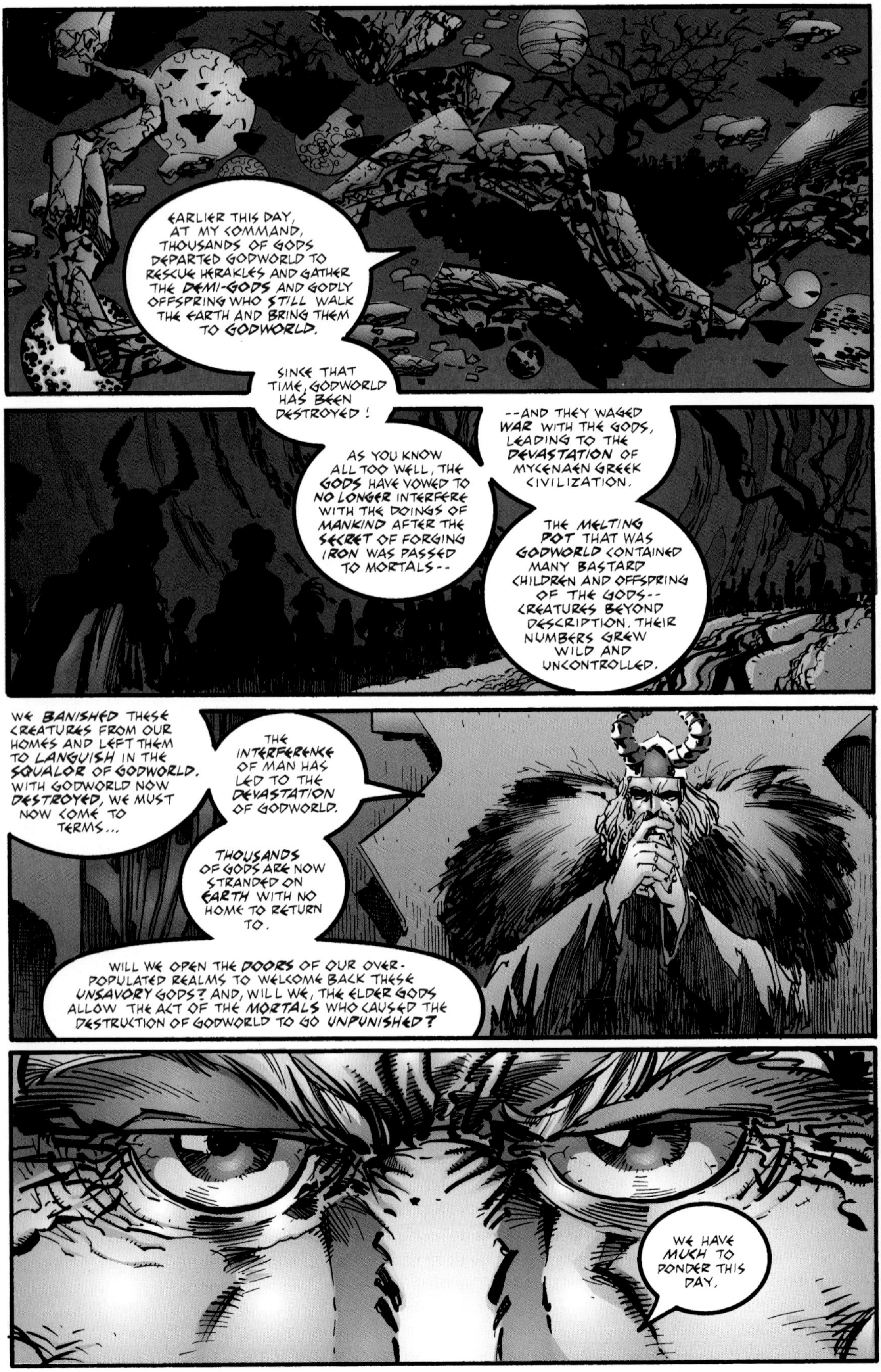
EARLIER THIS DAY, AT MY COMMAND, THOUSANDS OF GODS DEPARTED GODWORLD TO RESCUE HERAKLES AND GATHER THE DEMI-GODS AND GODLY OFFSPRING WHO STILL WALK THE EARTH AND BRING THEM TO GODWORLD.
SINCE THAT TIME, GODWORLD HAS BEEN DESTROYED!
AS YOU KNOW ALL TOO WELL, THE GODS HAVE VOWED TO NO LONGER INTERFERE WITH THE DOINGS OF MANKIND AFTER THE SECRET OF FORGING IRON WAS PASSED TO MORTALS--
--AND THEY WAGED WAR WITH THE GODS, LEADING TO THE DEVASTATION OF MYCENAEN GREEK CIVILIZATION.
THE MELTING POT THAT WAS GODWORLD CONTAINED MANY BASTARD CHILDREN AND OFFSPRING OF THE GODS-- CREATURES BEYOND DESCRIPTION. THEIR NUMBERS GREW WILD AND UNCONTROLLED.
WE BANISHED THESE CREATURES FROM OUR HOMES AND LEFT THEM TO LANGUISH IN THE SQUALOR OF GODWORLD. WITH GODWORLD NOW DESTROYED, WE MUST NOW COME TO TERMS...
THE INTERFERENCE OF MAN HAS LED TO THE DEVASTATION OF GODWORLD.
THOUSANDS OF GODS ARE NOW STRANDED ON EARTH WITH NO HOME TO RETURN TO.
WILL WE OPEN THE DOORS OF OUR OVER-POPULATED REALMS TO WELCOME BACK THESE UNSAVORY GODS? AND, WILL WE, THE ELDER GODS ALLOW THE ACT OF THE MORTALS WHO CAUSED THE DESTRUCTION OF GODWORLD TO GO UNPUNISHED?
WE HAVE MUCH TO PONDER THIS DAY.

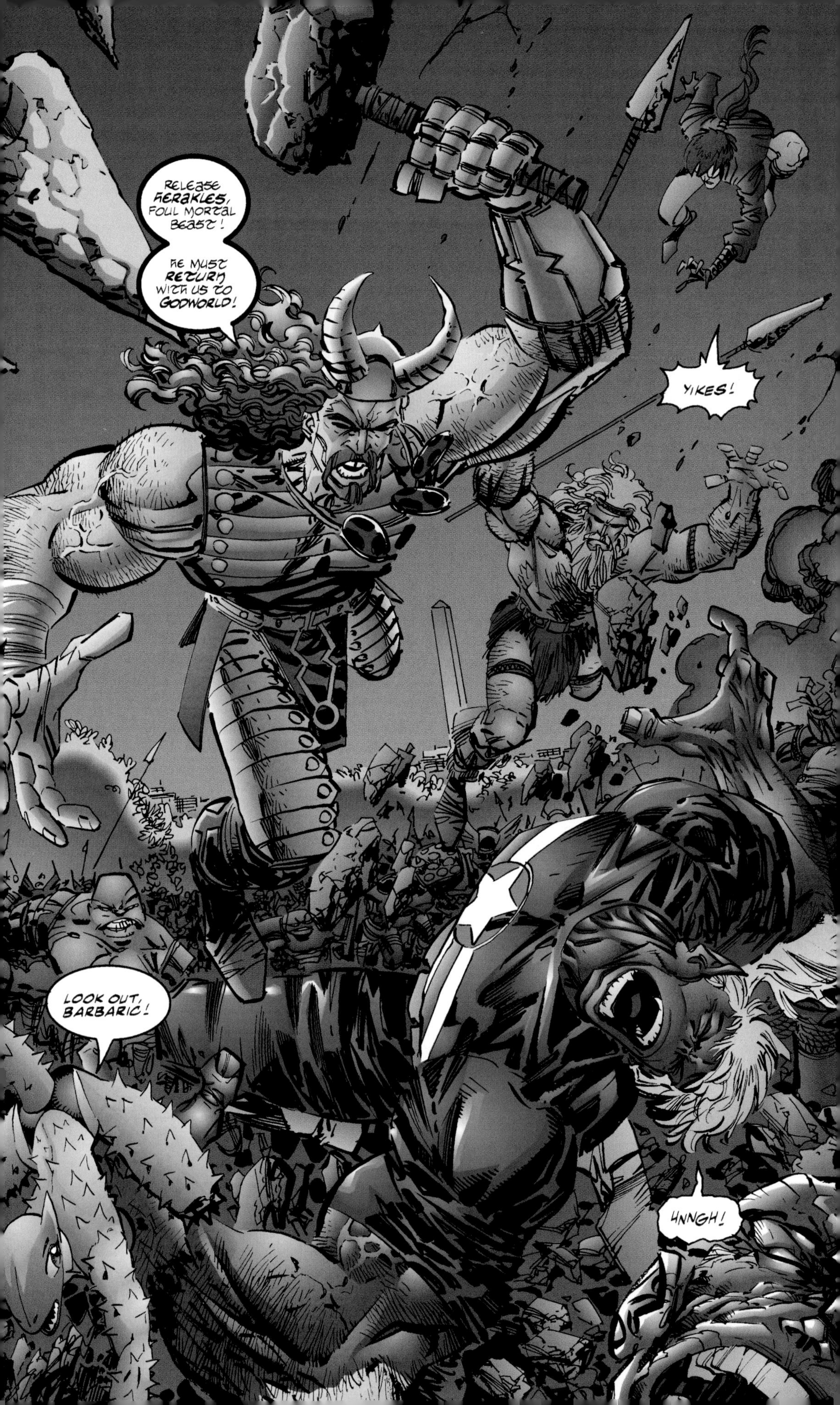
RELEASE HERAKLES, FOUL MORTAL BEAST!
HE MUST RETURN WITH US TO GODWORLD!
YIKES!
LOOK OUT, BARBARIC!
UNNGH!

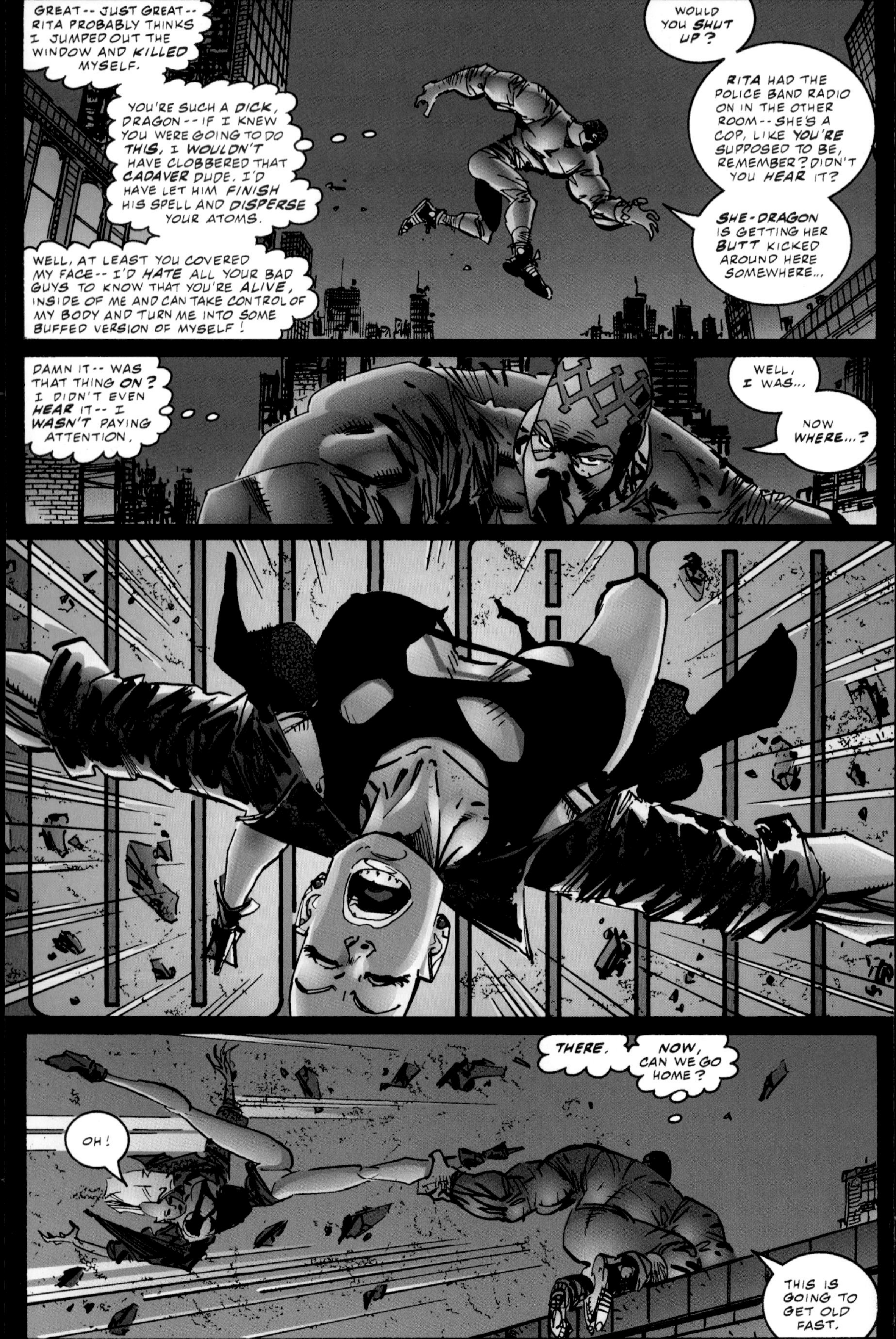
GREAT-- JUST GREAT-- RITA PROBABLY THINKS I JUMPED OUT THE WINDOW AND KILLED MYSELF.
YOU'RE SUCH A DICK, DRAGON-- IF I KNEW YOU WERE GOING TO DO THIS, I WOULDN'T HAVE CLOBBERED THAT CADAVER DUDE. I'D HAVE LET HIM FINISH HIS SPELL AND DISPERSE YOUR ATOMS.
WELL, AT LEAST YOU COVERED MY FACE-- I'D HATE ALL YOUR BAD GUYS TO KNOW THAT YOU'RE ALIVE, INSIDE OF ME AND CAN TAKE CONTROL OF MY BODY AND TURN ME INTO SOME BUFFED VERSION OF MYSELF!
WOULD YOU SHUT UP?
RITA HAD THE POLICE BAND RADIO ON IN THE OTHER ROOM-- SHE'S A COP, LIKE YOU'RE SUPPOSED TO BE, REMEMBER? DIDN'T YOU HEAR IT?
SHE-DRAGON IS GETTING HER BUTT KICKED AROUND HERE SOMEWHERE...
DAMN IT-- WAS THAT THING ON? I DIDN'T EVEN HEAR IT-- I WASN'T PAYING ATTENTION.
WELL, I WAS...
NOW WHERE...?
THERE.
NOW, CAN WE GO HOME?
OH!
THIS IS GOING TO GET OLD FAST.

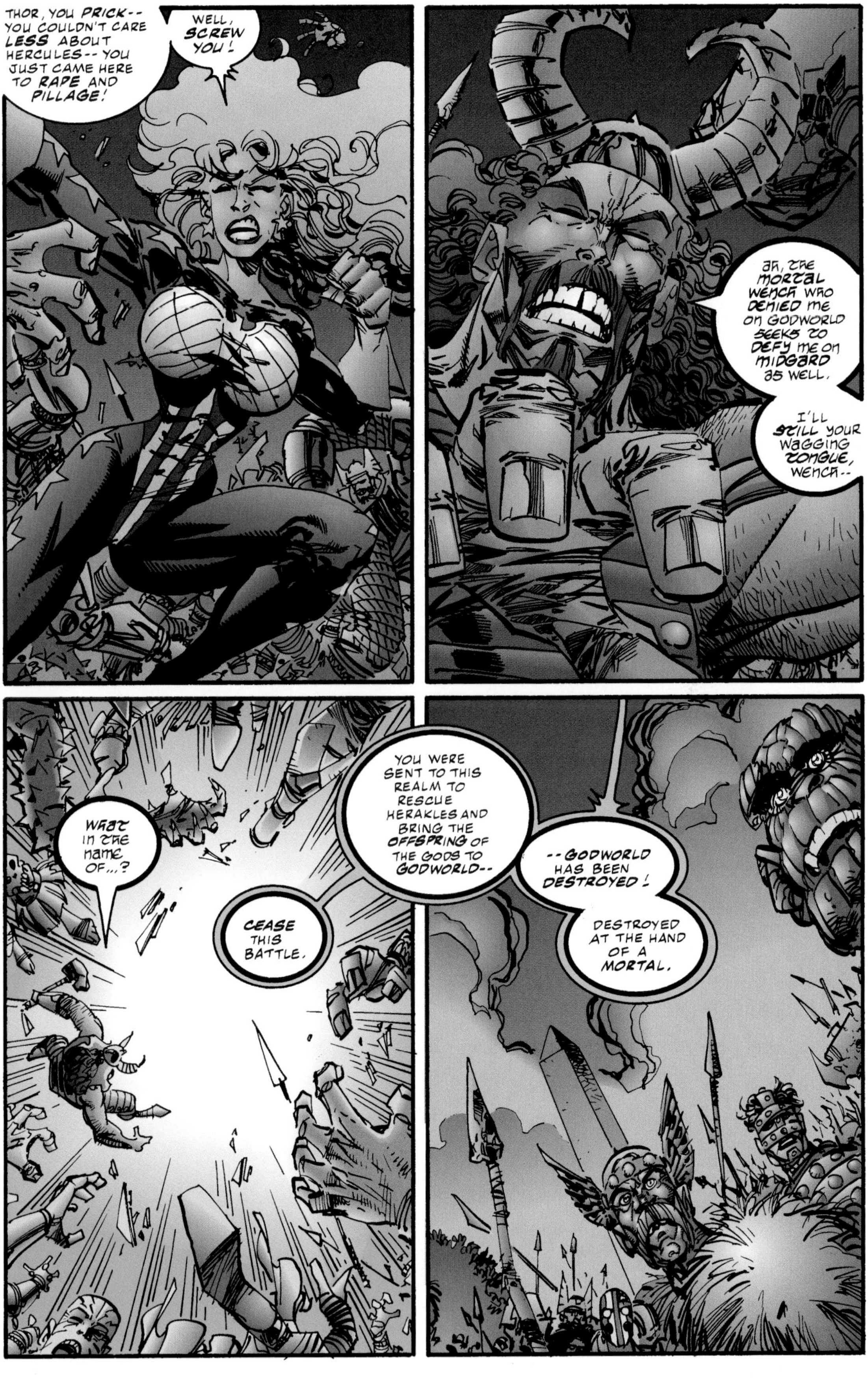
THOR, YOU PRICK-- YOU COULDN'T CARE LESS ABOUT HERCULES-- YOU JUST CAME HERE TO RAPE AND PILLAGE!
WELL, SCREW YOU!
AH, THE MORTAL WENCH WHO DENIED ME ON GODWORLD SEEKS TO DEFY ME ON MIDGARD AS WELL.
I'LL STILL YOUR WAGGING TONGUE, WENCH--
WHAT IN THE NAME OF...?
CEASE THIS BATTLE.
YOU WERE SENT TO THIS REALM TO RESCUE HERAKLES AND BRING THE OFFSPRING OF THE GODS TO GODWORLD--
--GODWORLD HAS BEEN DESTROYED!
DESTROYED AT THE HAND OF A MORTAL.

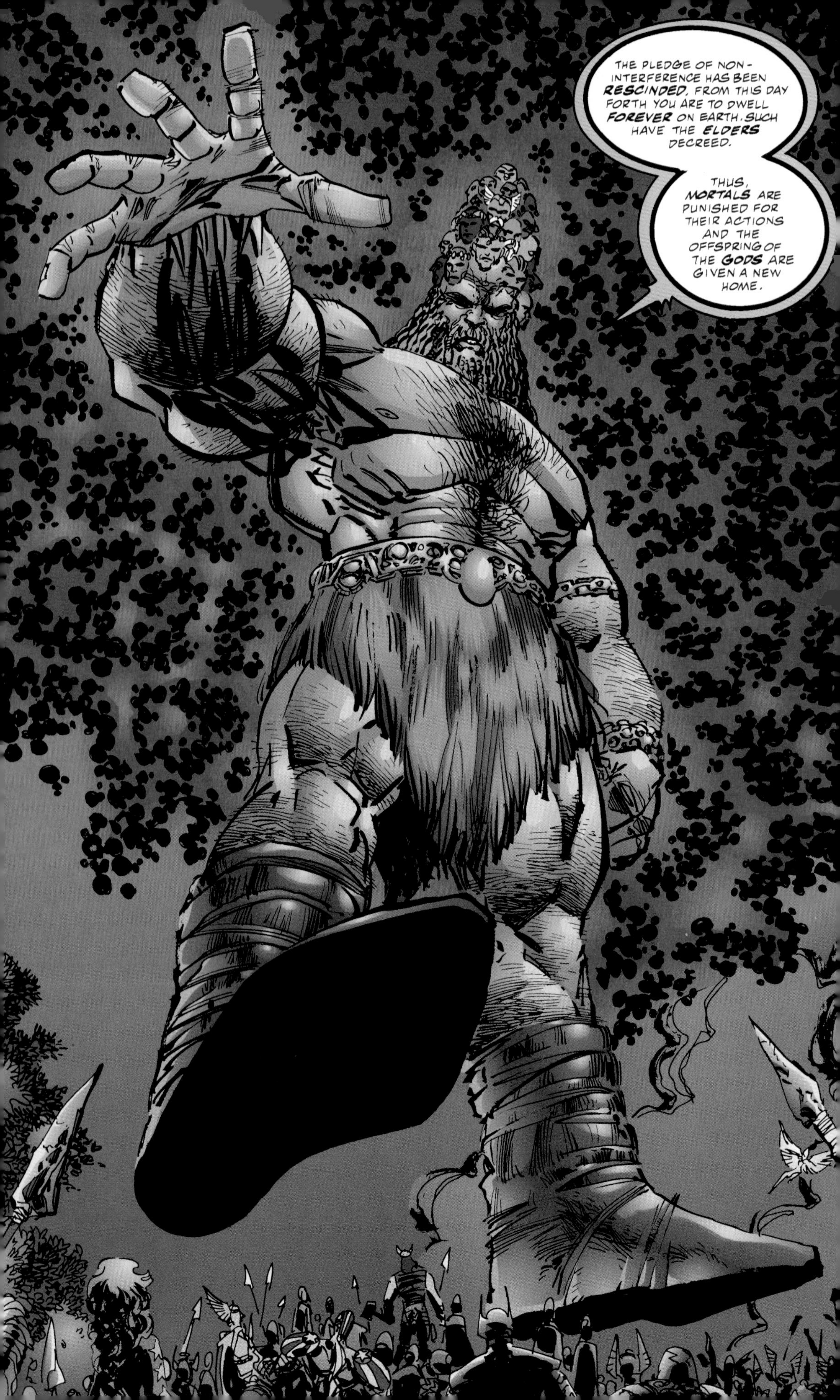
THE PLEDGE OF NON-INTERFERENCE HAS BEEN RESCINDED. FROM THIS DAY FORTH YOU ARE TO DWELL FOREVER ON EARTH. SUCH HAVE THE ELDERS DECREED.
THUS, MORTALS ARE PUNISHED FOR THEIR ACTIONS AND THE OFFSPRING OF THE GODS ARE GIVEN A NEW HOME.

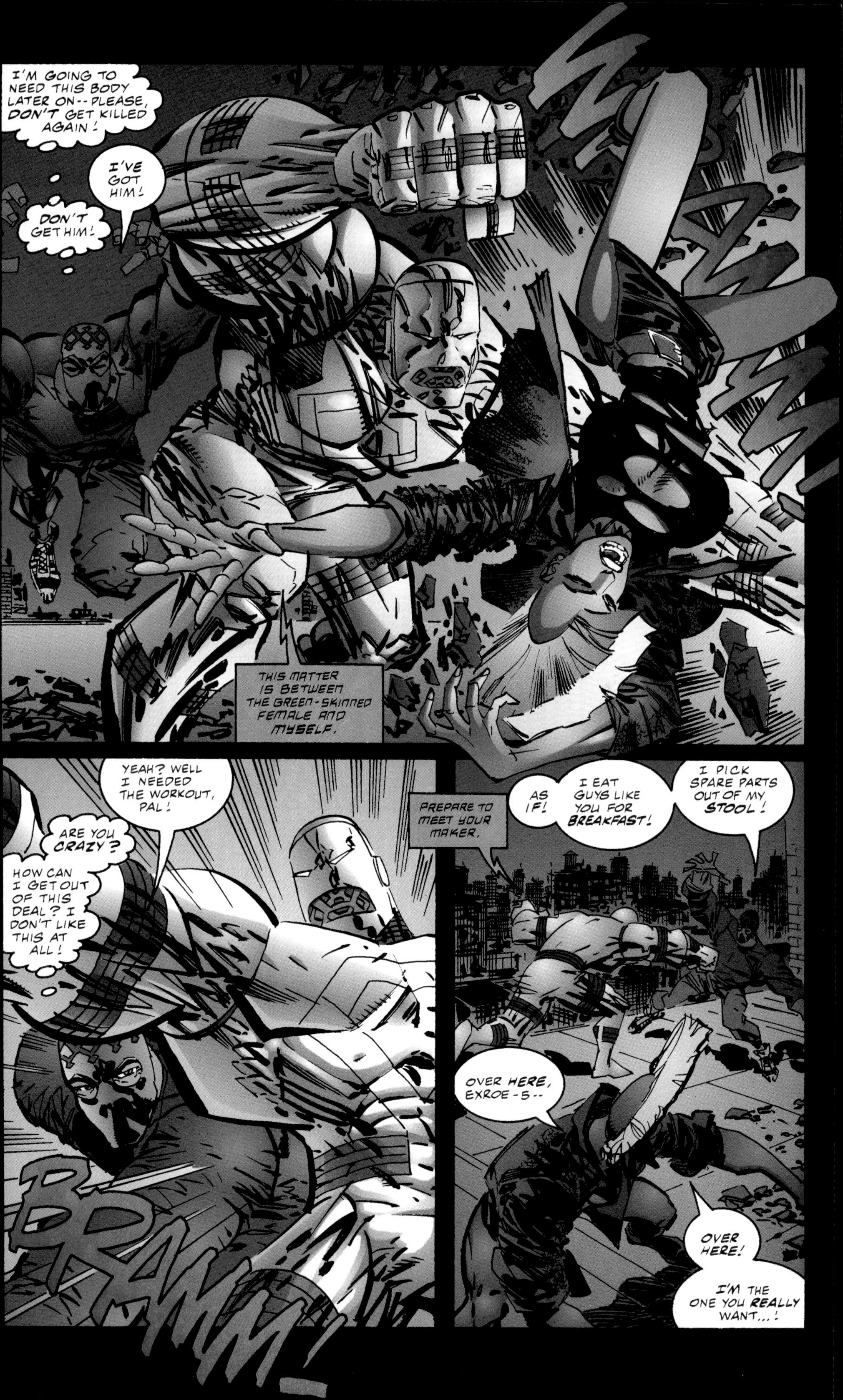
I'M GOING TO NEED THIS BODY LATER ON--PLEASE, DON'T GET KILLED AGAIN!
I'VE GOT HIM!
DON'T GET HIM!
THIS MATTER IS BETWEEN THE GREEN-SKINNED FEMALE AND MYSELF.
YEAH? WELL I NEEDED THE WORKOUT, PAL!
ARE YOU CRAZY?
HOW CAN I GET OUT OF THIS DEAL? I DON'T LIKE THIS AT ALL!
PREPARE TO MEET YOUR MAKER.
AS IF!
I EAT GUYS LIKE YOU FOR BREAKFAST!
I PICK SPARE PARTS OUT OF MY STOOL!
OVER HERE, EXROE-5--
OVER HERE!
I'M THE ONE YOU REALLY WANT...!

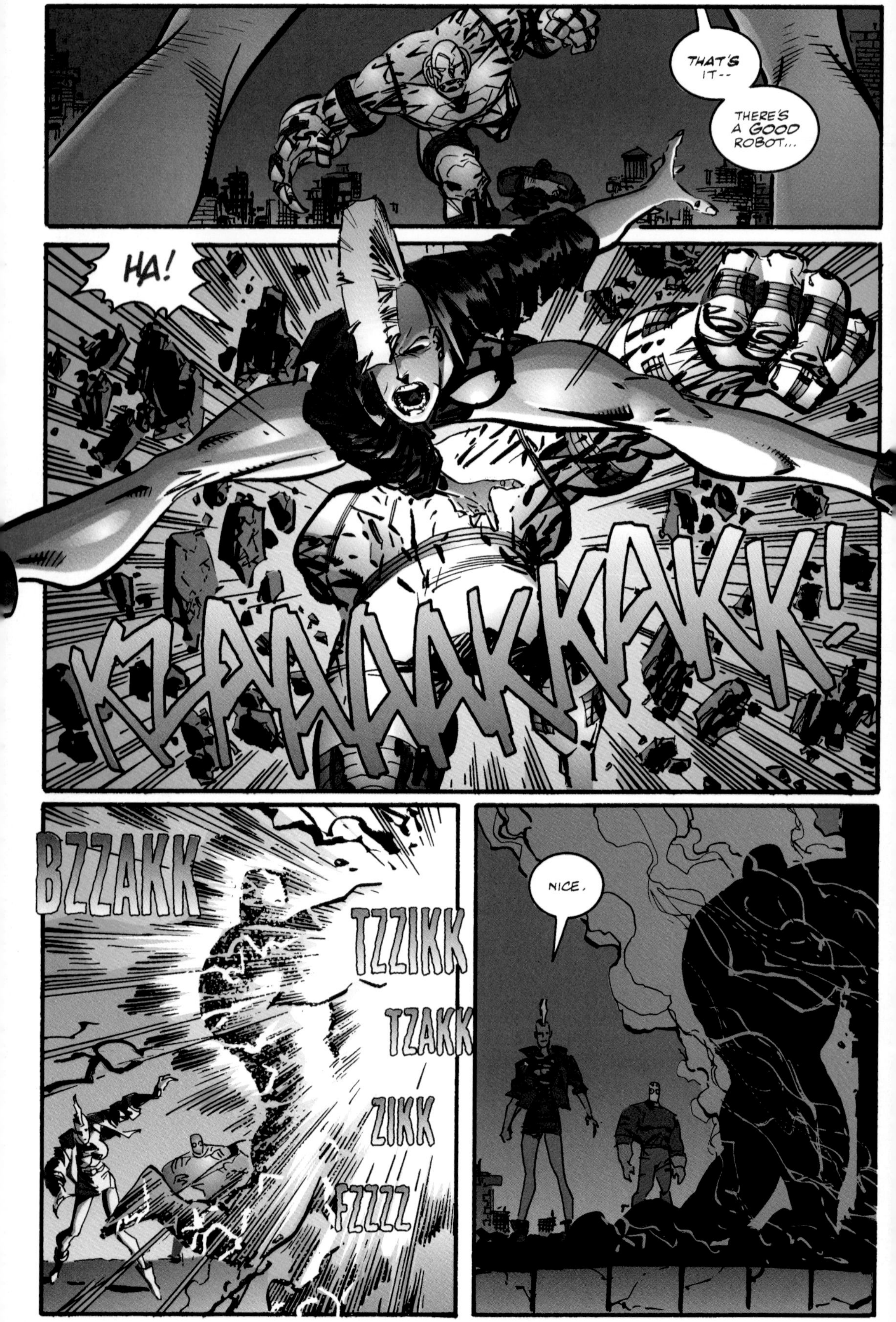

THAT'S IT--
THERE'S A GOOD ROBOT...
HA!
KRAAAAKKAKK!
BZZAKK
TZZIKK
TZAKK
ZIKK
FZZZZ
NICE.

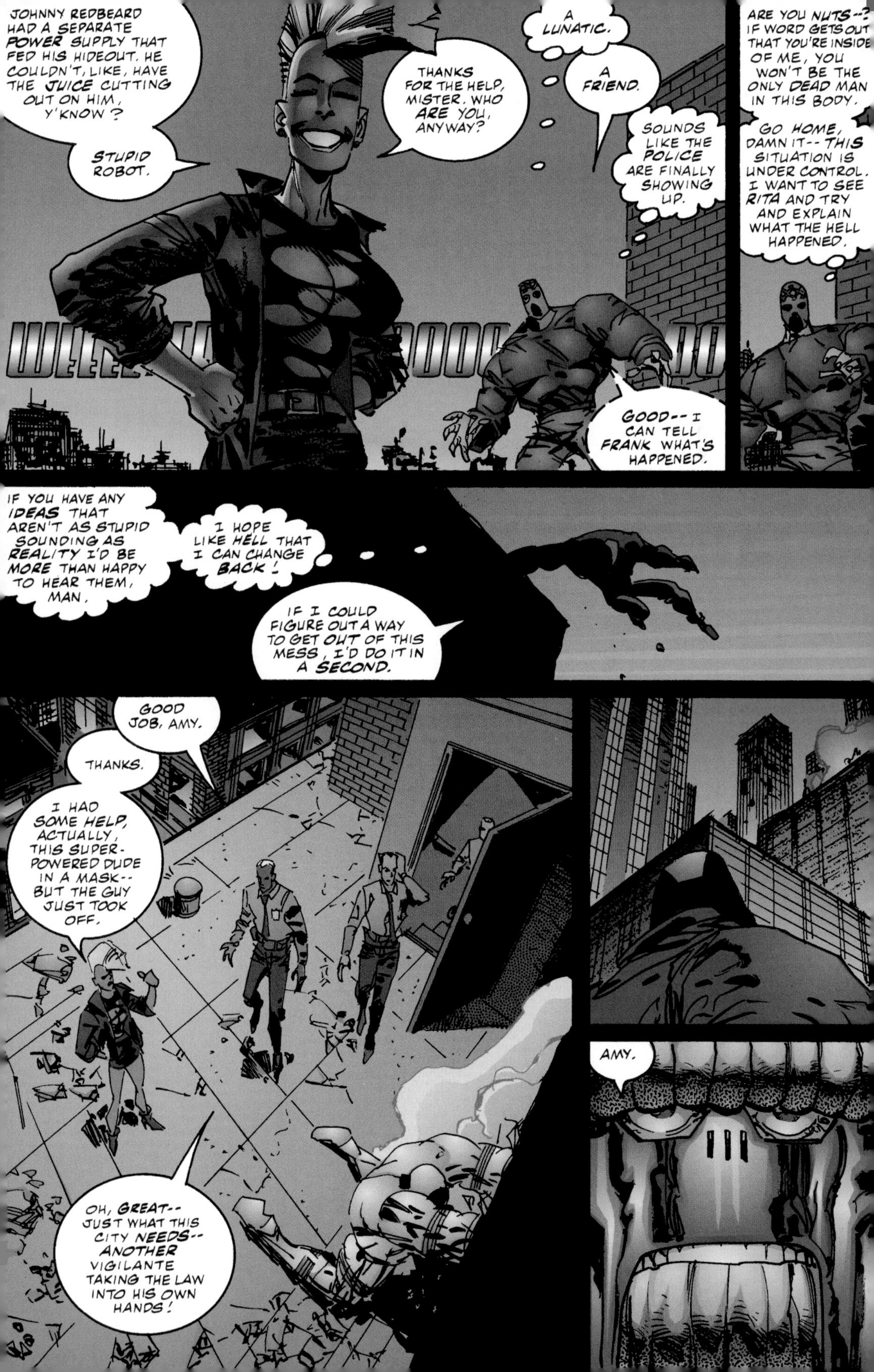
JOHNNY REDBEARD HAD A SEPARATE POWER SUPPLY THAT FED HIS HIDEOUT. HE COULDN'T, LIKE, HAVE THE JUICE CUTTING OUT ON HIM, Y'KNOW?
STUPID ROBOT.
THANKS FOR THE HELP, MISTER. WHO ARE YOU, ANYWAY?
A LUNATIC.
A FRIEND.
SOUNDS LIKE THE POLICE ARE FINALLY SHOWING UP.
GOOD-- I CAN TELL FRANK WHAT'S HAPPENED.
ARE YOU NUTS--? IF WORD GETS OUT THAT YOU'RE INSIDE OF ME, YOU WON'T BE THE ONLY DEAD MAN IN THIS BODY.
GO HOME, DAMN IT-- THIS SITUATION IS UNDER CONTROL. I WANT TO SEE RITA AND TRY AND EXPLAIN WHAT THE HELL HAPPENED.
IF YOU HAVE ANY IDEAS THAT AREN'T AS STUPID SOUNDING AS REALITY I'D BE MORE THAN HAPPY TO HEAR THEM, MAN.
I HOPE LIKE HELL THAT I CAN CHANGE BACK!
IF I COULD FIGURE OUT A WAY TO GET OUT OF THIS MESS, I'D DO IT IN A SECOND.
GOOD JOB, AMY.
THANKS.
I HAD SOME HELP, ACTUALLY, THIS SUPER-POWERED DUDE IN A MASK-- BUT THE GUY JUST TOOK OFF.
OH, GREAT-- JUST WHAT THIS CITY NEEDS-- ANOTHER VIGILANTE TAKING THE LAW INTO HIS OWN HANDS!
AMY.

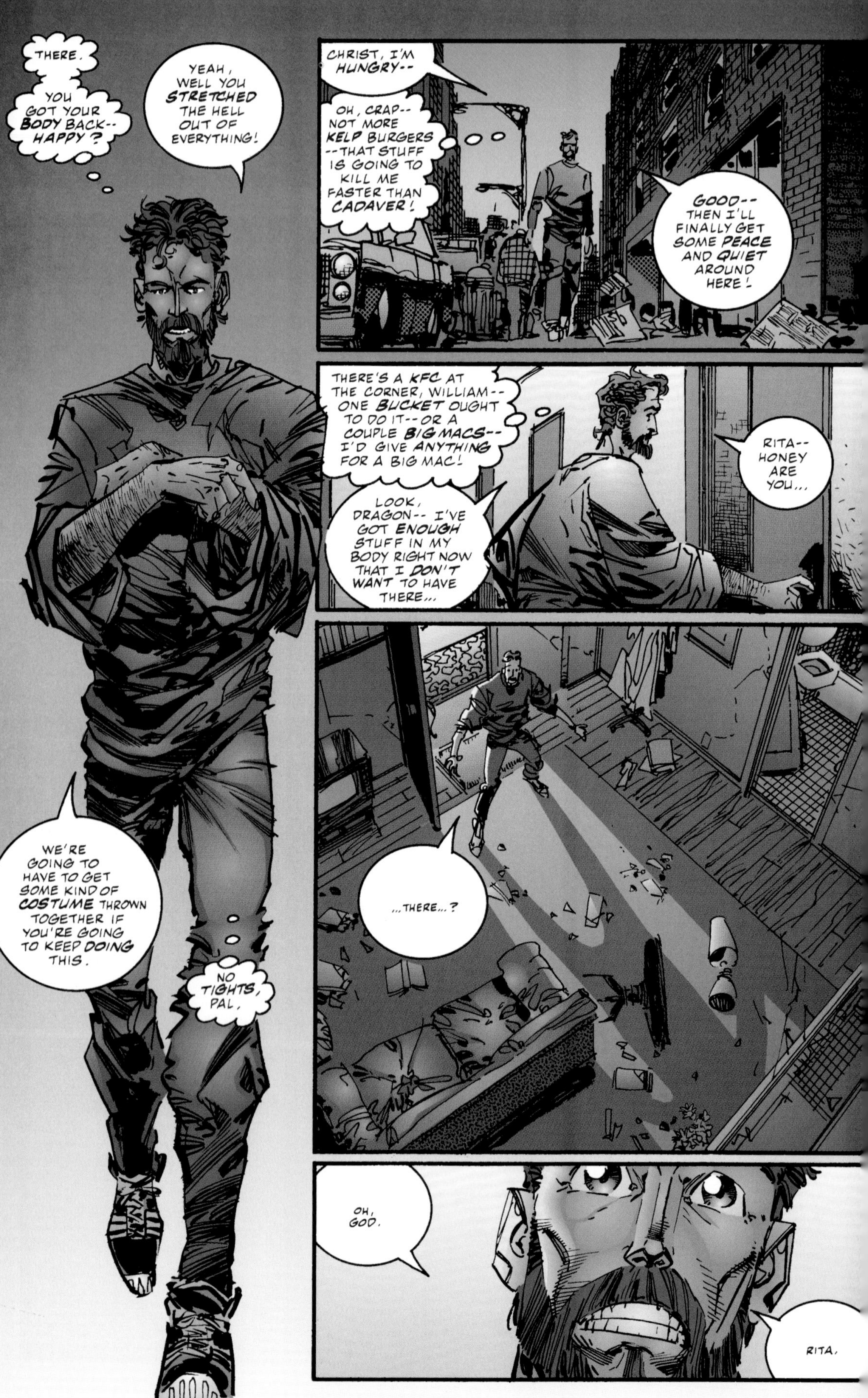
THERE.
YOU GOT YOUR BODY BACK-- HAPPY?
YEAH, WELL YOU STRETCHED THE HELL OUT OF EVERYTHING!
WE'RE GOING TO HAVE TO GET SOME KIND OF COSTUME THROWN TOGETHER IF YOU'RE GOING TO KEEP DOING THIS.
NO TIGHTS, PAL.
CHRIST, I'M HUNGRY--
OH, CRAP-- NOT MORE KELP BURGERS --THAT STUFF IS GOING TO KILL ME FASTER THAN CADAVER!
GOOD-- THEN I'LL FINALLY GET SOME PEACE AND QUIET AROUND HERE!
THERE'S A KFC AT THE CORNER, WILLIAM-- ONE BUCKET OUGHT TO DO IT--OR A COUPLE BIG MACS-- I'D GIVE ANYTHING FOR A BIG MAC!
LOOK, DRAGON-- I'VE GOT ENOUGH STUFF IN MY BODY RIGHT NOW THAT I DON'T WANT TO HAVE THERE...
RITA-- HONEY ARE YOU...
...THERE...?
OH, GOD.
RITA.

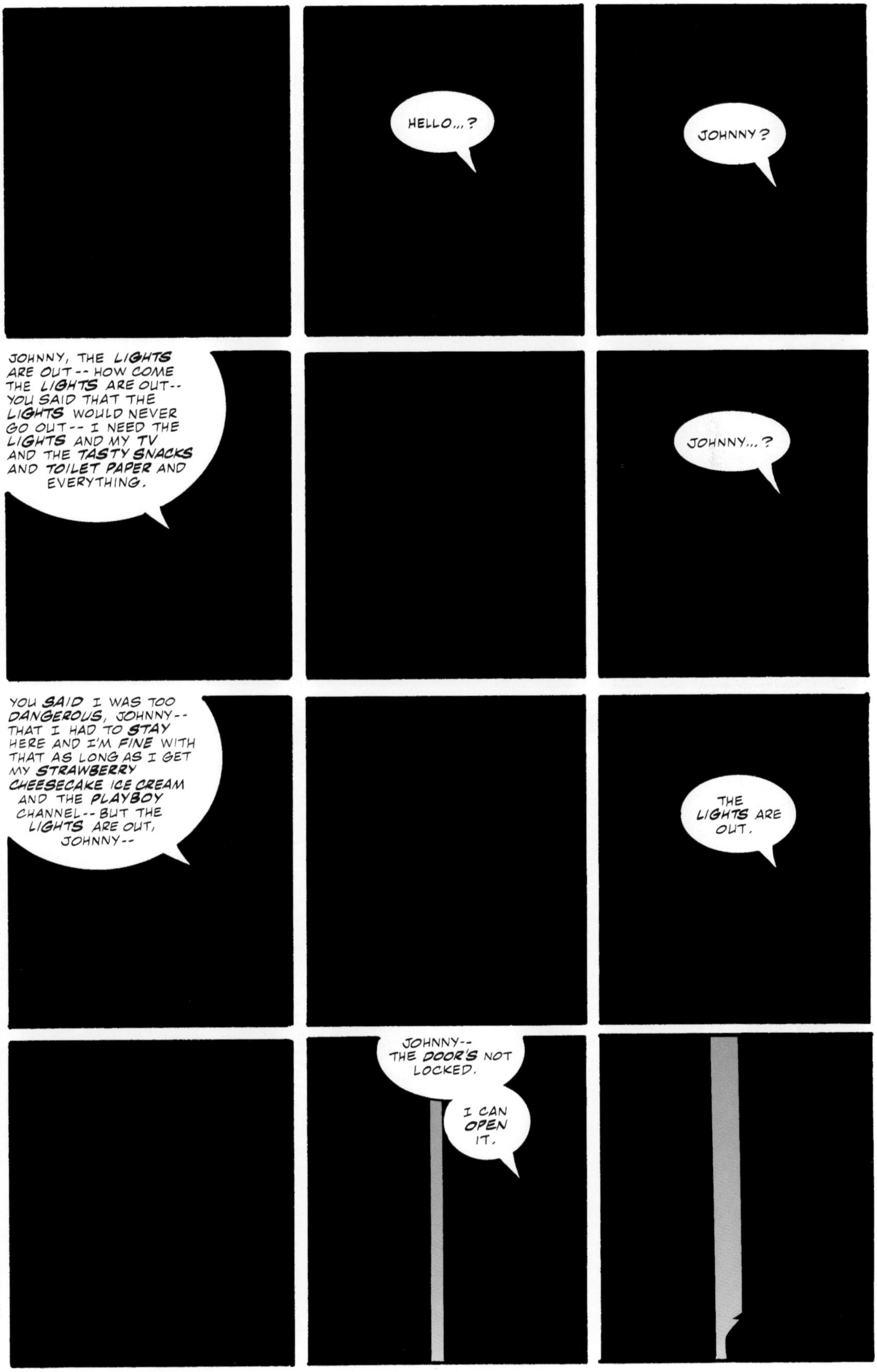
HELLO...?
JOHNNY?
JOHNNY, THE LIGHTS ARE OUT -- HOW COME THE LIGHTS ARE OUT -- YOU SAID THAT THE LIGHTS WOULD NEVER GO OUT -- I NEED THE LIGHTS AND MY TV AND THE TASTY SNACKS AND TOILET PAPER AND EVERYTHING.
JOHNNY...?
YOU SAID I WAS TOO DANGEROUS, JOHNNY -- THAT I HAD TO STAY HERE AND I'M FINE WITH THAT AS LONG AS I GET MY STRAWBERRY CHEESECAKE ICE CREAM AND THE PLAYBOY CHANNEL -- BUT THE LIGHTS ARE OUT, JOHNNY --
THE LIGHTS ARE OUT.
JOHNNY -- THE DOOR'S NOT LOCKED.
I CAN OPEN IT.

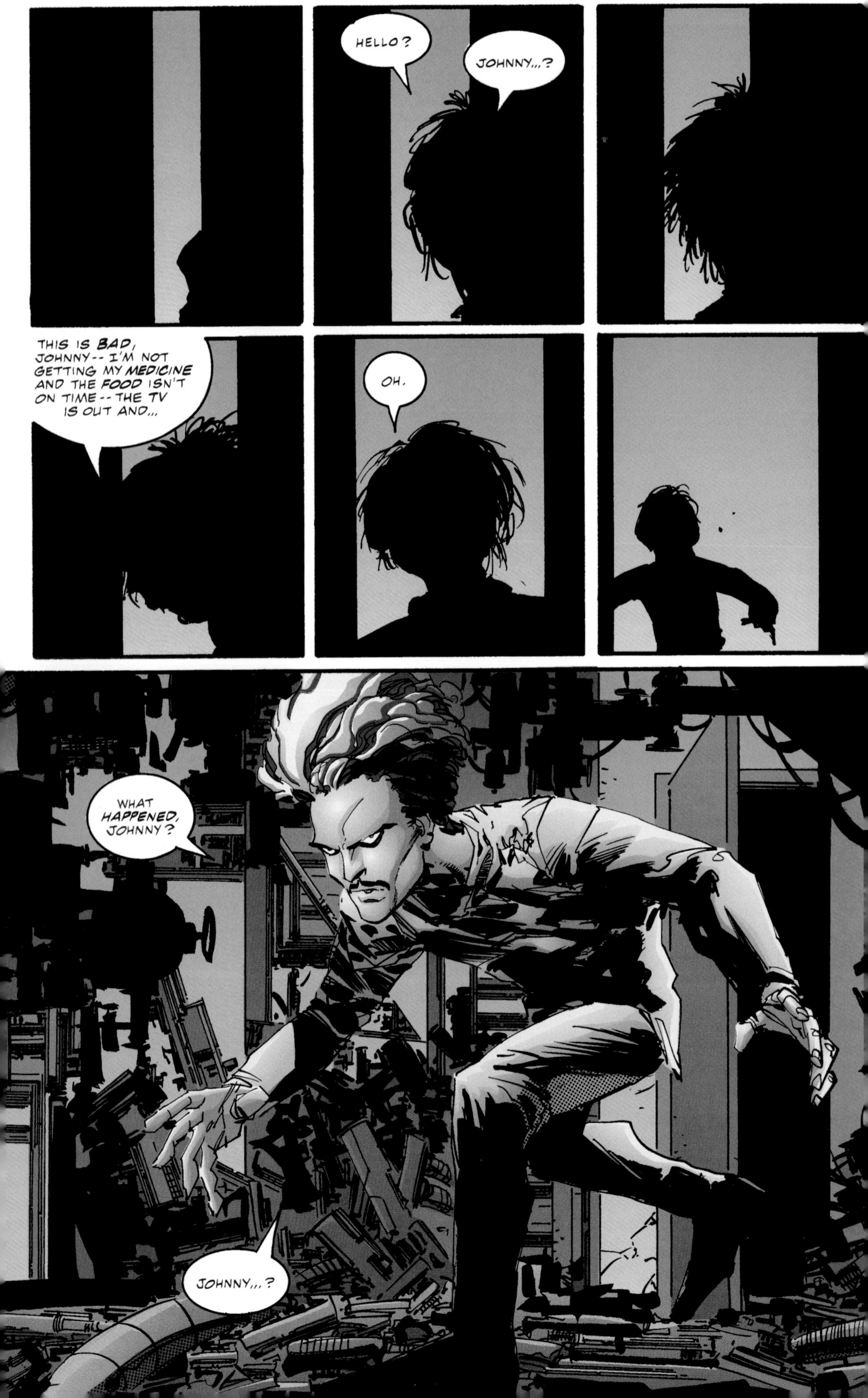
HELLO?
JOHNNY...?
THIS IS BAD, JOHNNY-- I'M NOT GETTING MY MEDICINE AND THE FOOD ISN'T ON TIME-- THE TV IS OUT AND...
OH.
WHAT HAPPENED, JOHNNY?
JOHNNY...?

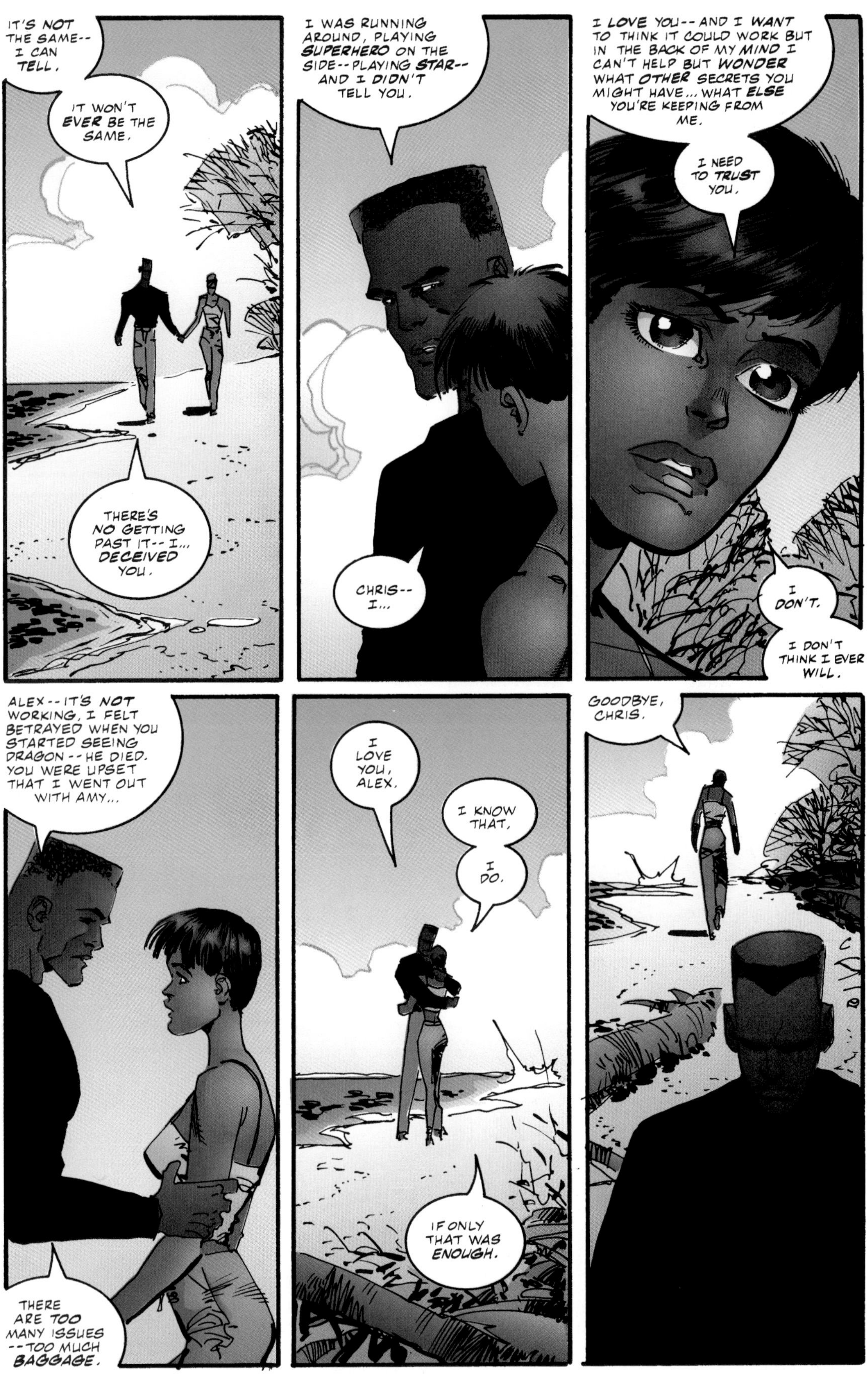
IT'S NOT THE SAME-- I CAN TELL.
IT WON'T EVER BE THE SAME.
THERE'S NO GETTING PAST IT-- I... DECEIVED YOU.
I WAS RUNNING AROUND, PLAYING SUPERHERO ON THE SIDE--PLAYING STAR-- AND I DIDN'T TELL YOU.
CHRIS-- I...
I LOVE YOU-- AND I WANT TO THINK IT COULD WORK BUT IN THE BACK OF MY MIND I CAN'T HELP BUT WONDER WHAT OTHER SECRETS YOU MIGHT HAVE... WHAT ELSE YOU'RE KEEPING FROM ME.
I NEED TO TRUST YOU.
I DON'T.
I DON'T THINK I EVER WILL.
ALEX--IT'S NOT WORKING. I FELT BETRAYED WHEN YOU STARTED SEEING DRAGON--HE DIED. YOU WERE UPSET THAT I WENT OUT WITH AMY...
THERE ARE TOO MANY ISSUES --TOO MUCH BAGGAGE.
I LOVE YOU, ALEX.
I KNOW THAT.
I DO.
IF ONLY THAT WAS ENOUGH.
GOODBYE, CHRIS.

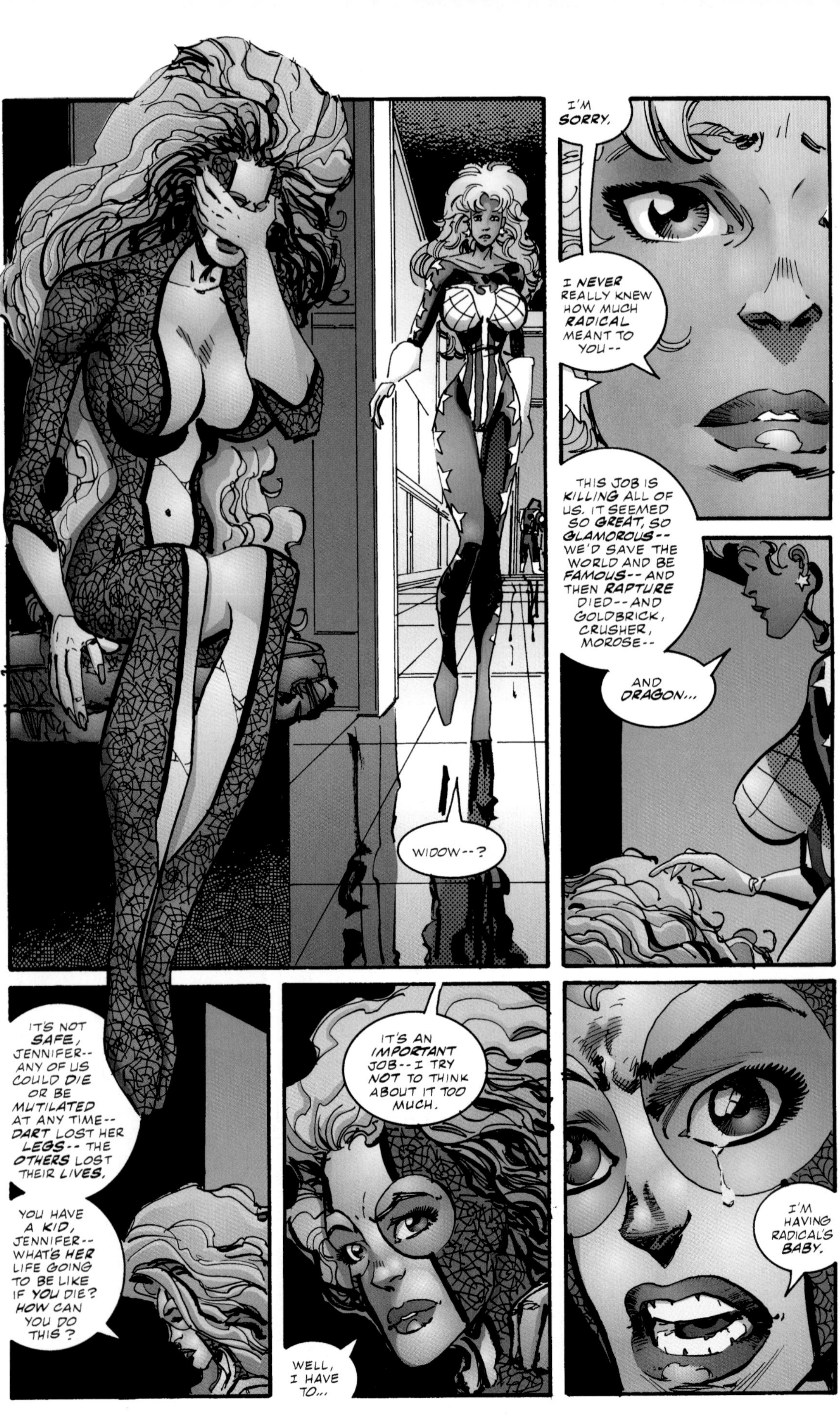
WIDOW--?
I'M SORRY.
I NEVER REALLY KNEW HOW MUCH RADICAL MEANT TO YOU--
THIS JOB IS KILLING ALL OF US. IT SEEMED SO GREAT, SO GLAMOROUS-- WE'D SAVE THE WORLD AND BE FAMOUS-- AND THEN RAPTURE DIED-- AND GOLDBRICK, CRUSHER, MOROSE--
AND DRAGON...
IT'S NOT SAFE, JENNIFER-- ANY OF US COULD DIE OR BE MUTILATED AT ANY TIME-- DART LOST HER LEGS-- THE OTHERS LOST THEIR LIVES.
YOU HAVE A KID, JENNIFER-- WHAT'S HER LIFE GOING TO BE LIKE IF YOU DIE? HOW CAN YOU DO THIS?
IT'S AN IMPORTANT JOB-- I TRY NOT TO THINK ABOUT IT TOO MUCH.
WELL, I HAVE TO...
I'M HAVING RADICAL'S BABY.

OKAY, WILLIAM--YOU'VE *DONE* YOUR BIT--DUSTED FOR FINGERPRINTS AND SEARCHED THE JOINT.

RITA'S *GONE*.

FROM ALL INDICATION-- SHE'S BEEN *ABDUCTED*.

MAY I *SUGGEST*-- SINCE YOU'RE CONVINCED THAT YOUR *BROTHER* TOOK HER-- THAT WE GET OUT THERE AND *ROUGH UP* SOME OF HIS 'VICIOUS CIRCLE PALS'?

SOMEBODY OUT THERE KNOWS *SOMETHING*.

WE'RE GETTING *NOWHERE* HANGING OUT THERE.

GREAT *VIEW*, WILLIAM.

YOU PAYING A *LOT* FOR THIS PLACE?

NICE *DOOR*. SHE MUST HAVE BEEN HIDING IN THE *BATHROOM*.

ACTUALLY, *RITA* BROKE THAT HERSELF.

IZZAT RIGHT?

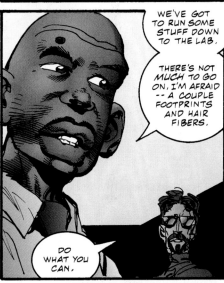

WE'VE GOT TO RUN SOME STUFF DOWN TO THE LAB.

THERE'S NOT *MUCH* TO GO ON, I'M AFRAID -- A COUPLE FOOTPRINTS AND HAIR FIBERS.

DO WHAT YOU CAN.

THESE GUYS ARE *MORONS*, WILLIAM-- CHANGE INTO ME AND LET'S GO BUST SOME HEADS.

NOT UNTIL I SCRAPE TOGETHER SOME KIND OF *DISGUISE* AND OVERSEE SOME OF THE *LAB* WORK.

I WANT TO BE *SURE* THIS IS DONE *RIGHT*.

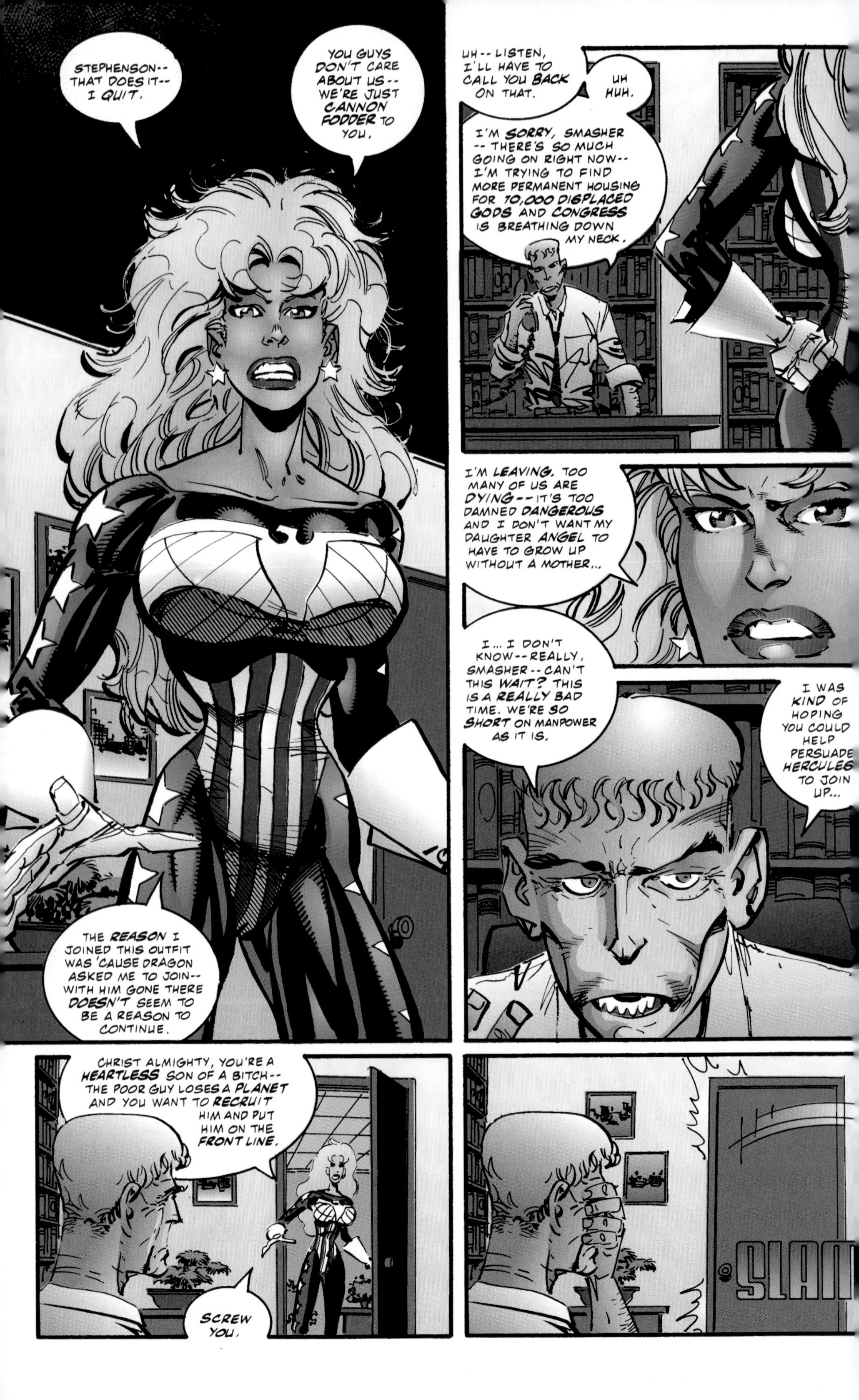
STEPHENSON--
THAT DOES IT--
I QUIT.
YOU GUYS DON'T CARE ABOUT US--WE'RE JUST CANNON FODDER TO YOU.
THE REASON I JOINED THIS OUTFIT WAS 'CAUSE DRAGON ASKED ME TO JOIN--WITH HIM GONE THERE DOESN'T SEEM TO BE A REASON TO CONTINUE.
UH--LISTEN, I'LL HAVE TO CALL YOU BACK ON THAT.
UH HUH.
I'M SORRY, SMASHER--THERE'S SO MUCH GOING ON RIGHT NOW--I'M TRYING TO FIND MORE PERMANENT HOUSING FOR 10,000 DISPLACED GODS AND CONGRESS IS BREATHING DOWN MY NECK.
I'M LEAVING. TOO MANY OF US ARE DYING--IT'S TOO DAMNED DANGEROUS AND I DON'T WANT MY DAUGHTER ANGEL TO HAVE TO GROW UP WITHOUT A MOTHER...
I... I DON'T KNOW--REALLY, SMASHER--CAN'T THIS WAIT? THIS IS A REALLY BAD TIME. WE'RE SO SHORT ON MANPOWER AS IT IS.
I WAS KIND OF HOPING YOU COULD HELP PERSUADE HERCULES TO JOIN UP...
CHRIST ALMIGHTY, YOU'RE A HEARTLESS SON OF A BITCH--THE POOR GUY LOSES A PLANET AND YOU WANT TO RECRUIT HIM AND PUT HIM ON THE FRONT LINE.
SCREW YOU.
SLAM

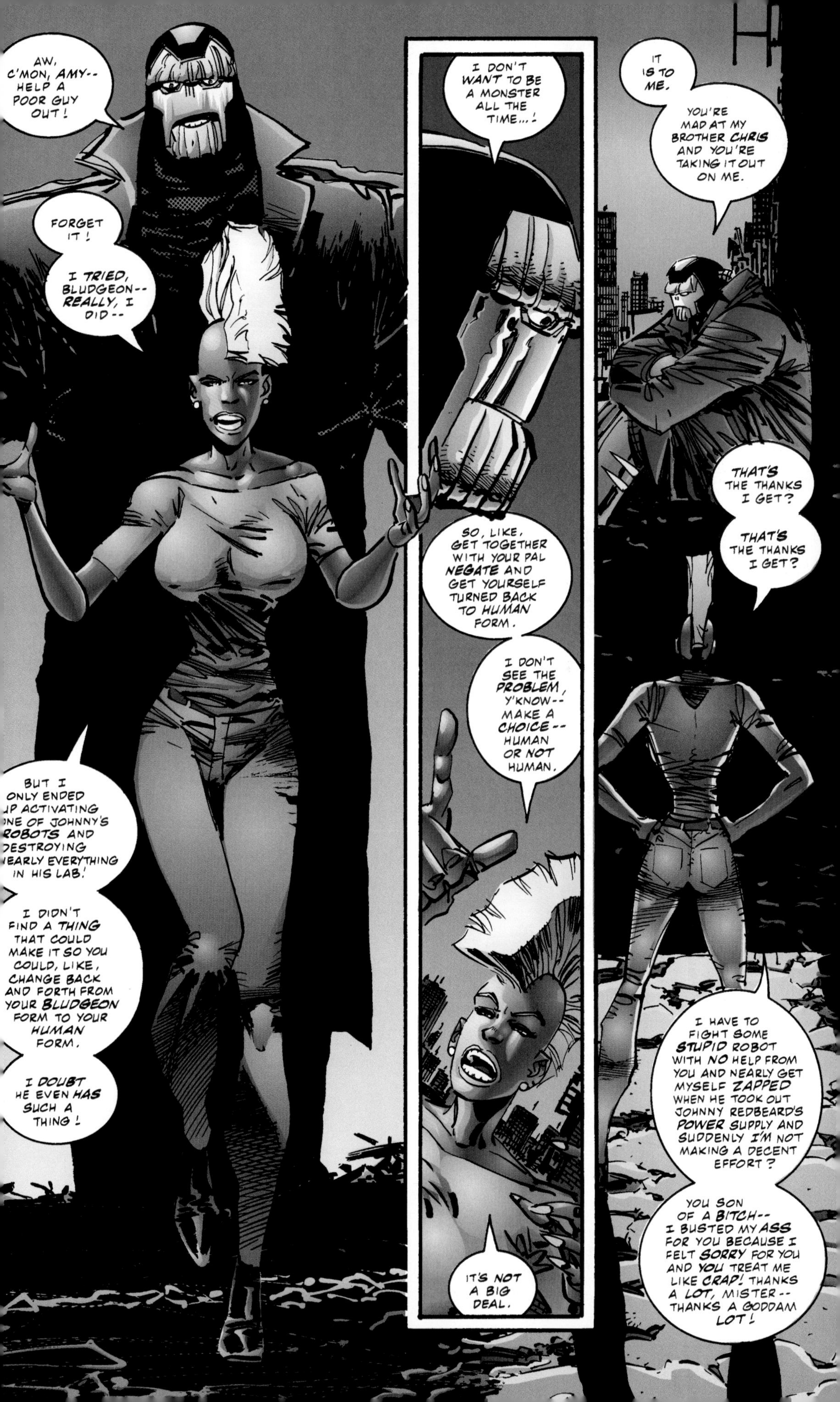
AW, C'MON, AMY-- HELP A POOR GUY OUT!
FORGET IT!
I TRIED, BLUDGEON-- REALLY, I DID--
BUT I ONLY ENDED UP ACTIVATING ONE OF JOHNNY'S ROBOTS AND DESTROYING NEARLY EVERYTHING IN HIS LAB!
I DIDN'T FIND A THING THAT COULD MAKE IT SO YOU COULD, LIKE, CHANGE BACK AND FORTH FROM YOUR BLUDGEON FORM TO YOUR HUMAN FORM.
I DOUBT HE EVEN HAS SUCH A THING!
I DON'T WANT TO BE A MONSTER ALL THE TIME...!
SO, LIKE, GET TOGETHER WITH YOUR PAL NEGATE AND GET YOURSELF TURNED BACK TO HUMAN FORM.
I DON'T SEE THE PROBLEM, Y'KNOW-- MAKE A CHOICE-- HUMAN OR NOT HUMAN.
IT'S NOT A BIG DEAL.
IT IS TO ME.
YOU'RE MAD AT MY BROTHER CHRIS AND YOU'RE TAKING IT OUT ON ME.
THAT'S THE THANKS I GET?
THAT'S THE THANKS I GET?
I HAVE TO FIGHT SOME STUPID ROBOT WITH NO HELP FROM YOU AND NEARLY GET MYSELF ZAPPED WHEN HE TOOK OUT JOHNNY REDBEARD'S POWER SUPPLY AND SUDDENLY I'M NOT MAKING A DECENT EFFORT?
YOU SON OF A BITCH-- I BUSTED MY ASS FOR YOU BECAUSE I FELT SORRY FOR YOU AND YOU TREAT ME LIKE CRAP! THANKS A LOT, MISTER-- THANKS A GODDAM LOT!

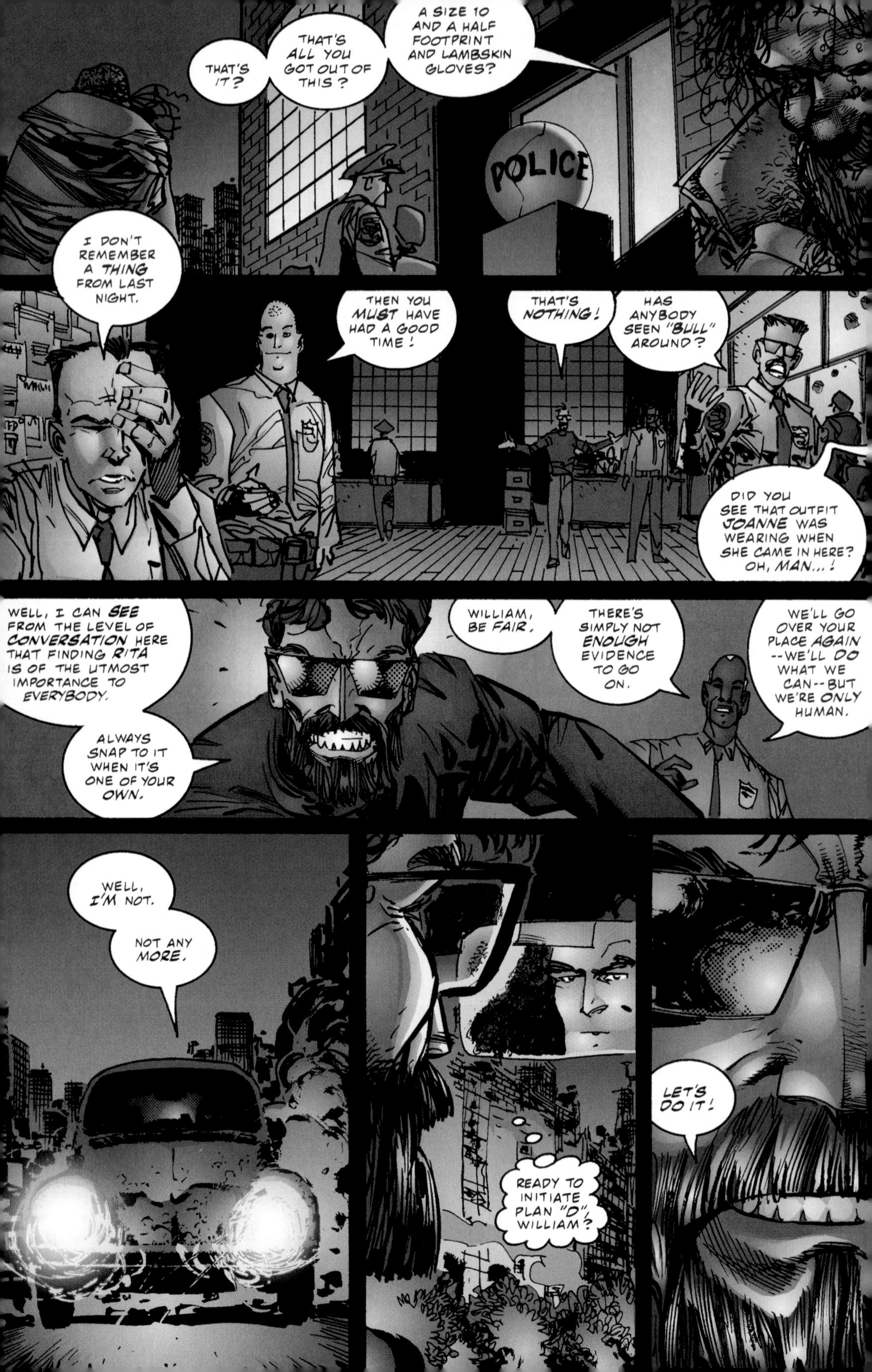
THAT'S IT?
THAT'S ALL YOU GOT OUT OF THIS?
A SIZE 10 AND A HALF FOOTPRINT AND LAMBSKIN GLOVES?
POLICE
I DON'T REMEMBER A THING FROM LAST NIGHT.
THEN YOU MUST HAVE HAD A GOOD TIME!
THAT'S NOTHING!
HAS ANYBODY SEEN "BULL" AROUND?
DID YOU SEE THAT OUTFIT JOANNE WAS WEARING WHEN SHE CAME IN HERE? OH, MAN...!
WELL, I CAN SEE FROM THE LEVEL OF CONVERSATION HERE THAT FINDING RITA IS OF THE UTMOST IMPORTANCE TO EVERYBODY.
ALWAYS SNAP TO IT WHEN IT'S ONE OF YOUR OWN.
WILLIAM, BE FAIR.
THERE'S SIMPLY NOT ENOUGH EVIDENCE TO GO ON.
WE'LL GO OVER YOUR PLACE AGAIN --WE'LL DO WHAT WE CAN--BUT WE'RE ONLY HUMAN.
WELL, I'M NOT.
NOT ANY MORE.
READY TO INITIATE PLAN "D", WILLIAM?
LET'S DO IT!

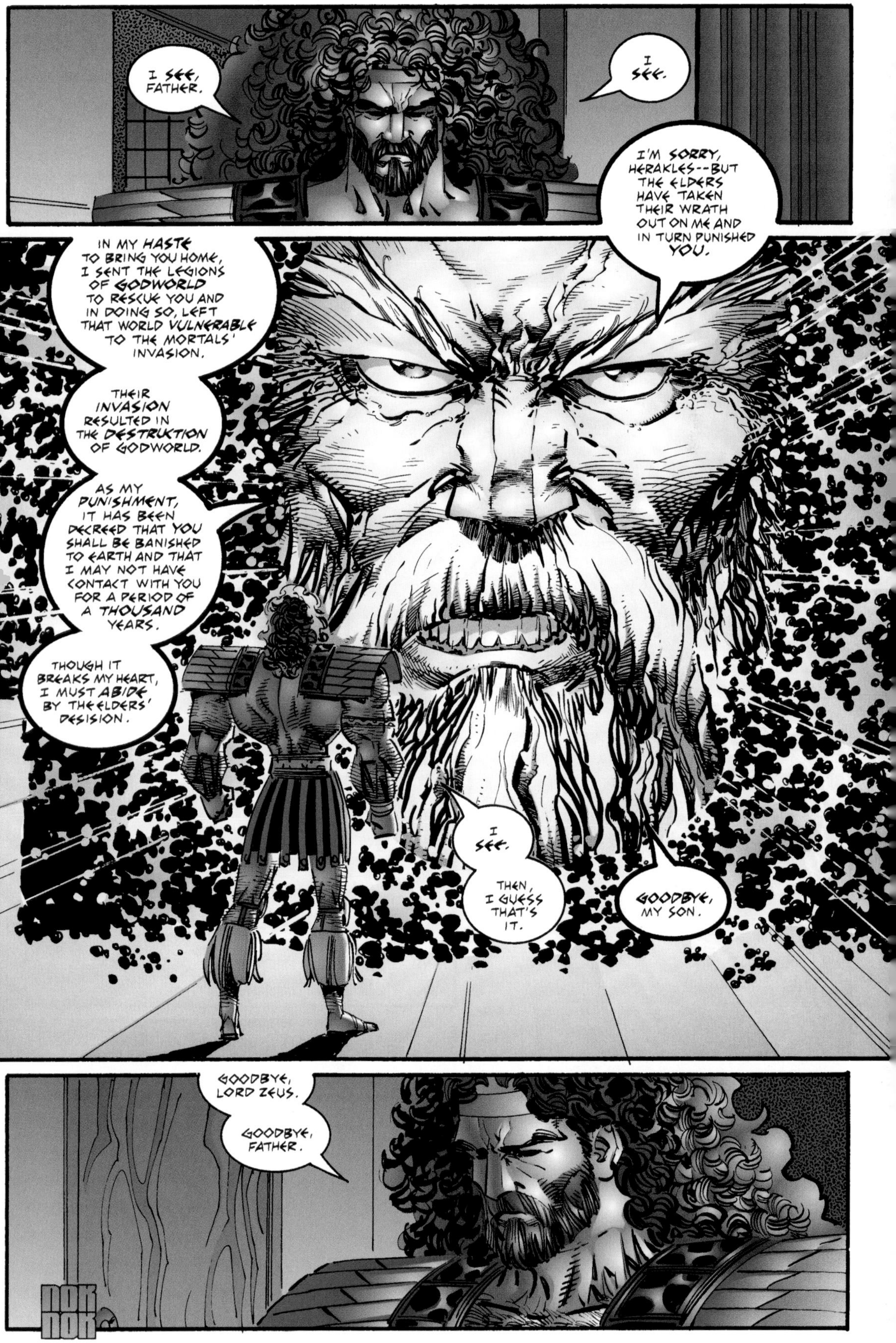

I SEE, FATHER.
I SEE.
I'M SORRY, HERAKLES--BUT THE ELDERS HAVE TAKEN THEIR WRATH OUT ON ME AND IN TURN PUNISHED YOU.
IN MY HASTE TO BRING YOU HOME, I SENT THE LEGIONS OF GODWORLD TO RESCUE YOU AND IN DOING SO, LEFT THAT WORLD VULNERABLE TO THE MORTALS' INVASION.
THEIR INVASION RESULTED IN THE DESTRUKTION OF GODWORLD.
AS MY PUNISHMENT, IT HAS BEEN DECREED THAT YOU SHALL BE BANISHED TO EARTH AND THAT I MAY NOT HAVE CONTACT WITH YOU FOR A PERIOD OF A THOUSAND YEARS.
THOUGH IT BREAKS MY HEART, I MUST ABIDE BY THE ELDERS' DESISION.
I SEE.
THEN, I GUESS THAT'S IT.
GOODBYE, MY SON.
GOODBYE, LORD ZEUS.
GOODBYE, FATHER.

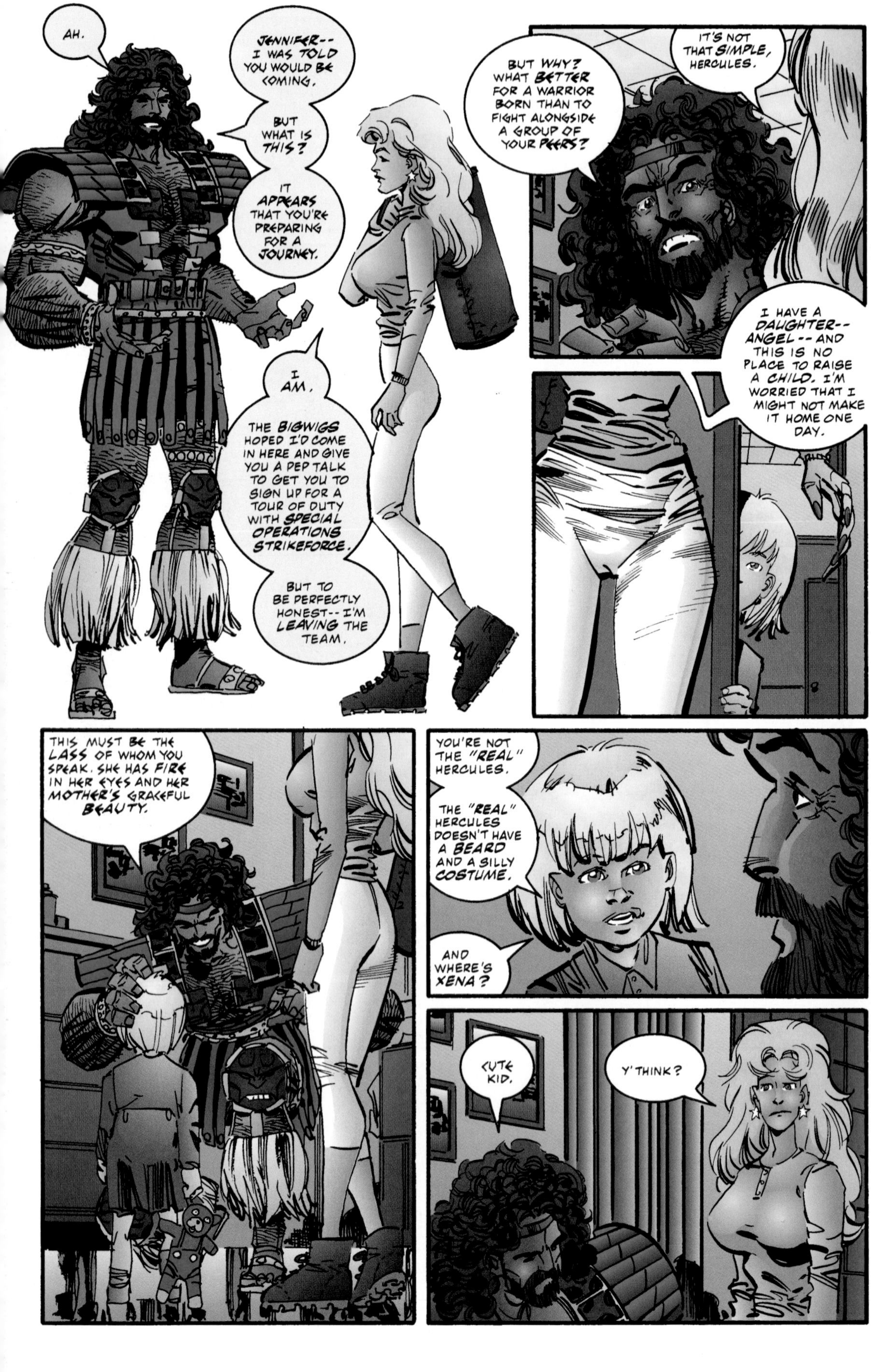
AH.
JENNIFER-- I WAS TOLD YOU WOULD BE COMING.
BUT WHAT IS THIS?
IT APPEARS THAT YOU'RE PREPARING FOR A JOURNEY.
I AM.
THE BIGWIGS HOPED I'D COME IN HERE AND GIVE YOU A PEP TALK TO GET YOU TO SIGN UP FOR A TOUR OF DUTY WITH SPECIAL OPERATIONS STRIKEFORCE.
BUT TO BE PERFECTLY HONEST-- I'M LEAVING THE TEAM.
BUT WHY? WHAT BETTER FOR A WARRIOR BORN THAN TO FIGHT ALONGSIDE A GROUP OF YOUR PEERS?
IT'S NOT THAT SIMPLE, HERCULES.
I HAVE A DAUGHTER-- ANGEL -- AND THIS IS NO PLACE TO RAISE A CHILD. I'M WORRIED THAT I MIGHT NOT MAKE IT HOME ONE DAY.
THIS MUST BE THE LASS OF WHOM YOU SPEAK. SHE HAS FIRE IN HER EYES AND HER MOTHER'S GRACEFUL BEAUTY.
YOU'RE NOT THE "REAL" HERCULES.
THE "REAL" HERCULES DOESN'T HAVE A BEARD AND A SILLY COSTUME.
AND WHERE'S XENA?
CUTE KID.
Y'THINK?

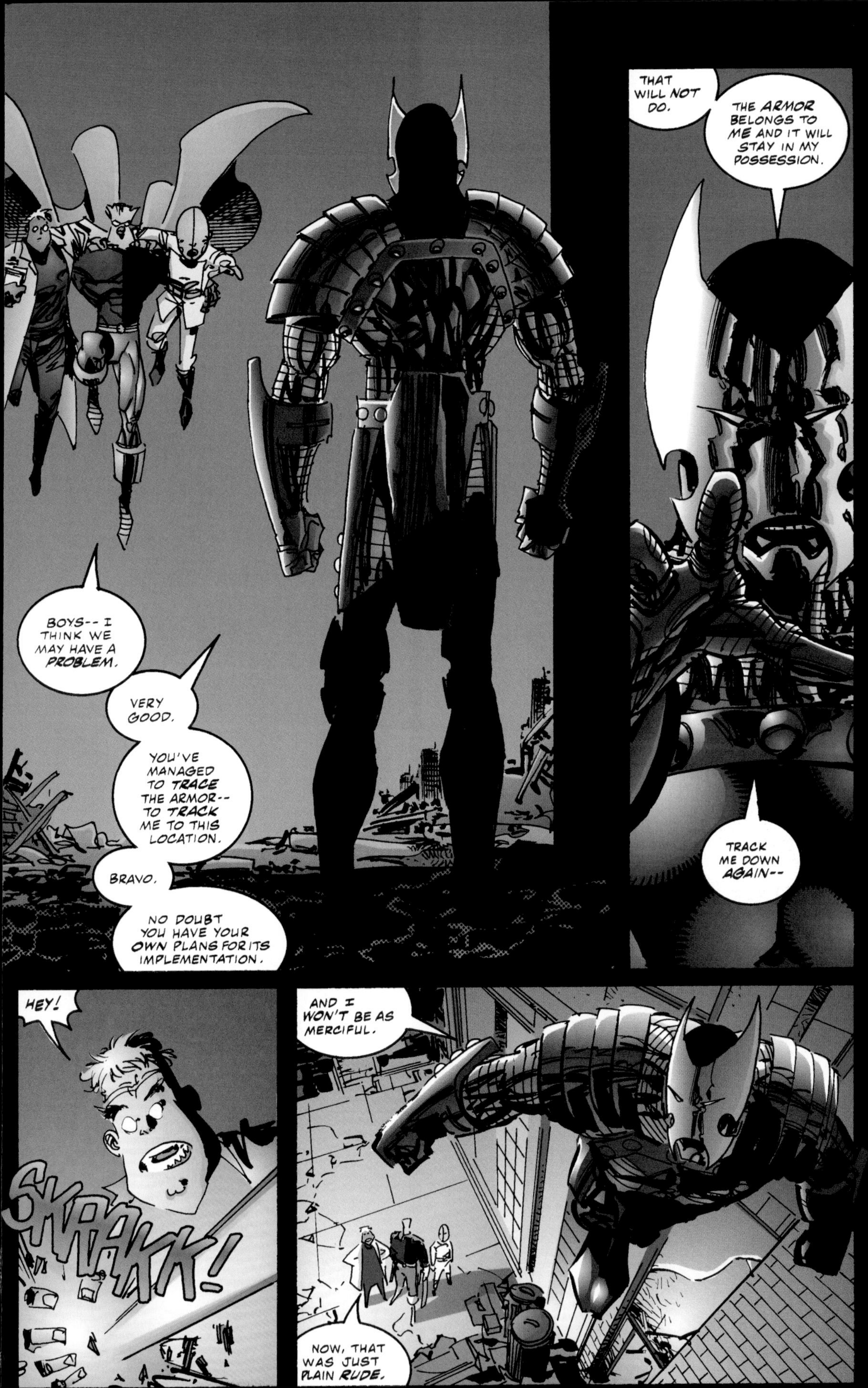

BOYS-- I THINK WE MAY HAVE A PROBLEM.
VERY GOOD.
YOU'VE MANAGED TO TRACE THE ARMOR-- TO TRACK ME TO THIS LOCATION.
BRAVO.
NO DOUBT YOU HAVE YOUR OWN PLANS FOR ITS IMPLEMENTATION.
THAT WILL NOT DO.
THE ARMOR BELONGS TO ME AND IT WILL STAY IN MY POSSESSION.
TRACK ME DOWN AGAIN--
HEY!
SKRAKK!
AND I WON'T BE AS MERCIFUL.
NOW, THAT WAS JUST PLAIN RUDE.

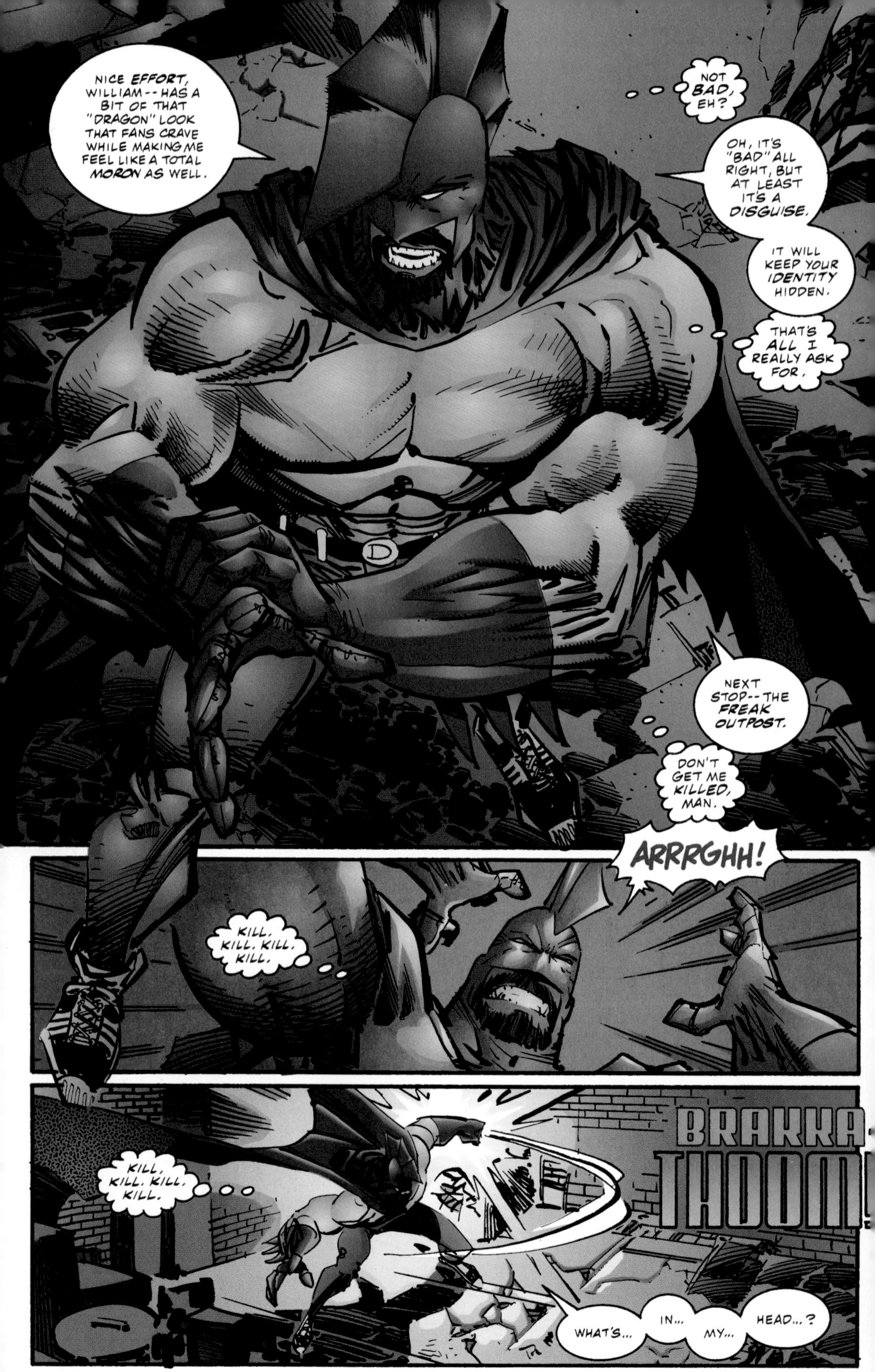
NICE EFFORT, WILLIAM--HAS A BIT OF THAT "DRAGON" LOOK THAT FANS CRAVE WHILE MAKING ME FEEL LIKE A TOTAL MORON AS WELL.
NOT BAD, EH?
OH, IT'S "BAD" ALL RIGHT, BUT AT LEAST IT'S A DISGUISE.
IT WILL KEEP YOUR IDENTITY HIDDEN.
THAT'S ALL I REALLY ASK FOR.
NEXT STOP--THE FREAK OUTPOST.
DON'T GET ME KILLED, MAN.
ARRRGHH!
KILL. KILL. KILL. KILL.
BRAKKA THOOM!
KILL, KILL. KILL. KILL.
WHAT'S...
IN...
MY...
HEAD...?

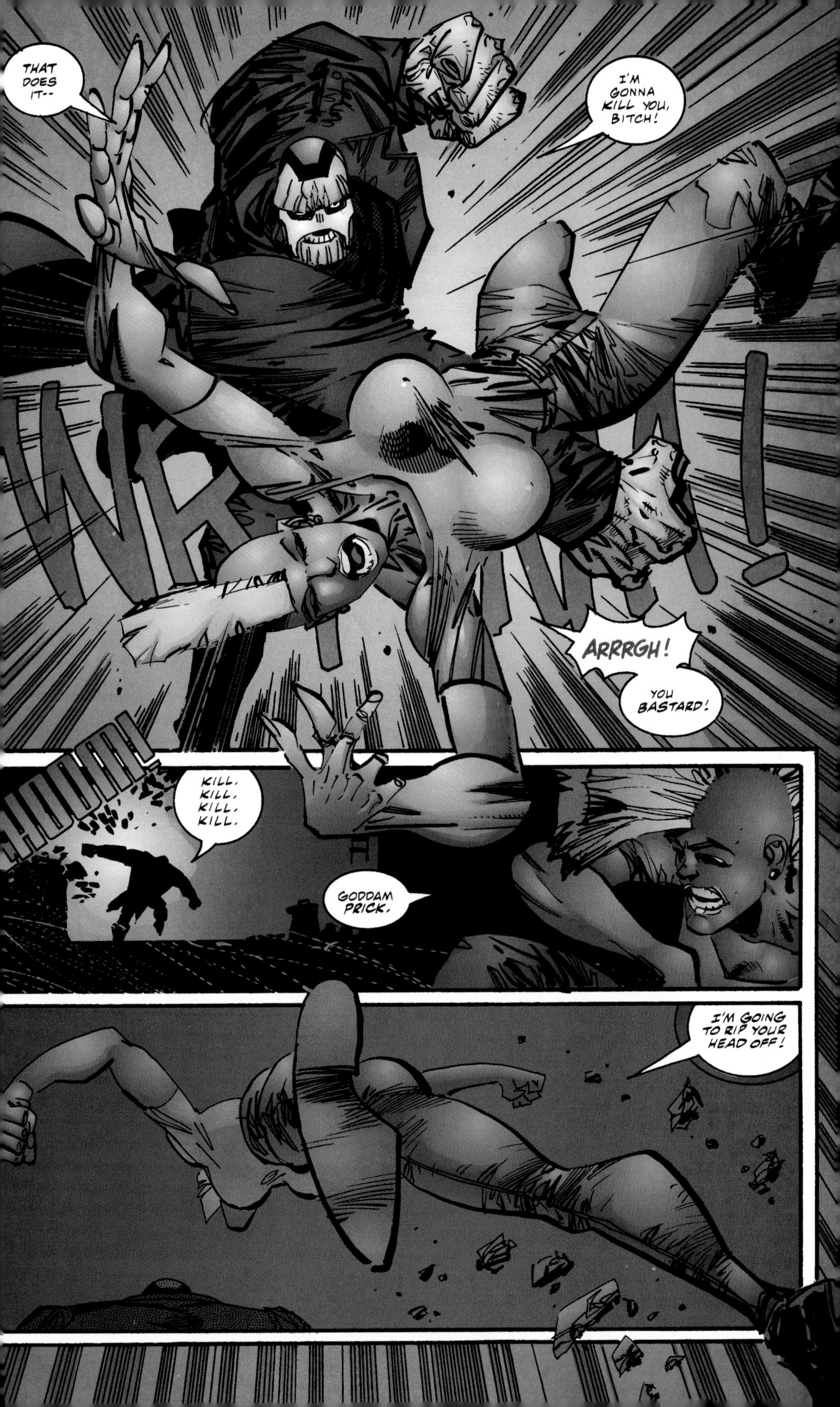

THAT DOES IT--
I'M GONNA KILL YOU, BITCH!
ARRRGH!
YOU BASTARD!
KILL. KILL. KILL. KILL.
GODDAM PRICK.
I'M GOING TO RIP YOUR HEAD OFF!

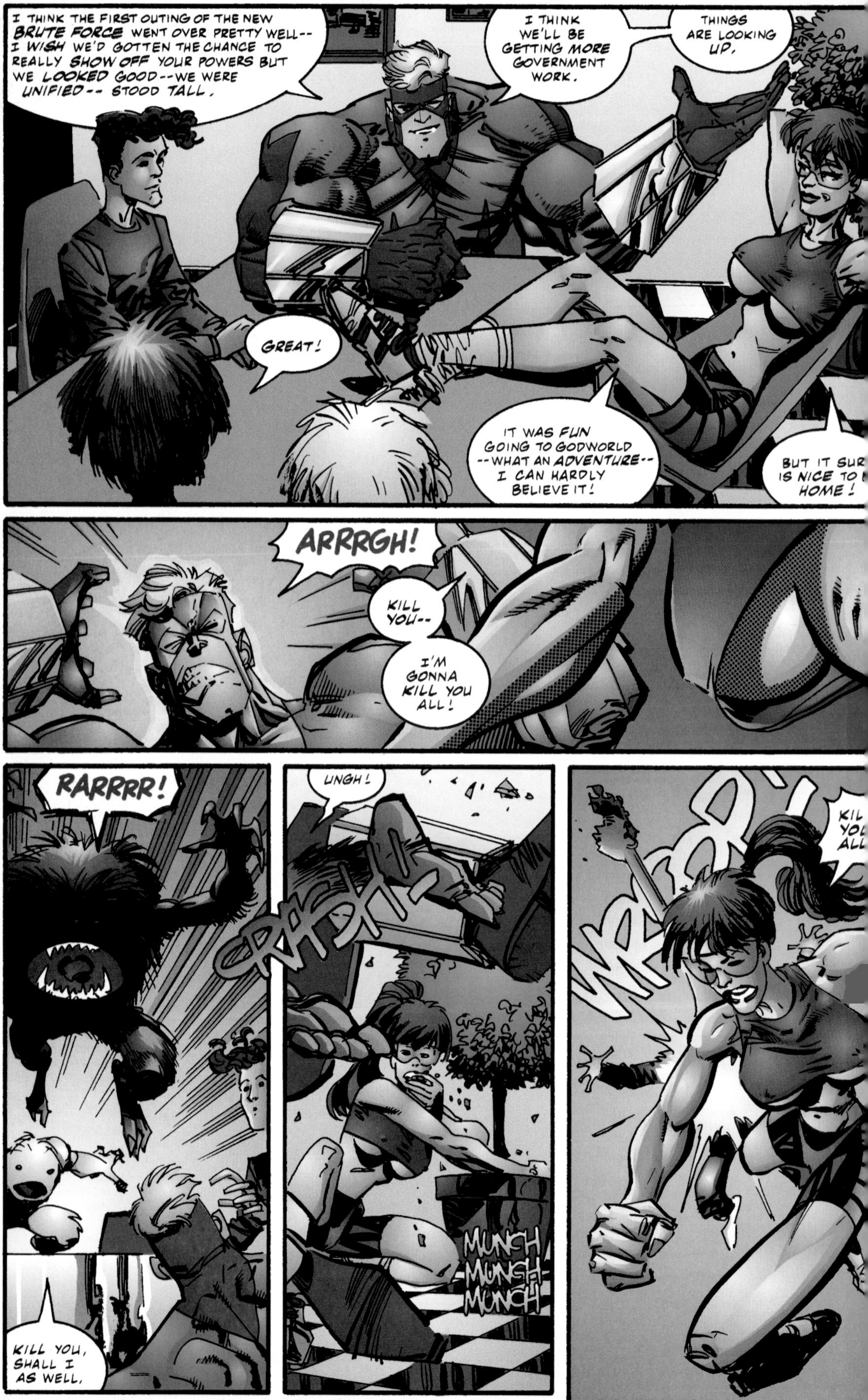

I THINK THE FIRST OUTING OF THE NEW BRUTE FORCE WENT OVER PRETTY WELL-- I WISH WE'D GOTTEN THE CHANCE TO REALLY SHOW OFF YOUR POWERS BUT WE LOOKED GOOD--WE WERE UNIFIED-- STOOD TALL.
I THINK WE'LL BE GETTING MORE GOVERNMENT WORK.
THINGS ARE LOOKING UP.
GREAT!
IT WAS FUN GOING TO GODWORLD --WHAT AN ADVENTURE-- I CAN HARDLY BELIEVE IT!
BUT IT SUR IS NICE TO HOME!
ARRRGH!
KILL YOU--
I'M GONNA KILL YOU ALL!
RARRRR!
KILL YOU, SHALL I AS WELL.
UNGH!
CRASH
MUNCH MUNCH MUNCH
KIL YO AL

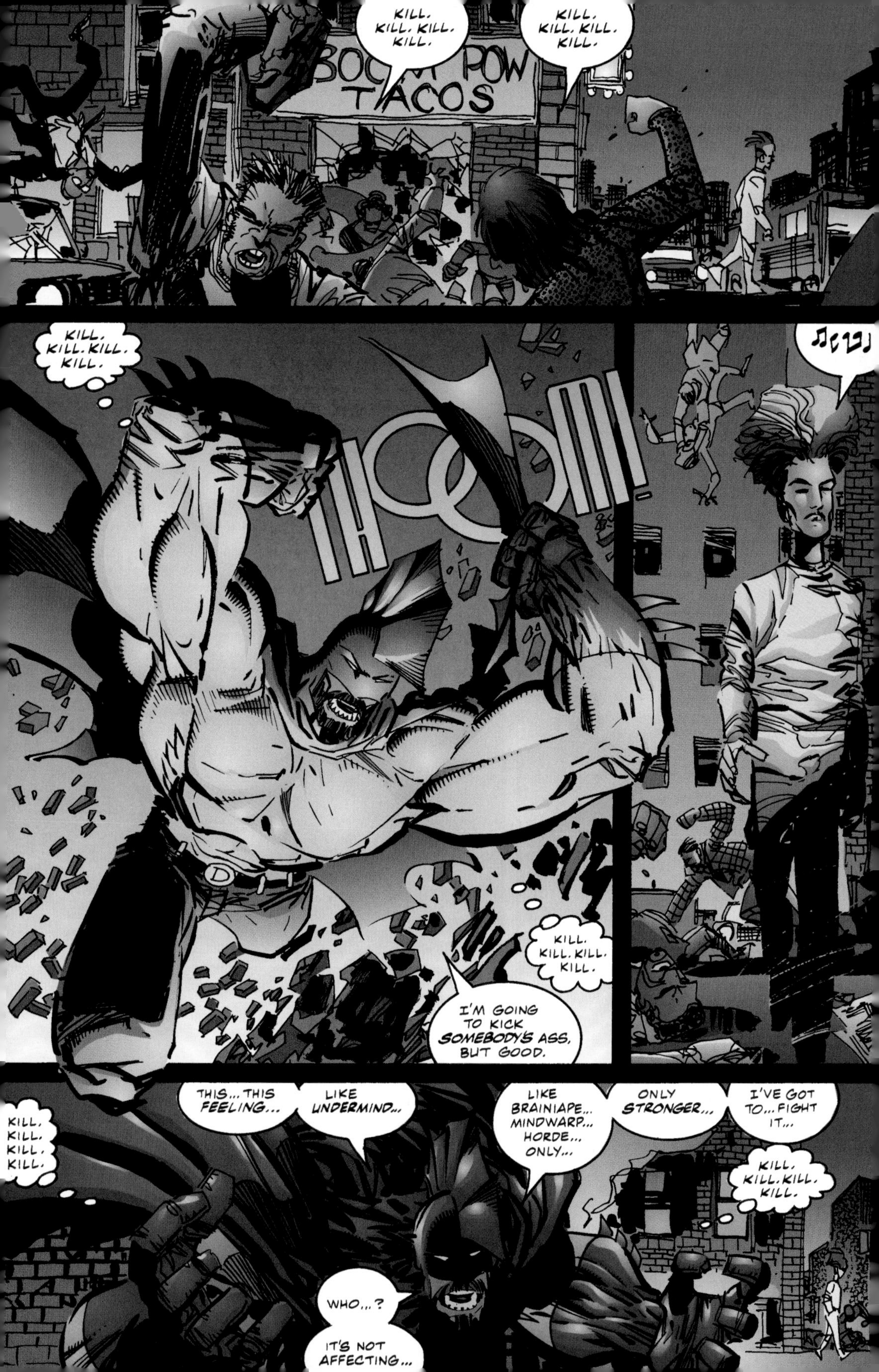
KILL. KILL. KILL. KILL.
KILL. KILL. KILL. KILL.
BOOM POW TACOS
KILL. KILL. KILL. KILL.
♫♪♫♪
KILL. KILL. KILL. KILL.
I'M GOING TO KICK SOMEBODY'S ASS, BUT GOOD.
KILL. KILL. KILL. KILL.
THIS... THIS FEELING...
LIKE UNDERMIND...
LIKE BRAINIAPE... MINDWARP... HORDE... ONLY...
ONLY STRONGER...
I'VE GOT TO... FIGHT IT...
KILL. KILL. KILL. KILL.
WHO...?
IT'S NOT AFFECTING...

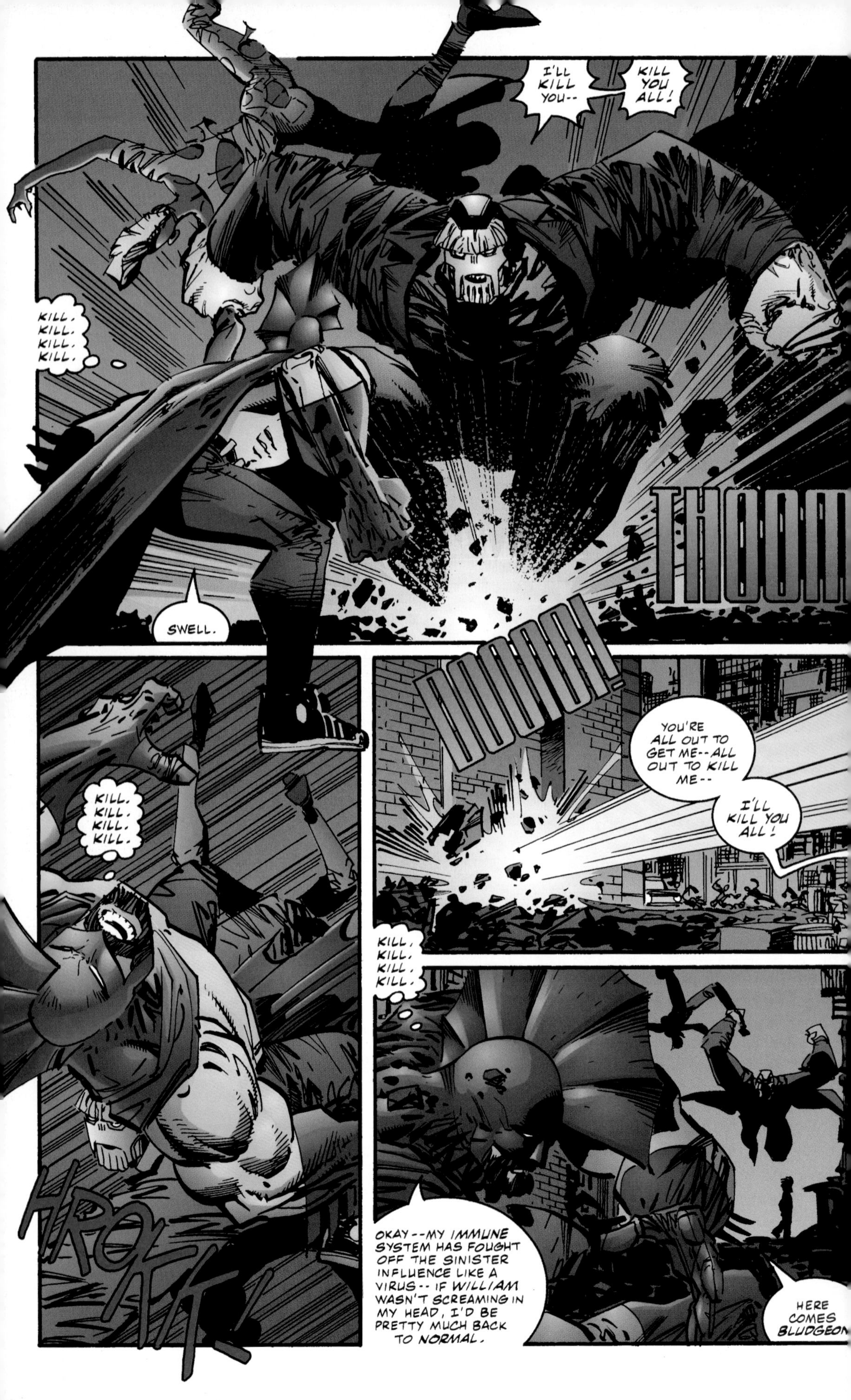
I'LL KILL YOU--
KILL YOU ALL!
KILL. KILL. KILL. KILL.
THOOM
SWELL.
KILL. KILL. KILL. KILL.
HROKK!
DOOOOM!
YOU'RE ALL OUT TO GET ME--ALL OUT TO KILL ME--
I'LL KILL YOU ALL!
KILL, KILL. KILL. KILL.
OKAY--MY IMMUNE SYSTEM HAS FOUGHT OFF THE SINISTER INFLUENCE LIKE A VIRUS--IF WILLIAM WASN'T SCREAMING IN MY HEAD, I'D BE PRETTY MUCH BACK TO NORMAL.
HERE COMES BLUDGEON

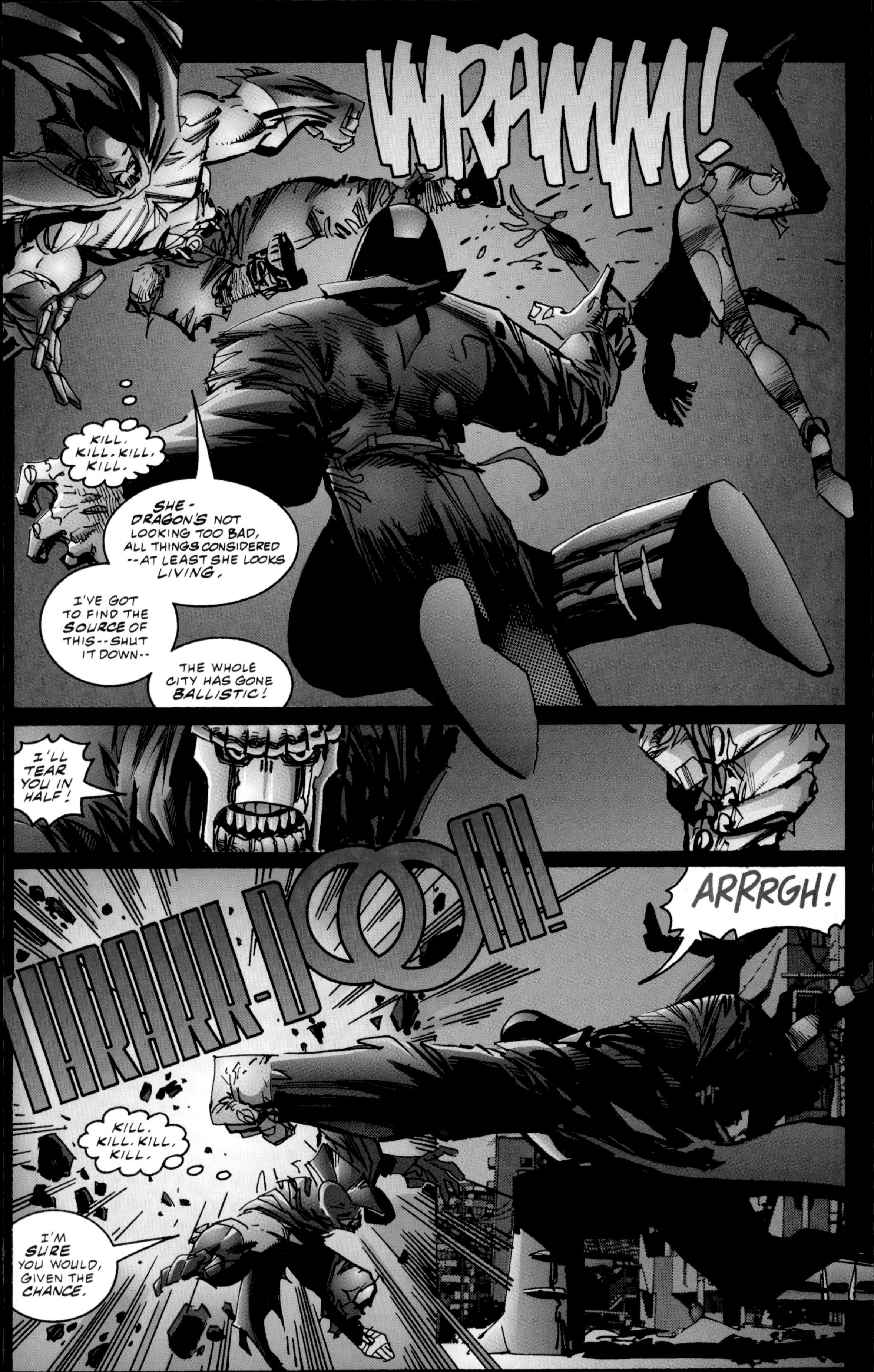
WRAMM!
KILL. KILL. KILL. KILL.
SHE-DRAGON'S NOT LOOKING TOO BAD, ALL THINGS CONSIDERED --AT LEAST SHE LOOKS LIVING.
I'VE GOT TO FIND THE SOURCE OF THIS--SHUT IT DOWN--
THE WHOLE CITY HAS GONE BALLISTIC!
I'LL TEAR YOU IN HALF!
WHAKK-DOOM!
ARRRGH!
KILL. KILL. KILL. KILL.
I'M SURE YOU WOULD, GIVEN THE CHANCE.

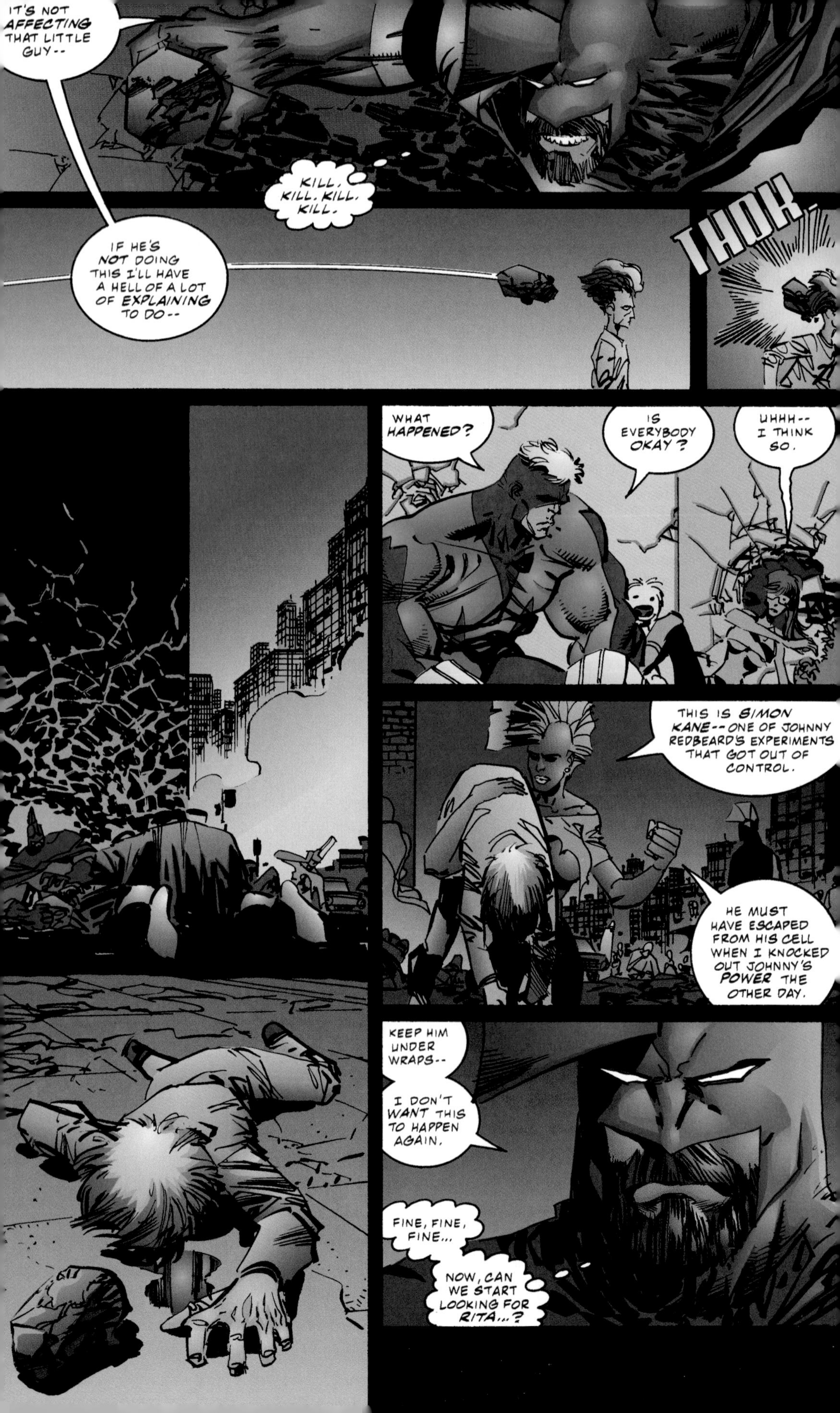
IT'S NOT AFFECTING THAT LITTLE GUY--
KILL. KILL. KILL. KILL.
IF HE'S NOT DOING THIS I'LL HAVE A HELL OF A LOT OF EXPLAINING TO DO--
THOK
WHAT HAPPENED?
IS EVERYBODY OKAY?
UHHH-- I THINK SO.
THIS IS SIMON KANE-- ONE OF JOHNNY REDBEARD'S EXPERIMENTS THAT GOT OUT OF CONTROL.
HE MUST HAVE ESCAPED FROM HIS CELL WHEN I KNOCKED OUT JOHNNY'S POWER THE OTHER DAY.
KEEP HIM UNDER WRAPS--
I DON'T WANT THIS TO HAPPEN AGAIN.
FINE, FINE, FINE...
NOW, CAN WE START LOOKING FOR RITA...?

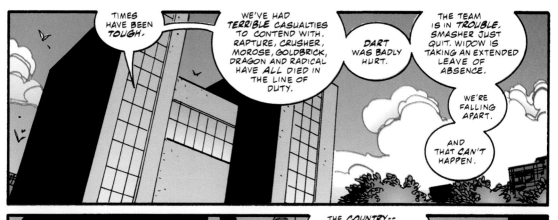

TIMES HAVE BEEN *TOUGH.*

WE'VE HAD *TERRIBLE* CASUALTIES TO CONTEND WITH. RAPTURE, CRUSHER, MOROSE, GOLDBRICK, DRAGON AND RADICAL HAVE *ALL* DIED IN THE LINE OF DUTY.

DART WAS BADLY HURT.

THE TEAM IS IN *TROUBLE.* SMASHER JUST QUIT. WIDOW IS TAKING AN EXTENDED LEAVE OF ABSENCE.

WE'RE FALLING APART.

AND THAT *CAN'T* HAPPEN.

THE *COUNTRY--* THE *WORLD--*DEPENDS ON US. WE *NEED* AN INCREDIBLE, CAPABLE, *EXTRAORDINARY* FIGHTING FORCE TO CONTEND WITH THE OPPONENTS THAT WE FACE.

NO *CRAP,* STEPHENSON.

WHAT ARE WE GOING TO *DO* ABOUT IT?

WE NEED TO *REBUILD.* TO GET *NEW* HEROES INTO THE FOLD. AND IN *THAT* EFFORT, I'VE MADE A SPECIAL *APPEAL* TO GET OUR *NEWEST* MEMBER ON BOARD...

THE FIRST OF *MANY* NEW MEMBERS. *ONCE* CONSIDERED FOR MEMBERSHIP IN *YOUNGBLOOD--*

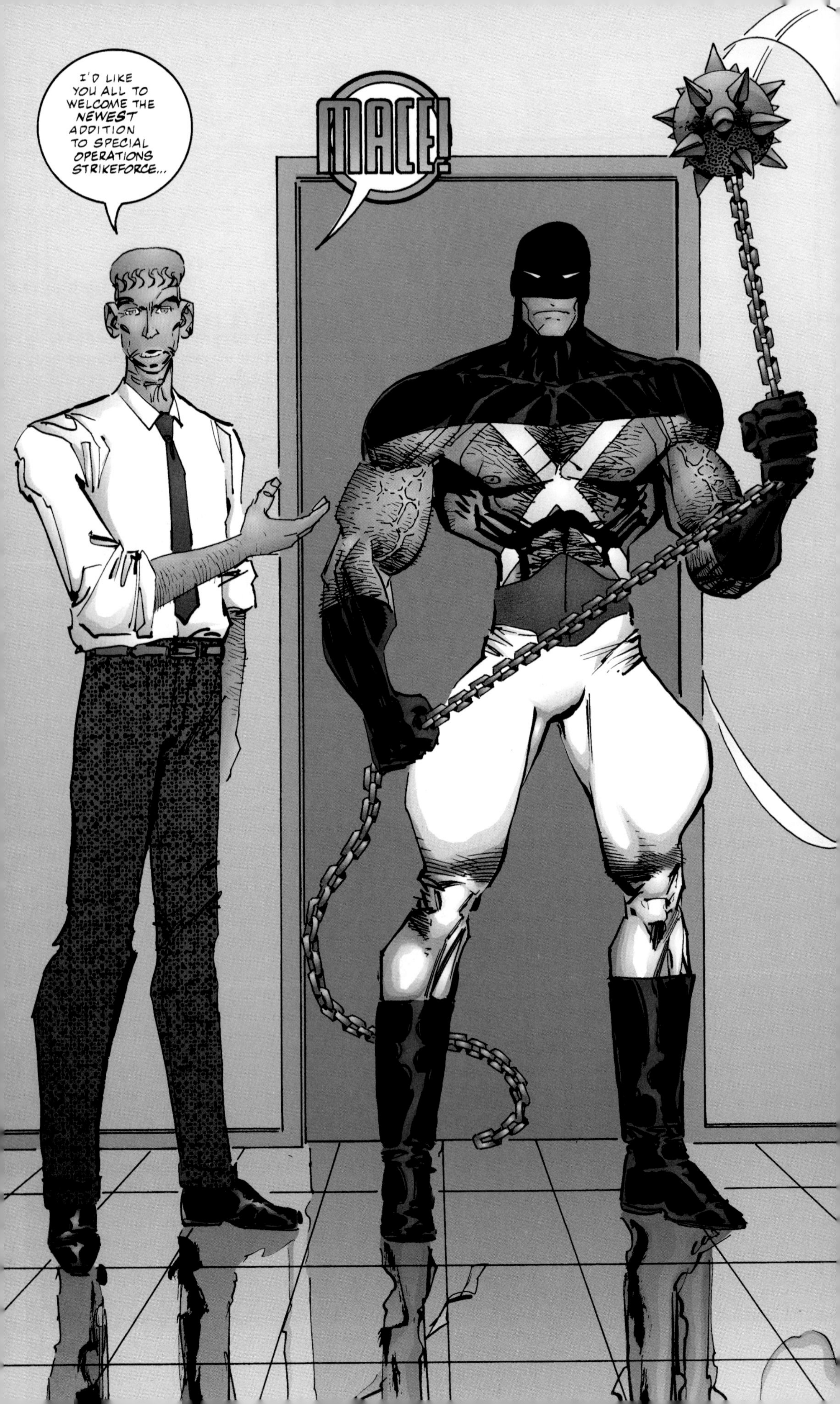
I'D LIKE YOU ALL TO WELCOME THE NEWEST ADDITION TO SPECIAL OPERATIONS STRIKEFORCE...
MACE!

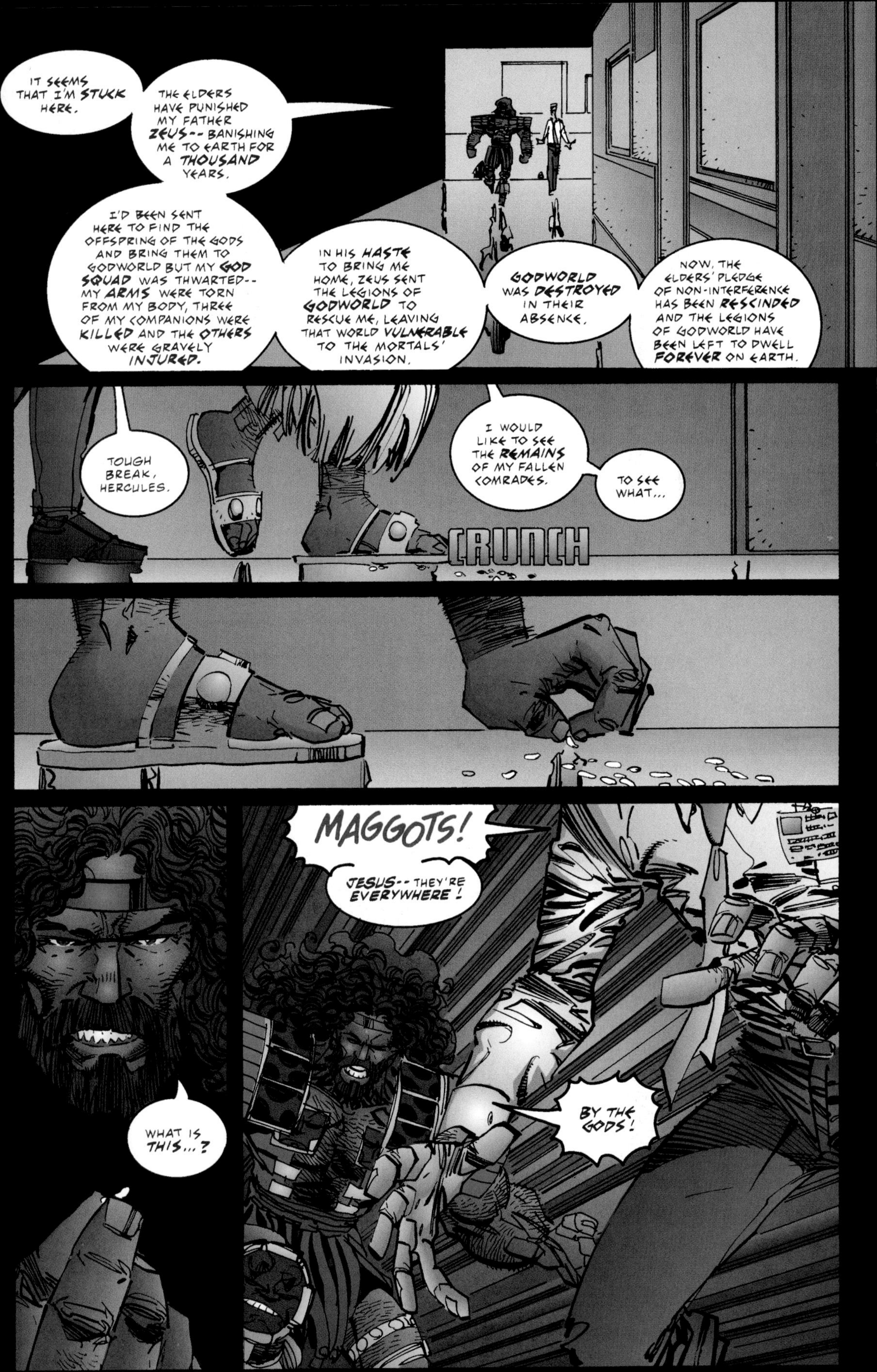

IT SEEMS THAT I'M STUCK HERE.
THE ELDERS HAVE PUNISHED MY FATHER ZEUS-- BANISHING ME TO EARTH FOR A THOUSAND YEARS.
I'D BEEN SENT HERE TO FIND THE OFFSPRING OF THE GODS AND BRING THEM TO GODWORLD BUT MY GOD SQUAD WAS THWARTED-- MY ARMS WERE TORN FROM MY BODY, THREE OF MY COMPANIONS WERE KILLED AND THE OTHERS WERE GRAVELY INJURED.
IN HIS HASTE TO BRING ME HOME, ZEUS SENT THE LEGIONS OF GODWORLD TO RESCUE ME, LEAVING THAT WORLD VULNERABLE TO THE MORTALS' INVASION.
GODWORLD WAS DESTROYED IN THEIR ABSENCE.
NOW, THE ELDERS' PLEDGE OF NON-INTERFERENCE HAS BEEN RESCINDED AND THE LEGIONS OF GODWORLD HAVE BEEN LEFT TO DWELL FOREVER ON EARTH.
TOUGH BREAK, HERCULES.
I WOULD LIKE TO SEE THE REMAINS OF MY FALLEN COMRADES.
TO SEE WHAT...
CRUNCH
WHAT IS THIS...?
MAGGOTS!
JESUS-- THEY'RE EVERYWHERE!
BY THE GODS!

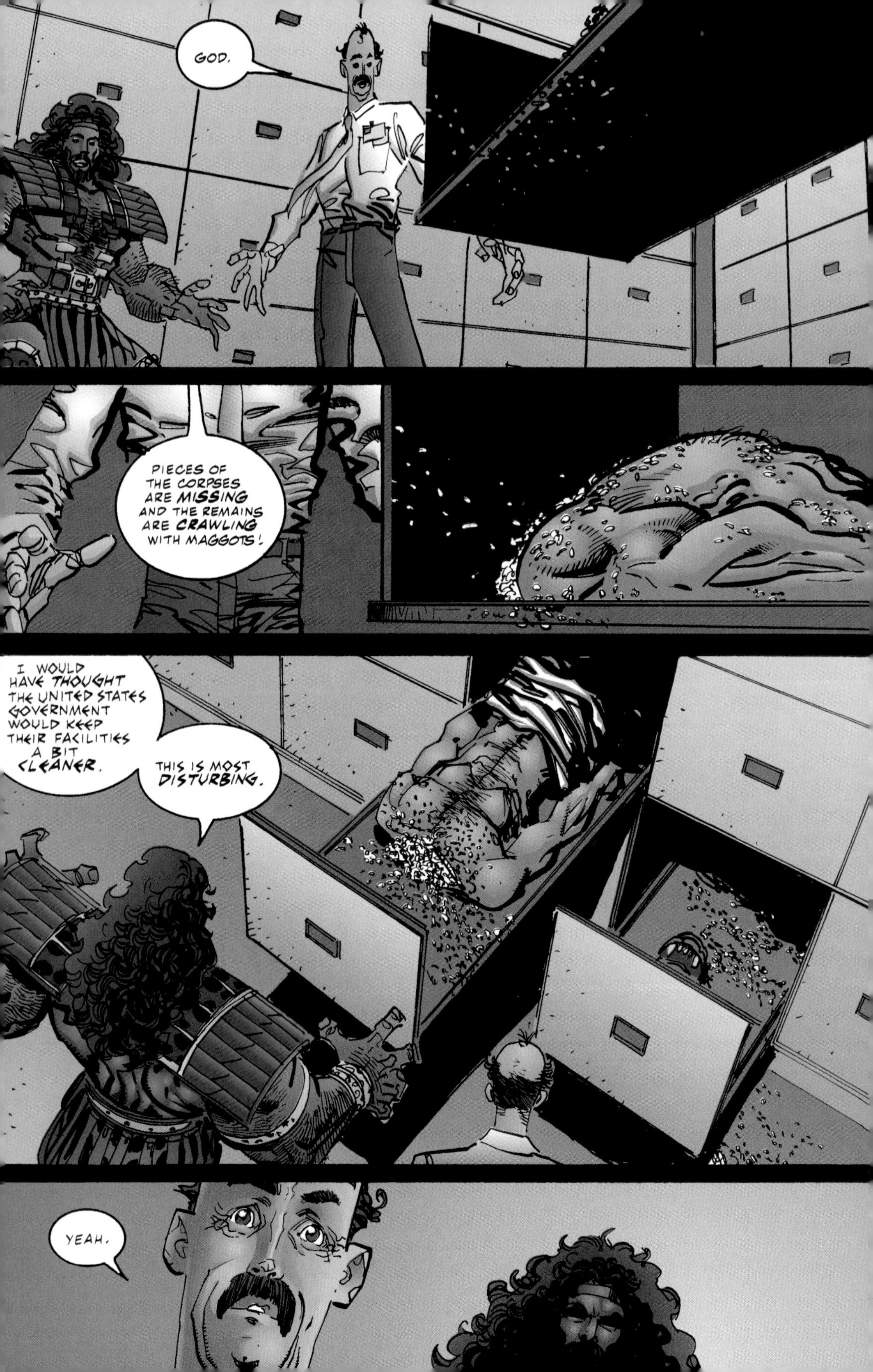
GOD.
PIECES OF THE CORPSES ARE MISSING AND THE REMAINS ARE CRAWLING WITH MAGGOTS!
I WOULD HAVE THOUGHT THE UNITED STATES GOVERNMENT WOULD KEEP THEIR FACILITIES A BIT CLEANER.
THIS IS MOST DISTURBING.
YEAH.

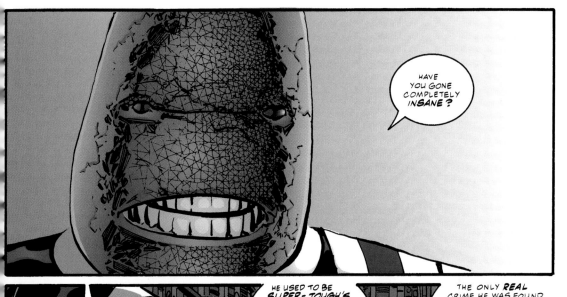

HAVE YOU GONE COMPLETELY *INSANE*?

MACE IS A COLD-BLOODED *KILLER*, STEPHENSON --HAVING HIM JOIN *SPECIAL OPERATIONS STRIKEFORCE* IS A *BIG* MISTAKE.

I CAN'T *BELIEVE* YOU ACTUALLY RECRUITED THE SON OF A BITCH-- AND THAT YOU THOUGHT WE'D THINK THAT YOUR DOING SO WAS A *GOOD* THING!

HE USED TO BE *SUPER-TOUGH'S* SIDEKICK, ROCK-- HE'S HAD A FEW LOUSY BREAKS-- HE THOUGHT HIS PARTNER WAS KILLED, FOR CRYING OUT LOUD --CUT HIM SOME SLACK.

THE ONLY *REAL* CRIME HE WAS FOUND GUILTY OF IS ASSAULTING A *POLICE OFFICER* AND FRANKLY, THEN-OFFICER DRAGON HAD JUST GONE ON A RAMPAGE THROUGH CHICAGO AND MACE'S ASSAULT ON HIM *STOPPED* THAT RAMPAGE.

YOU *KNOW* THERE'S MORE TO IT THAN THAT.

IN *ANY* CASE, MACE HAD EARLIER ATTACKED THE SHREW-- BACK WHEN HE WAS A HOMELESS FREAK.

HE'S *BAD NEWS*, STEPHENSON, *YOU* KNOW IT AND *I* KNOW IT.

YOU CAN'T *BEGIN* TO KNOW HOW TOUGH THIS JOB IS -- HOW MANY *FACTORS* ARE INVOLVED HERE --HOW MUCH *POLITICS*.

THIS IS NO EASY TASK, ROCK.

THERE ARE A LOT OF *TOUGH* CHOICES TO BE MADE HERE...

WE MAY *FINALLY* BE IMPLEMENTING OUR ORIGINAL PLAN OF EXPANDING TO SEVERAL *BRANCHES* FOR SPECIAL OPERATIONS STRIKEFORCE-- SEVERAL *COMPLEXES* AND I *NEED* TO INCREASE THE SIZE OF THE TEAM.

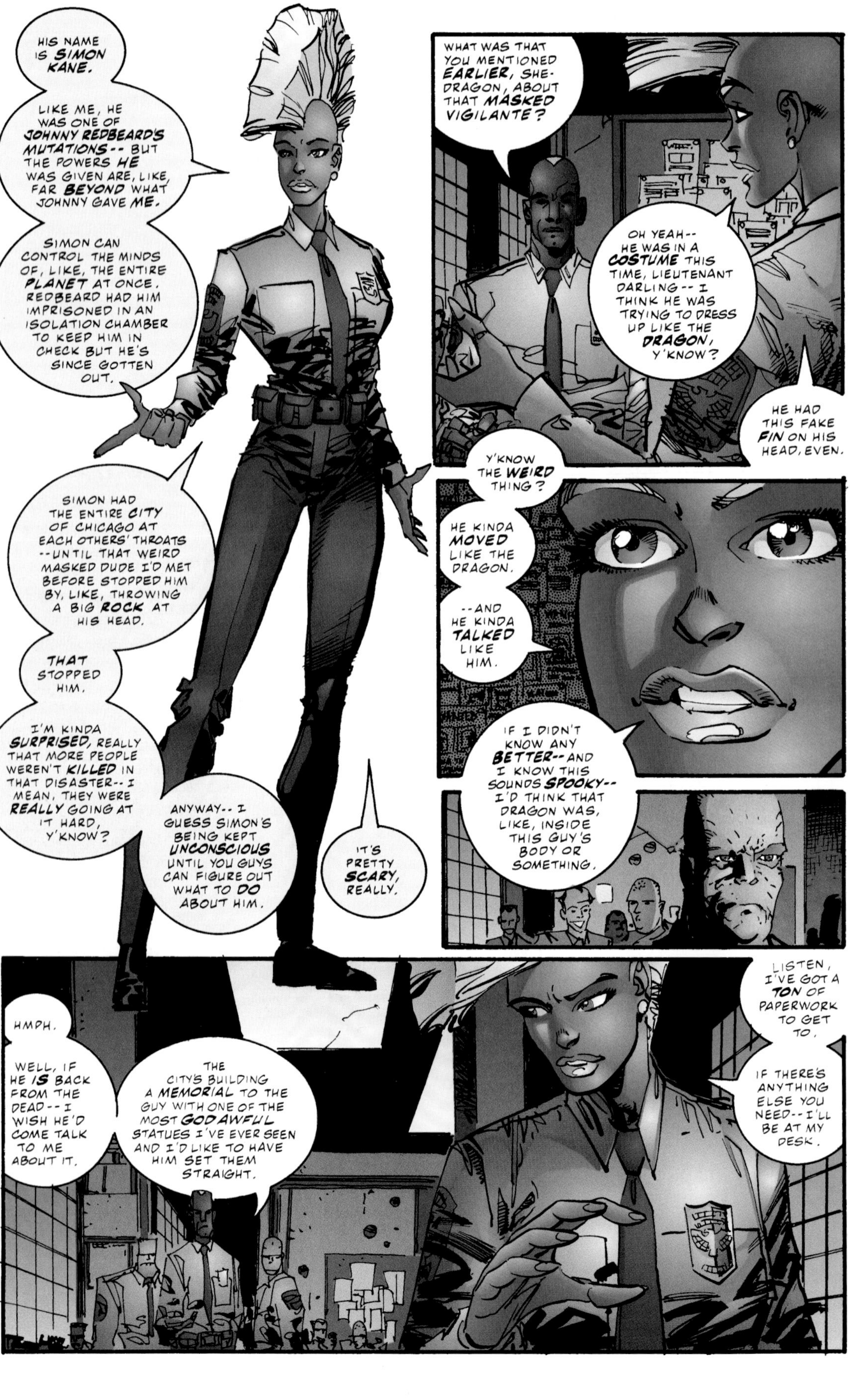
HIS NAME IS SIMON KANE.
LIKE ME, HE WAS ONE OF JOHNNY REDBEARD'S MUTATIONS-- BUT THE POWERS HE WAS GIVEN ARE, LIKE, FAR BEYOND WHAT JOHNNY GAVE ME.
SIMON CAN CONTROL THE MINDS OF, LIKE, THE ENTIRE PLANET AT ONCE. REDBEARD HAD HIM IMPRISONED IN AN ISOLATION CHAMBER TO KEEP HIM IN CHECK BUT HE'S SINCE GOTTEN OUT.
SIMON HAD THE ENTIRE CITY OF CHICAGO AT EACH OTHERS' THROATS --UNTIL THAT WEIRD MASKED DUDE I'D MET BEFORE STOPPED HIM BY, LIKE, THROWING A BIG ROCK AT HIS HEAD.
THAT STOPPED HIM.
I'M KINDA SURPRISED, REALLY THAT MORE PEOPLE WEREN'T KILLED IN THAT DISASTER-- I MEAN, THEY WERE REALLY GOING AT IT HARD, Y'KNOW?
ANYWAY-- I GUESS SIMON'S BEING KEPT UNCONSCIOUS UNTIL YOU GUYS CAN FIGURE OUT WHAT TO DO ABOUT HIM.
IT'S PRETTY SCARY, REALLY.
WHAT WAS THAT YOU MENTIONED EARLIER, SHE-DRAGON, ABOUT THAT MASKED VIGILANTE?
OH YEAH-- HE WAS IN A COSTUME THIS TIME, LIEUTENANT DARLING-- I THINK HE WAS TRYING TO DRESS UP LIKE THE DRAGON, Y'KNOW?
HE HAD THIS FAKE FIN ON HIS HEAD, EVEN.
Y'KNOW THE WEIRD THING?
HE KINDA MOVED LIKE THE DRAGON.
--AND HE KINDA TALKED LIKE HIM.
IF I DIDN'T KNOW ANY BETTER-- AND I KNOW THIS SOUNDS SPOOKY-- I'D THINK THAT DRAGON WAS, LIKE, INSIDE THIS GUY'S BODY OR SOMETHING.
HMPH.
WELL, IF HE IS BACK FROM THE DEAD-- I WISH HE'D COME TALK TO ME ABOUT IT.
THE CITY'S BUILDING A MEMORIAL TO THE GUY WITH ONE OF THE MOST GODAWFUL STATUES I'VE EVER SEEN AND I'D LIKE TO HAVE HIM SET THEM STRAIGHT.
LISTEN, I'VE GOT A TON OF PAPERWORK TO GET TO.
IF THERE'S ANYTHING ELSE YOU NEED-- I'LL BE AT MY DESK.

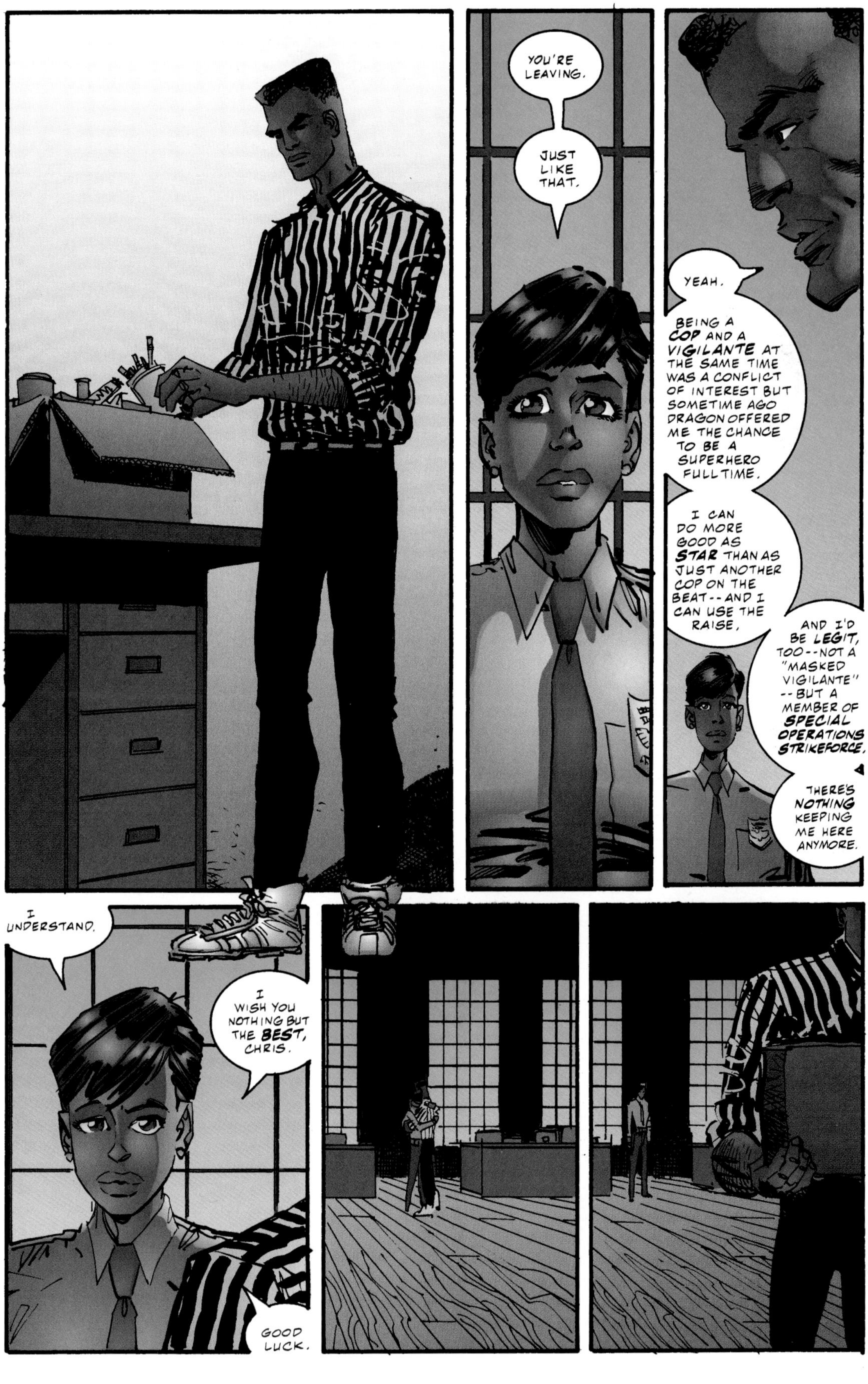
YOU'RE LEAVING.
JUST LIKE THAT.
YEAH.
BEING A COP AND A VIGILANTE AT THE SAME TIME WAS A CONFLICT OF INTEREST BUT SOMETIME AGO DRAGON OFFERED ME THE CHANCE TO BE A SUPERHERO FULLTIME.
I CAN DO MORE GOOD AS STAR THAN AS JUST ANOTHER COP ON THE BEAT--AND I CAN USE THE RAISE.
AND I'D BE LEGIT, TOO--NOT A "MASKED VIGILANTE" --BUT A MEMBER OF SPECIAL OPERATIONS STRIKEFORCE.
THERE'S NOTHING KEEPING ME HERE ANYMORE.
I UNDERSTAND.
I WISH YOU NOTHING BUT THE BEST, CHRIS.
GOOD LUCK.

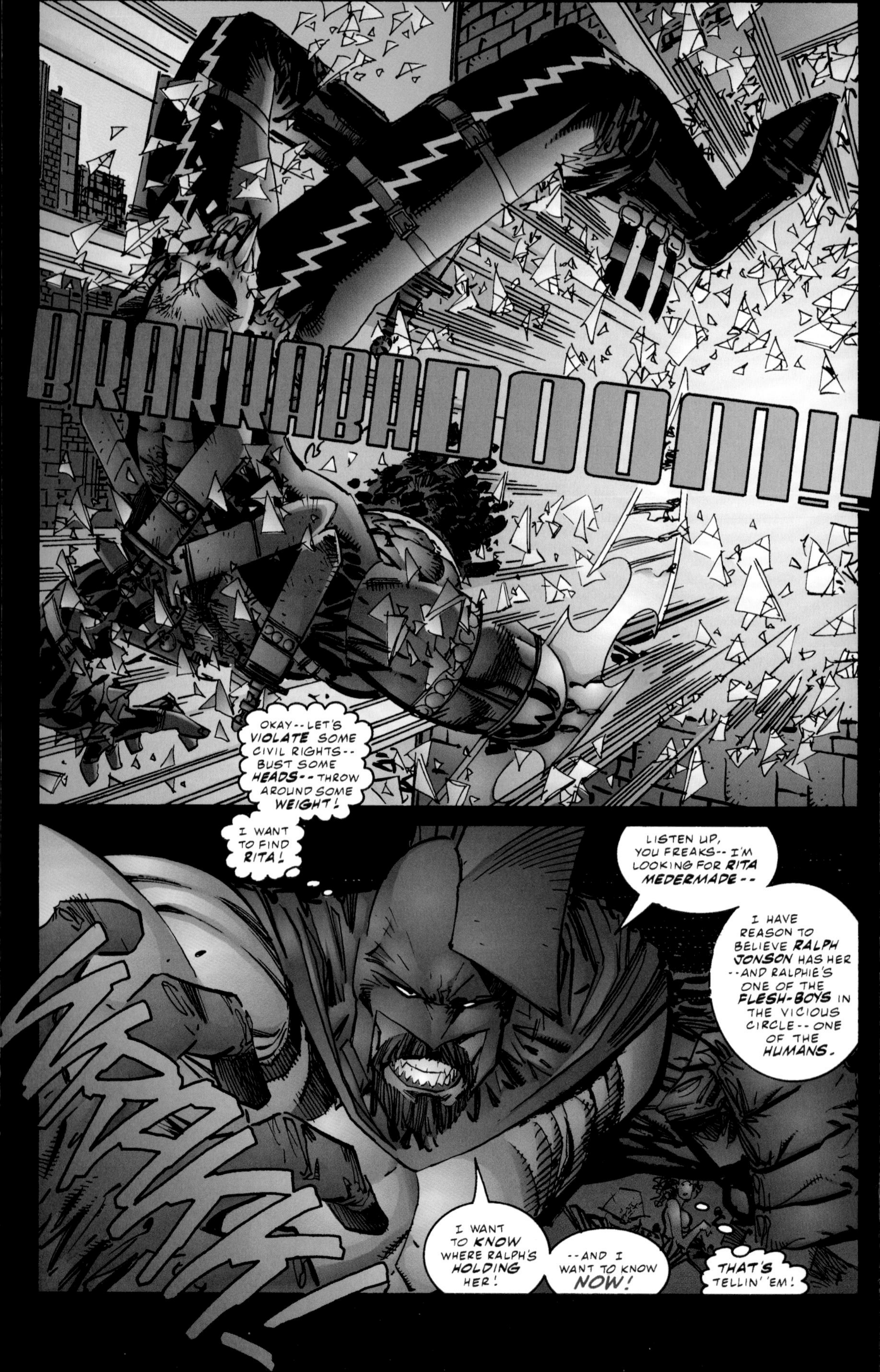

BRAKKABADOOM!!
OKAY--LET'S VIOLATE SOME CIVIL RIGHTS--BUST SOME HEADS--THROW AROUND SOME WEIGHT!
I WANT TO FIND RITA!
LISTEN UP, YOU FREAKS--I'M LOOKING FOR RITA MEDERMADE--
I HAVE REASON TO BELIEVE RALPH JONSON HAS HER--AND RALPHIE'S ONE OF THE FLESH-BOYS IN THE VICIOUS CIRCLE--ONE OF THE HUMANS.
I WANT TO KNOW WHERE RALPH'S HOLDING HER!
--AND I WANT TO KNOW NOW!
THAT'S TELLIN' 'EM!

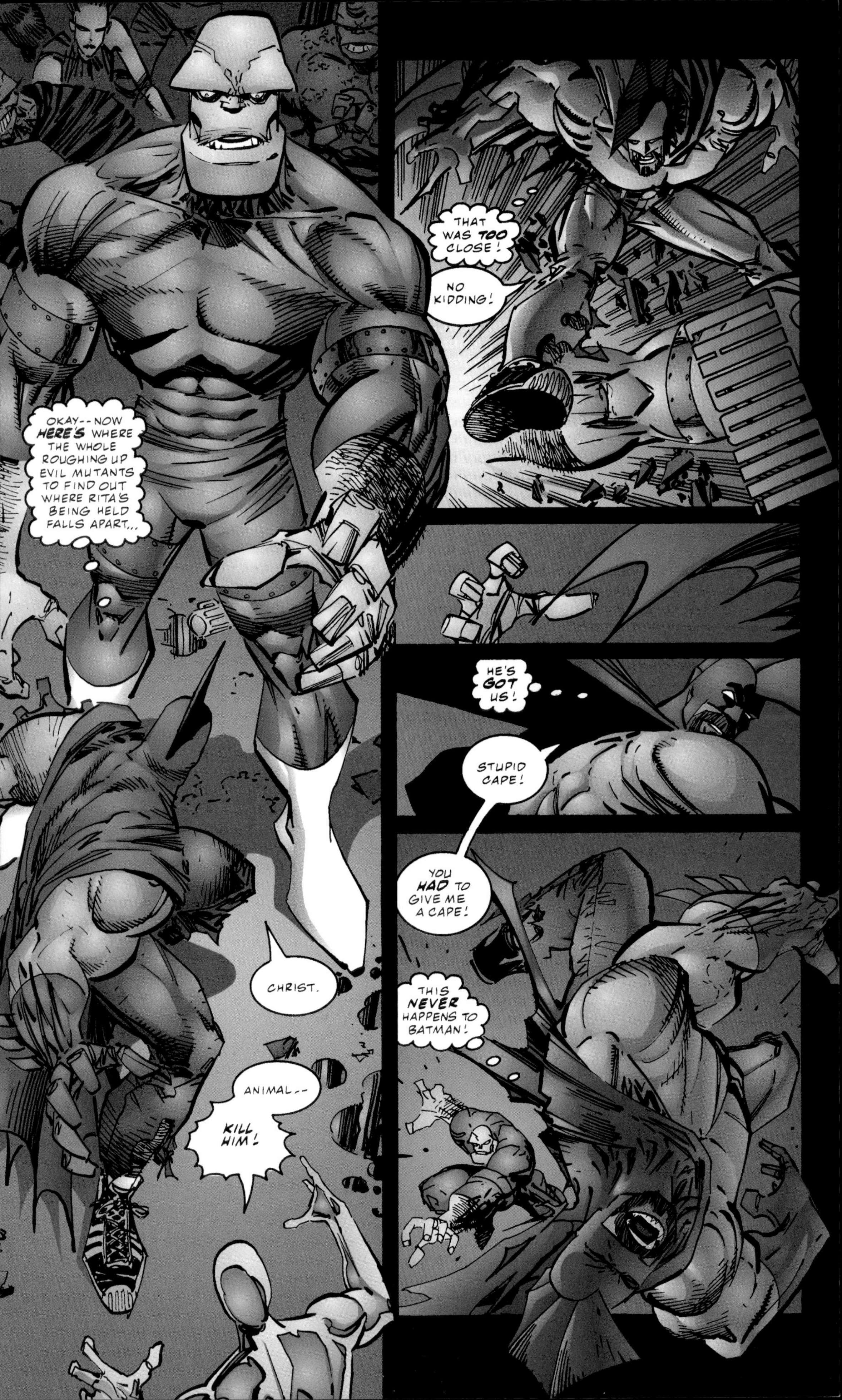
OKAY--NOW HERE'S WHERE THE WHOLE ROUGHING UP EVIL MUTANTS TO FIND OUT WHERE RITA'S BEING HELD FALLS APART...
CHRIST.
ANIMAL--
KILL HIM!
THAT WAS TOO CLOSE!
NO KIDDING!
HE'S GOT US!
STUPID CAPE!
YOU HAD TO GIVE ME A CAPE!
THIS NEVER HAPPENS TO BATMAN!

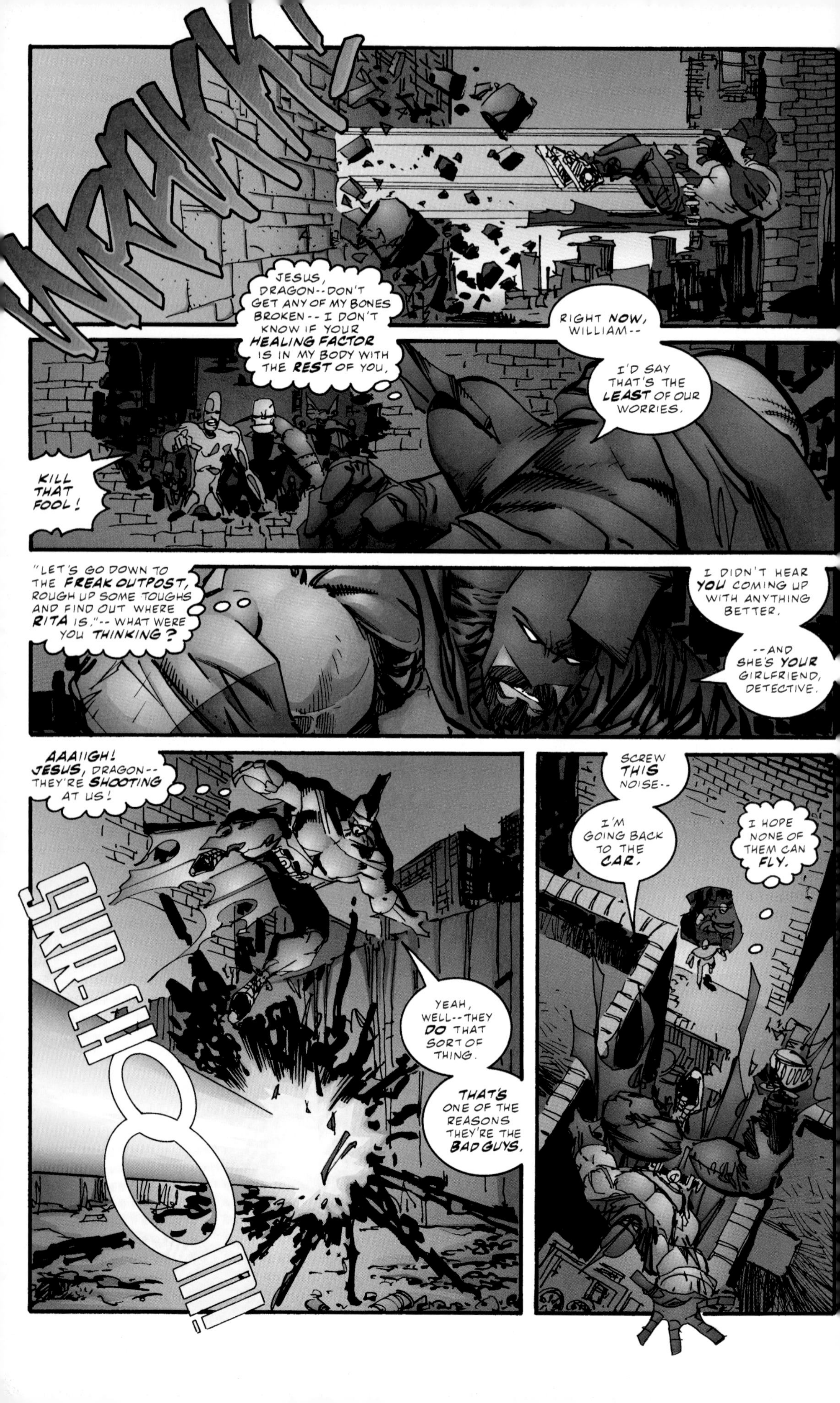
WRAKK!
JESUS, DRAGON--DON'T GET ANY OF MY BONES BROKEN-- I DON'T KNOW IF YOUR HEALING FACTOR IS IN MY BODY WITH THE REST OF YOU.
RIGHT NOW, WILLIAM--
I'D SAY THAT'S THE LEAST OF OUR WORRIES.
KILL THAT FOOL!
"LET'S GO DOWN TO THE FREAK OUTPOST, ROUGH UP SOME TOUGHS AND FIND OUT WHERE RITA IS."-- WHAT WERE YOU THINKING?
I DIDN'T HEAR YOU COMING UP WITH ANYTHING BETTER.
--AND SHE'S YOUR GIRLFRIEND, DETECTIVE.
AAAIIGH! JESUS, DRAGON-- THEY'RE SHOOTING AT US!
SKR-CHOOM!
YEAH, WELL--THEY DO THAT SORT OF THING.
THAT'S ONE OF THE REASONS THEY'RE THE BAD GUYS.
SCREW THIS NOISE--
I'M GOING BACK TO THE CAR.
I HOPE NONE OF THEM CAN FLY.

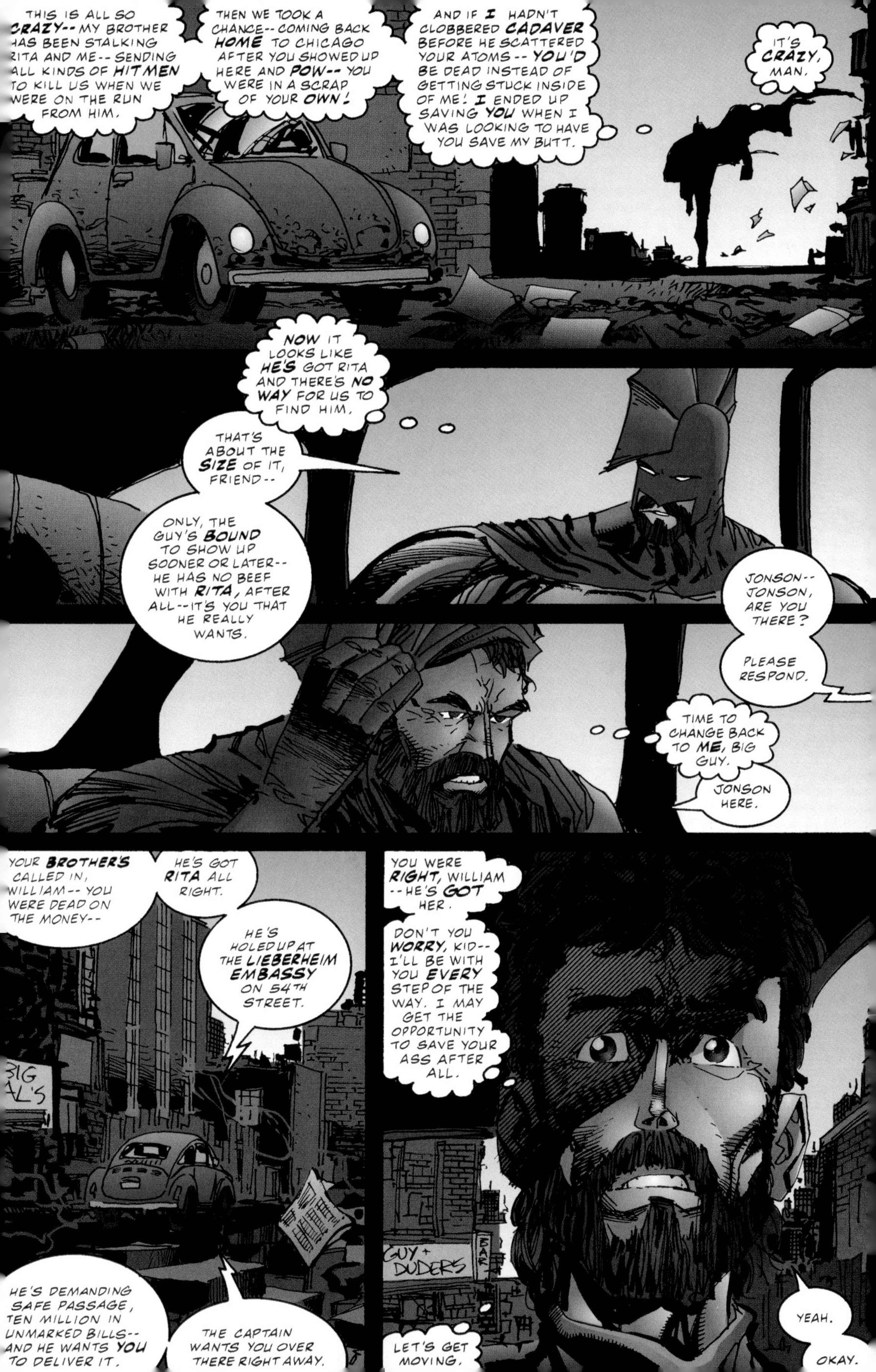

THIS IS ALL SO CRAZY-- MY BROTHER HAS BEEN STALKING RITA AND ME-- SENDING ALL KINDS OF HITMEN TO KILL US WHEN WE WERE ON THE RUN FROM HIM.
THEN WE TOOK A CHANCE-- COMING BACK HOME TO CHICAGO AFTER YOU SHOWED UP HERE AND POW-- YOU WERE IN A SCRAP OF YOUR OWN!
AND IF I HADN'T CLOBBERED CADAVER BEFORE HE SCATTERED YOUR ATOMS -- YOU'D BE DEAD INSTEAD OF GETTING STUCK INSIDE OF ME! I ENDED UP SAVING YOU WHEN I WAS LOOKING TO HAVE YOU SAVE MY BUTT.
IT'S CRAZY, MAN.
NOW IT LOOKS LIKE HE'S GOT RITA AND THERE'S NO WAY FOR US TO FIND HIM.
THAT'S ABOUT THE SIZE OF IT, FRIEND--
ONLY, THE GUY'S BOUND TO SHOW UP SOONER OR LATER-- HE HAS NO BEEF WITH RITA, AFTER ALL--IT'S YOU THAT HE REALLY WANTS.
JONSON-- JONSON, ARE YOU THERE?
PLEASE RESPOND.
TIME TO CHANGE BACK TO ME, BIG GUY.
JONSON HERE.
YOUR BROTHER'S CALLED IN, WILLIAM-- YOU WERE DEAD ON THE MONEY--
HE'S GOT RITA ALL RIGHT.
HE'S HOLED UP AT THE LIEBERHEIM EMBASSY ON 54TH STREET.
BIG AL'S
HE'S DEMANDING SAFE PASSAGE, TEN MILLION IN UNMARKED BILLS-- AND HE WANTS YOU TO DELIVER IT.
THE CAPTAIN WANTS YOU OVER THERE RIGHT AWAY.
YOU WERE RIGHT, WILLIAM --HE'S GOT HER.
DON'T YOU WORRY, KID-- I'LL BE WITH YOU EVERY STEP OF THE WAY. I MAY GET THE OPPORTUNITY TO SAVE YOUR ASS AFTER ALL.
GUY + DUDERS
BAR
LET'S GET MOVING.
YEAH.
OKAY.

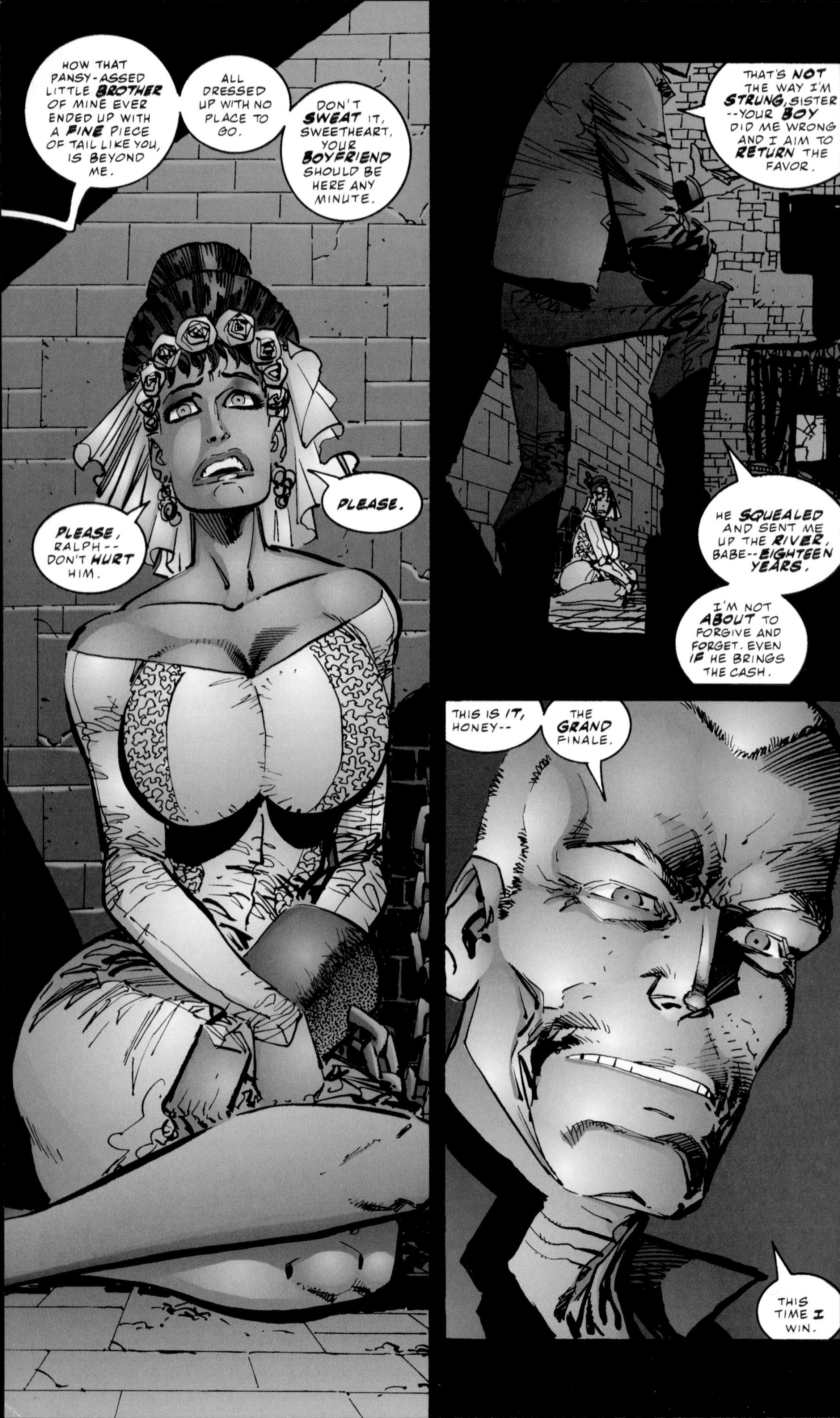
HOW THAT PANSY-ASSED LITTLE BROTHER OF MINE EVER ENDED UP WITH A FINE PIECE OF TAIL LIKE YOU, IS BEYOND ME.
ALL DRESSED UP WITH NO PLACE TO GO.
DON'T SWEAT IT, SWEETHEART, YOUR BOYFRIEND SHOULD BE HERE ANY MINUTE.
PLEASE.
PLEASE, RALPH-- DON'T HURT HIM.
THAT'S NOT THE WAY I'M STRUNG, SISTER --YOUR BOY DID ME WRONG AND I AIM TO RETURN THE FAVOR.
HE SQUEALED AND SENT ME UP THE RIVER, BABE--EIGHTEEN YEARS.
I'M NOT ABOUT TO FORGIVE AND FORGET. EVEN IF HE BRINGS THE CASH.
THIS IS IT, HONEY--
THE GRAND FINALE.
THIS TIME I WIN.

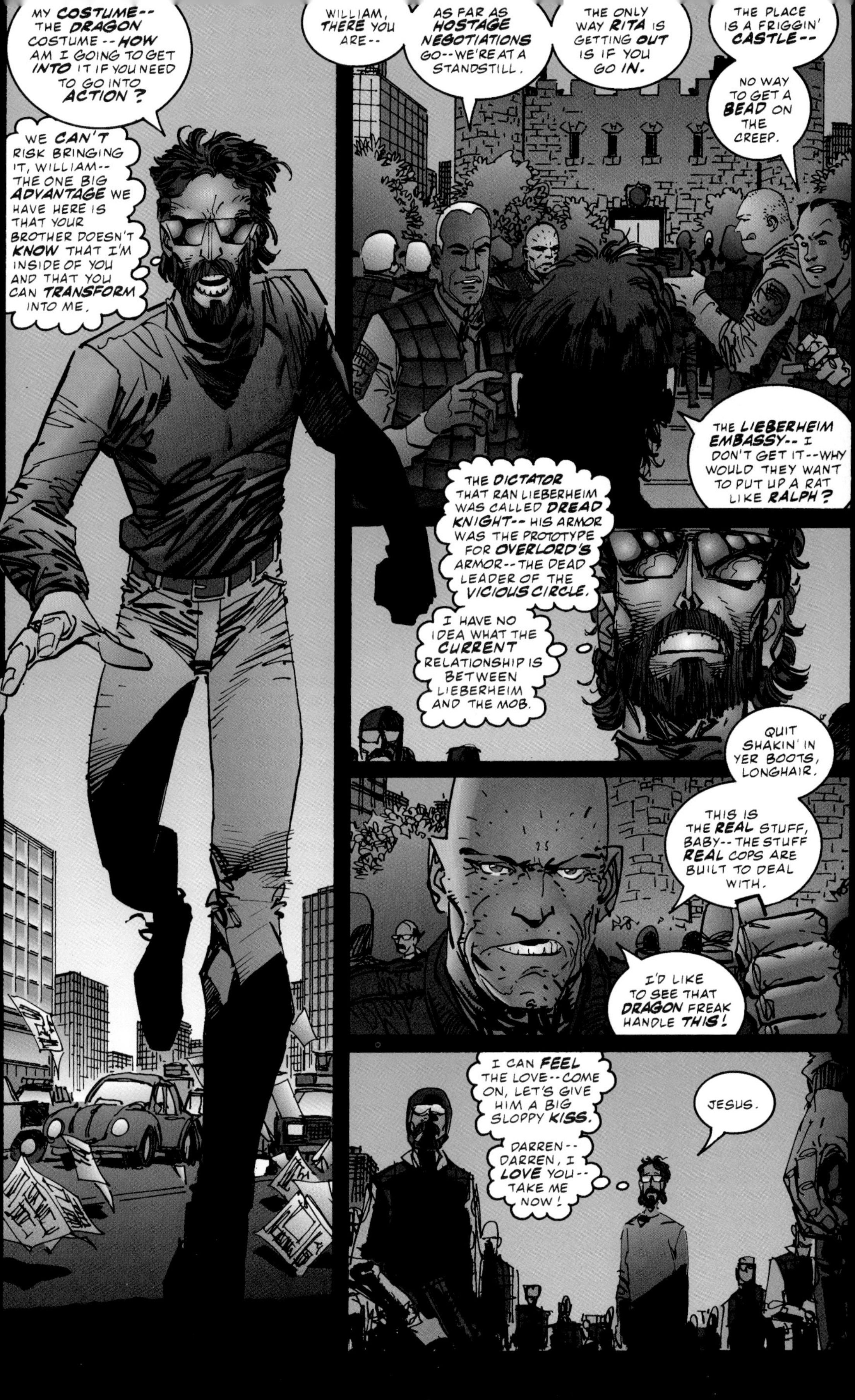
MY COSTUME-- THE DRAGON COSTUME--HOW AM I GOING TO GET INTO IT IF YOU NEED TO GO INTO ACTION?
WE CAN'T RISK BRINGING IT, WILLIAM-- THE ONE BIG ADVANTAGE WE HAVE HERE IS THAT YOUR BROTHER DOESN'T KNOW THAT I'M INSIDE OF YOU AND THAT YOU CAN TRANSFORM INTO ME.
WILLIAM, THERE YOU ARE--
AS FAR AS HOSTAGE NEGOTIATIONS GO--WE'RE AT A STANDSTILL.
THE ONLY WAY RITA IS GETTING OUT IS IF YOU GO IN.
THE PLACE IS A FRIGGIN' CASTLE--
NO WAY TO GET A BEAD ON THE CREEP.
THE LIEBERHEIM EMBASSY-- I DON'T GET IT--WHY WOULD THEY WANT TO PUT UP A RAT LIKE RALPH?
THE DICTATOR THAT RAN LIEBERHEIM WAS CALLED DREAD KNIGHT-- HIS ARMOR WAS THE PROTOTYPE FOR OVERLORD'S ARMOR--THE DEAD LEADER OF THE VICIOUS CIRCLE.
I HAVE NO IDEA WHAT THE CURRENT RELATIONSHIP IS BETWEEN LIEBERHEIM AND THE MOB.
QUIT SHAKIN' IN YER BOOTS, LONGHAIR.
THIS IS THE REAL STUFF, BABY--THE STUFF REAL COPS ARE BUILT TO DEAL WITH.
I'D LIKE TO SEE THAT DRAGON FREAK HANDLE THIS!
I CAN FEEL THE LOVE--COME ON, LET'S GIVE HIM A BIG SLOPPY KISS.
DARREN-- DARREN, I LOVE YOU-- TAKE ME NOW!
JESUS.

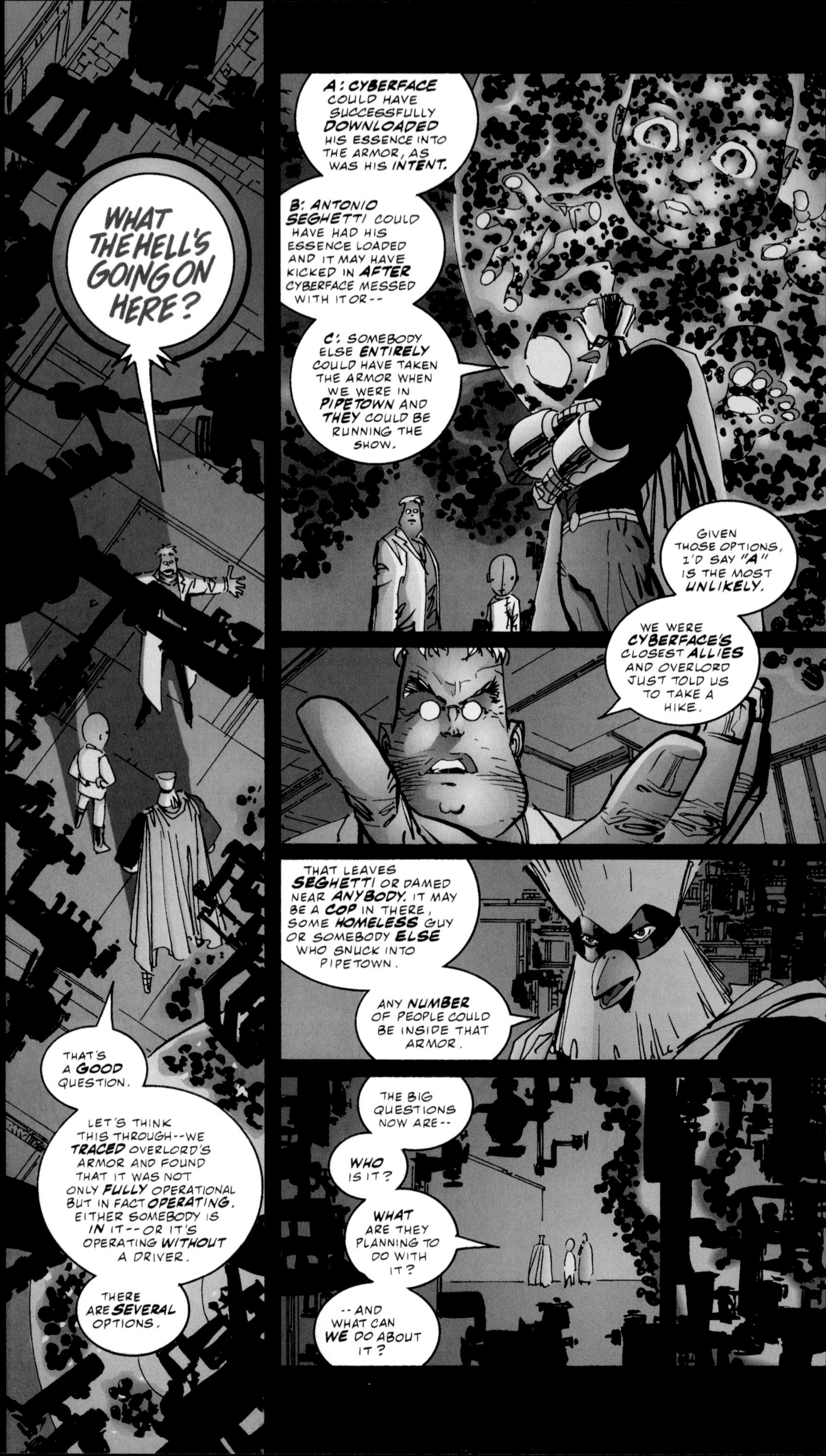

WHAT THE HELL'S GOING ON HERE?
THAT'S A GOOD QUESTION.
LET'S THINK THIS THROUGH--WE TRACED OVERLORD'S ARMOR AND FOUND THAT IT WAS NOT ONLY FULLY OPERATIONAL BUT IN FACT OPERATING. EITHER SOMEBODY IS IN IT--OR IT'S OPERATING WITHOUT A DRIVER.
THERE ARE SEVERAL OPTIONS.
A: CYBERFACE COULD HAVE SUCCESSFULLY DOWNLOADED HIS ESSENCE INTO THE ARMOR, AS WAS HIS INTENT.
B: ANTONIO SEGHETTI COULD HAVE HAD HIS ESSENCE LOADED AND IT MAY HAVE KICKED IN AFTER CYBERFACE MESSED WITH IT OR--
C: SOMEBODY ELSE ENTIRELY COULD HAVE TAKEN THE ARMOR WHEN WE WERE IN PIPETOWN AND THEY COULD BE RUNNING THE SHOW.
GIVEN THOSE OPTIONS, I'D SAY "A" IS THE MOST UNLIKELY.
WE WERE CYBERFACE'S CLOSEST ALLIES AND OVERLORD JUST TOLD US TO TAKE A HIKE.
THAT LEAVES SEGHETTI OR DAMED NEAR ANYBODY. IT MAY BE A COP IN THERE, SOME HOMELESS GUY OR SOMEBODY ELSE WHO SNUCK INTO PIPETOWN.
ANY NUMBER OF PEOPLE COULD BE INSIDE THAT ARMOR.
THE BIG QUESTIONS NOW ARE--
WHO IS IT?
WHAT ARE THEY PLANNING TO DO WITH IT?
--AND WHAT CAN WE DO ABOUT IT?

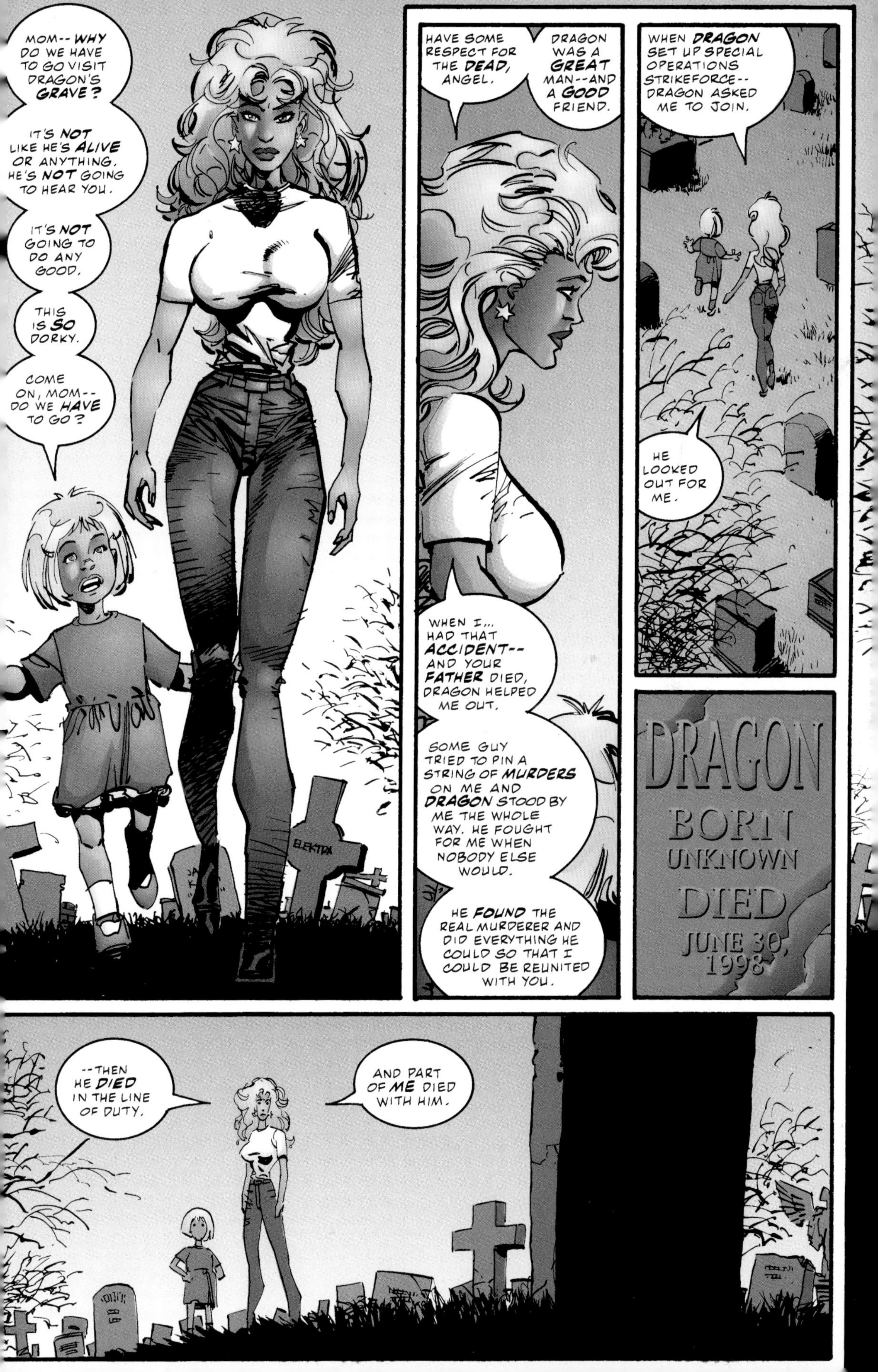
MOM--WHY DO WE HAVE TO GO VISIT DRAGON'S GRAVE?
IT'S NOT LIKE HE'S ALIVE OR ANYTHING. HE'S NOT GOING TO HEAR YOU.
IT'S NOT GOING TO DO ANY GOOD.
THIS IS SO DORKY.
COME ON, MOM--DO WE HAVE TO GO?
ELEKTRA
HAVE SOME RESPECT FOR THE DEAD, ANGEL.
DRAGON WAS A GREAT MAN--AND A GOOD FRIEND.
WHEN I... HAD THAT ACCIDENT--AND YOUR FATHER DIED, DRAGON HELPED ME OUT.
SOME GUY TRIED TO PIN A STRING OF MURDERS ON ME AND DRAGON STOOD BY ME THE WHOLE WAY. HE FOUGHT FOR ME WHEN NOBODY ELSE WOULD.
HE FOUND THE REAL MURDERER AND DID EVERYTHING HE COULD SO THAT I COULD BE REUNITED WITH YOU.
WHEN DRAGON SET UP SPECIAL OPERATIONS STRIKEFORCE--DRAGON ASKED ME TO JOIN.
HE LOOKED OUT FOR ME.
DRAGON
BORN
UNKNOWN
DIED
JUNE 30, 1998
--THEN HE DIED IN THE LINE OF DUTY.
AND PART OF ME DIED WITH HIM.

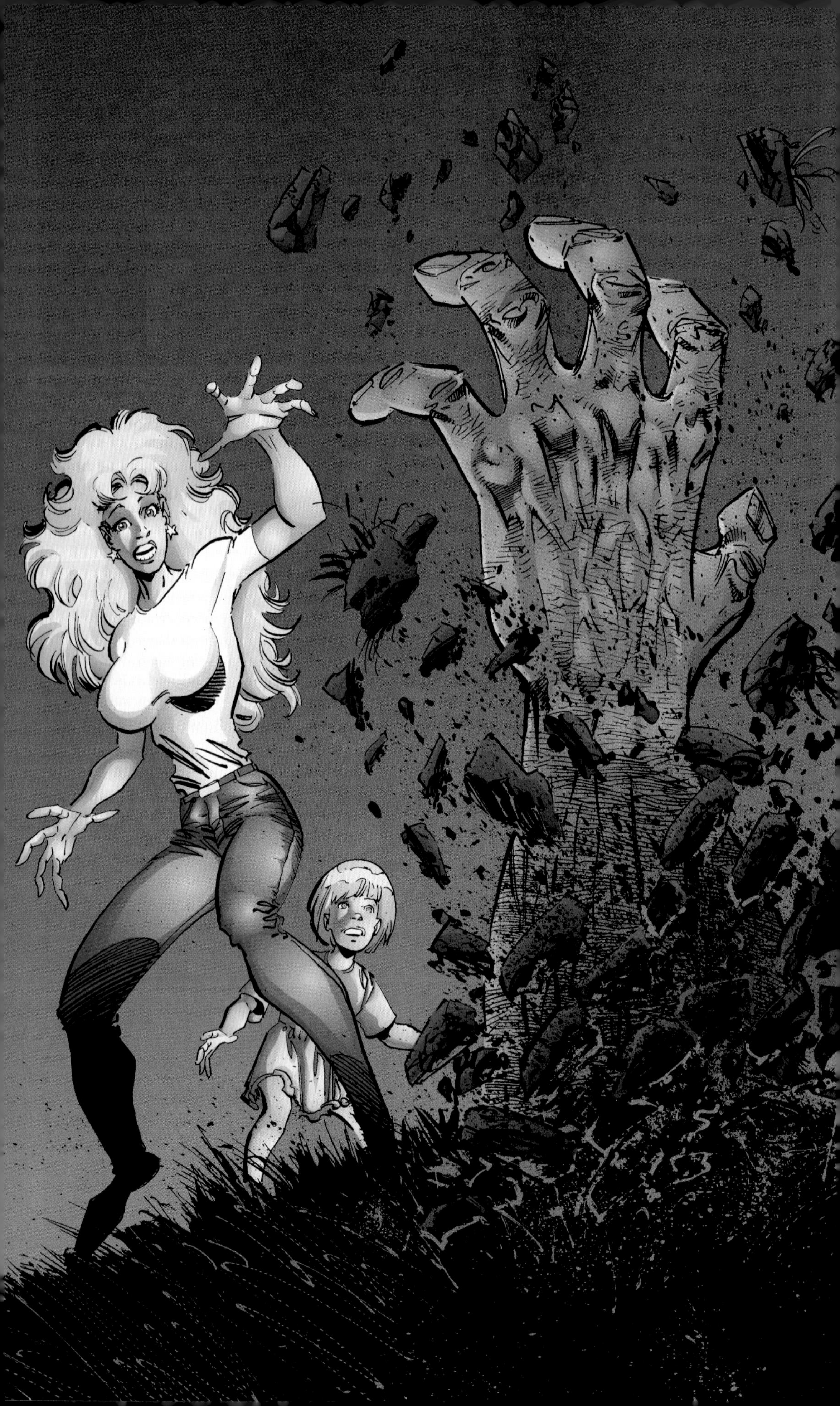

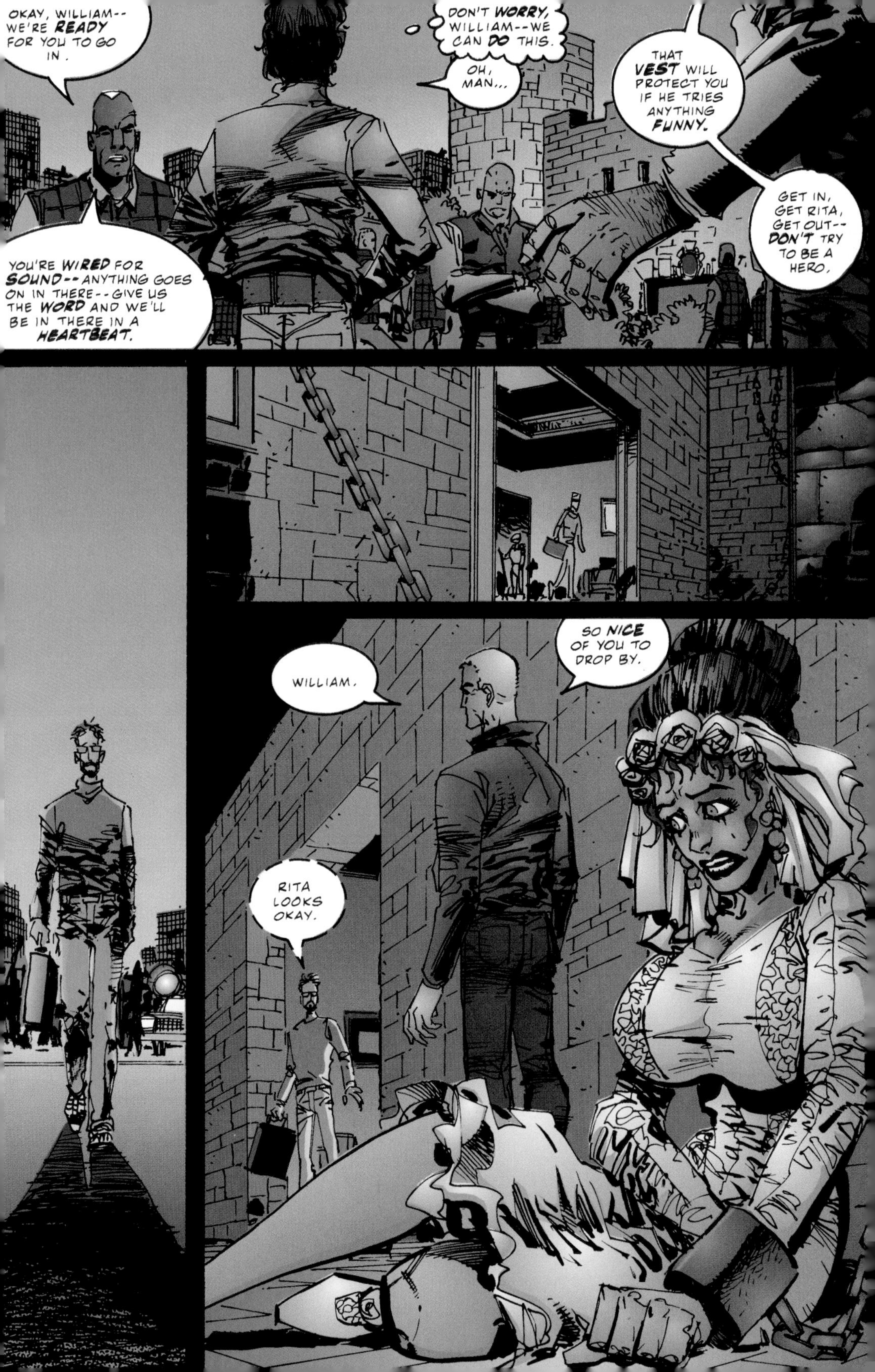
OKAY, WILLIAM-- WE'RE READY FOR YOU TO GO IN.
YOU'RE WIRED FOR SOUND-- ANYTHING GOES ON IN THERE-- GIVE US THE WORD AND WE'LL BE IN THERE IN A HEARTBEAT.
DON'T WORRY, WILLIAM--WE CAN DO THIS.
OH, MAN...
THAT VEST WILL PROTECT YOU IF HE TRIES ANYTHING FUNNY.
GET IN, GET RITA, GET OUT-- DON'T TRY TO BE A HERO.
WILLIAM.
SO NICE OF YOU TO DROP BY.
RITA LOOKS OKAY.

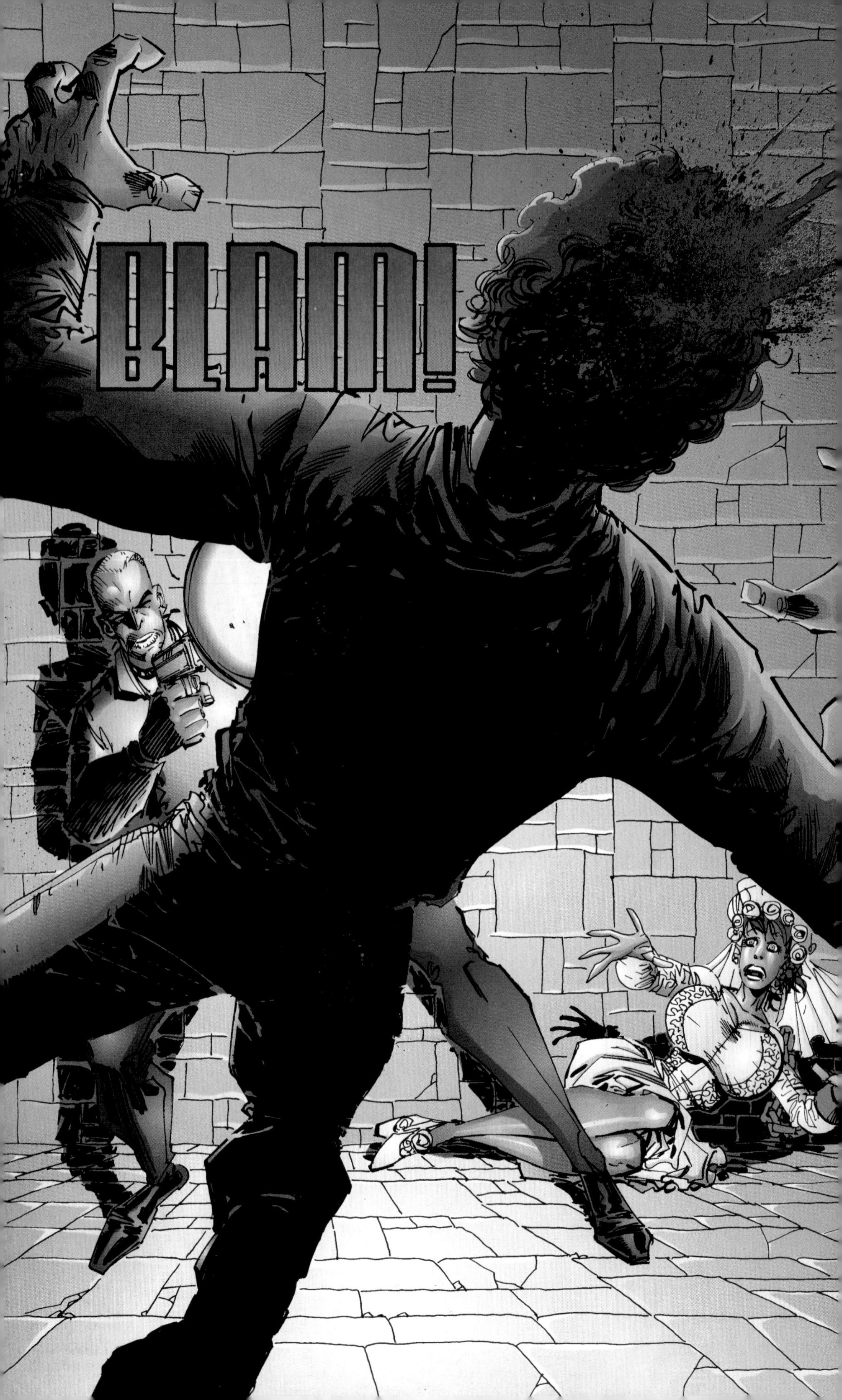
BLAM!

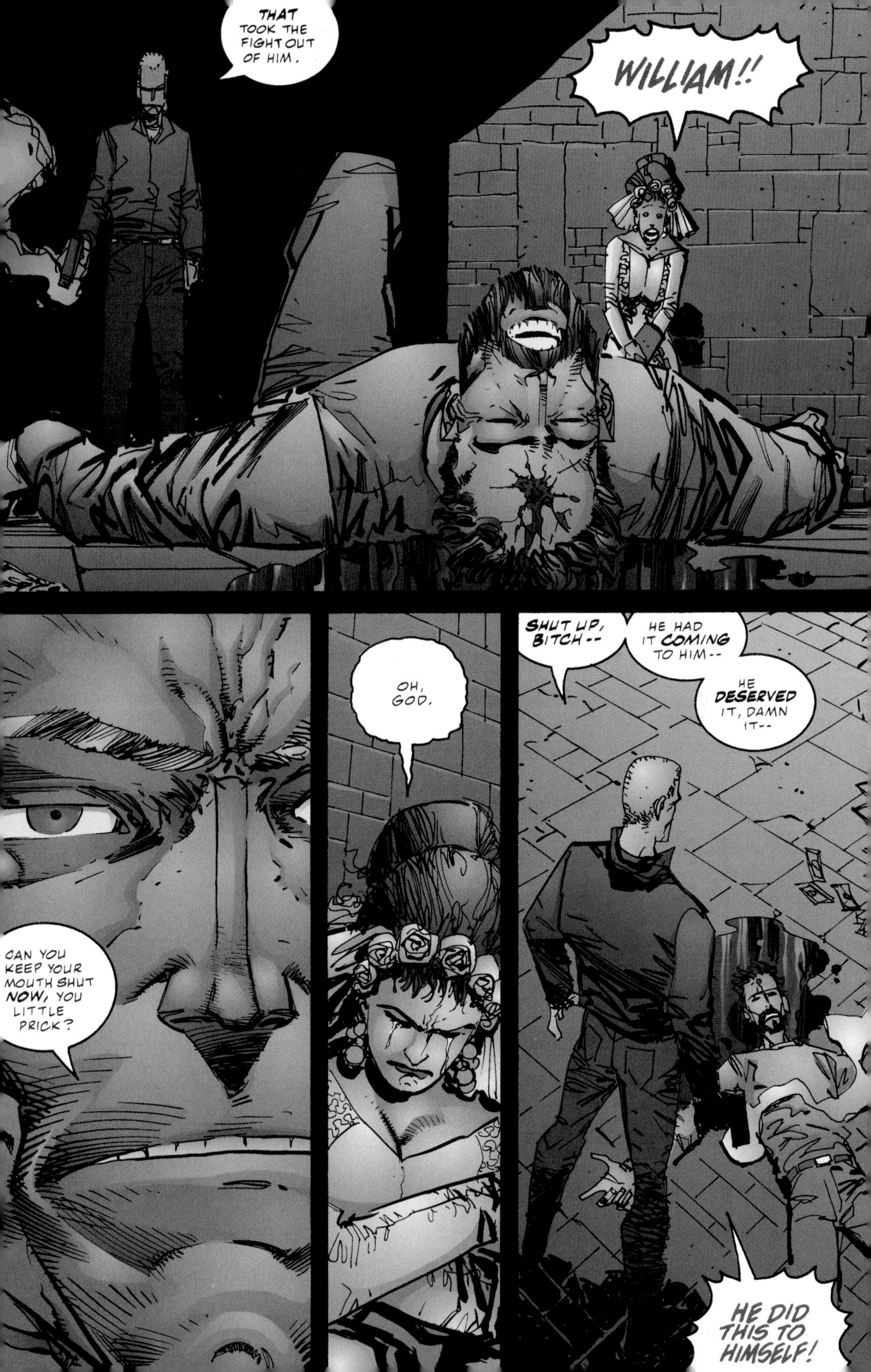
THAT TOOK THE FIGHT OUT OF HIM.
WILLIAM!!
CAN YOU KEEP YOUR MOUTH SHUT NOW, YOU LITTLE PRICK?
OH, GOD.
SHUT UP, BITCH--
HE HAD IT COMING TO HIM--
HE DESERVED IT, DAMN IT--
HE DID THIS TO HIMSELF!

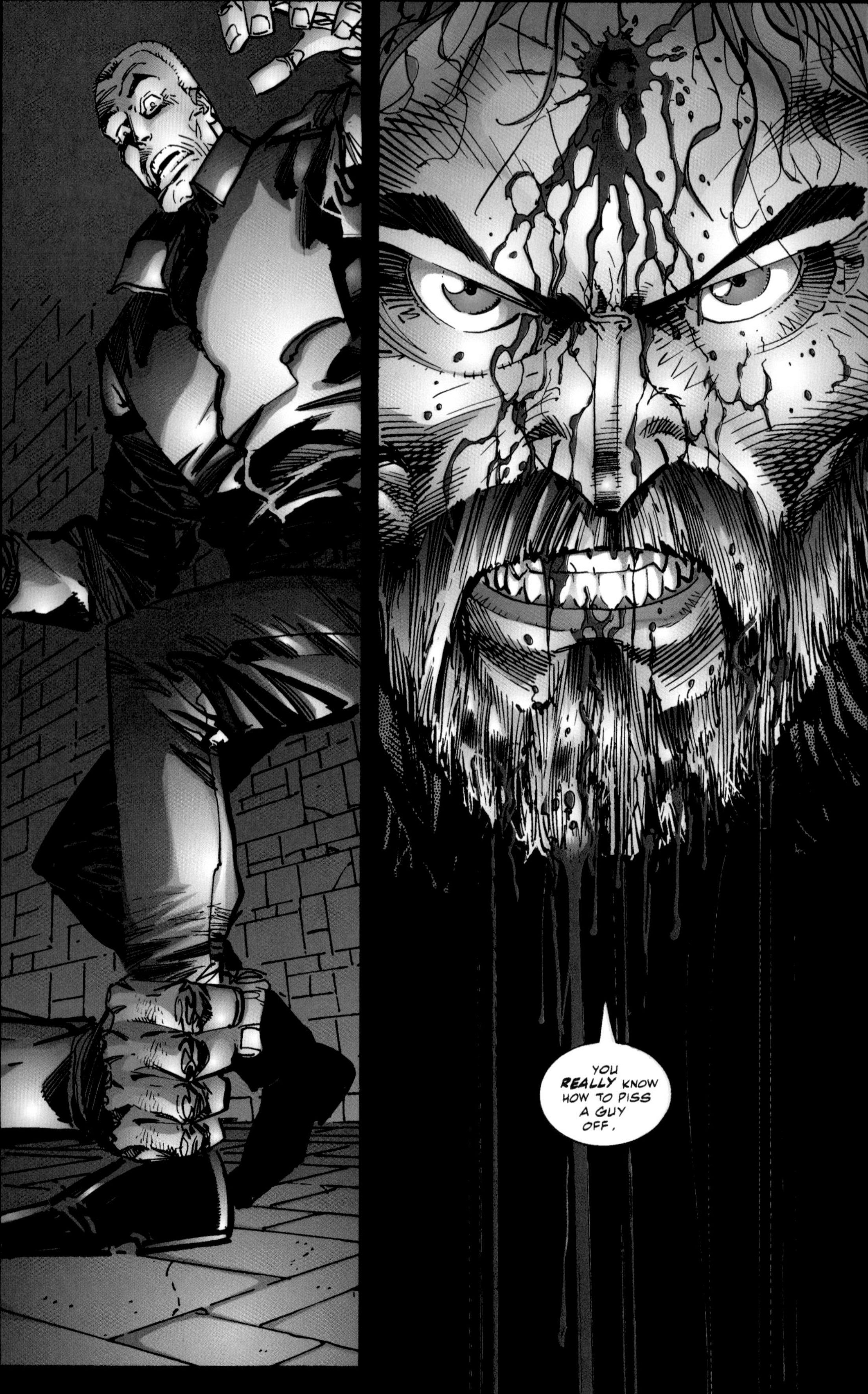
YOU REALLY KNOW HOW TO PISS A GUY OFF.

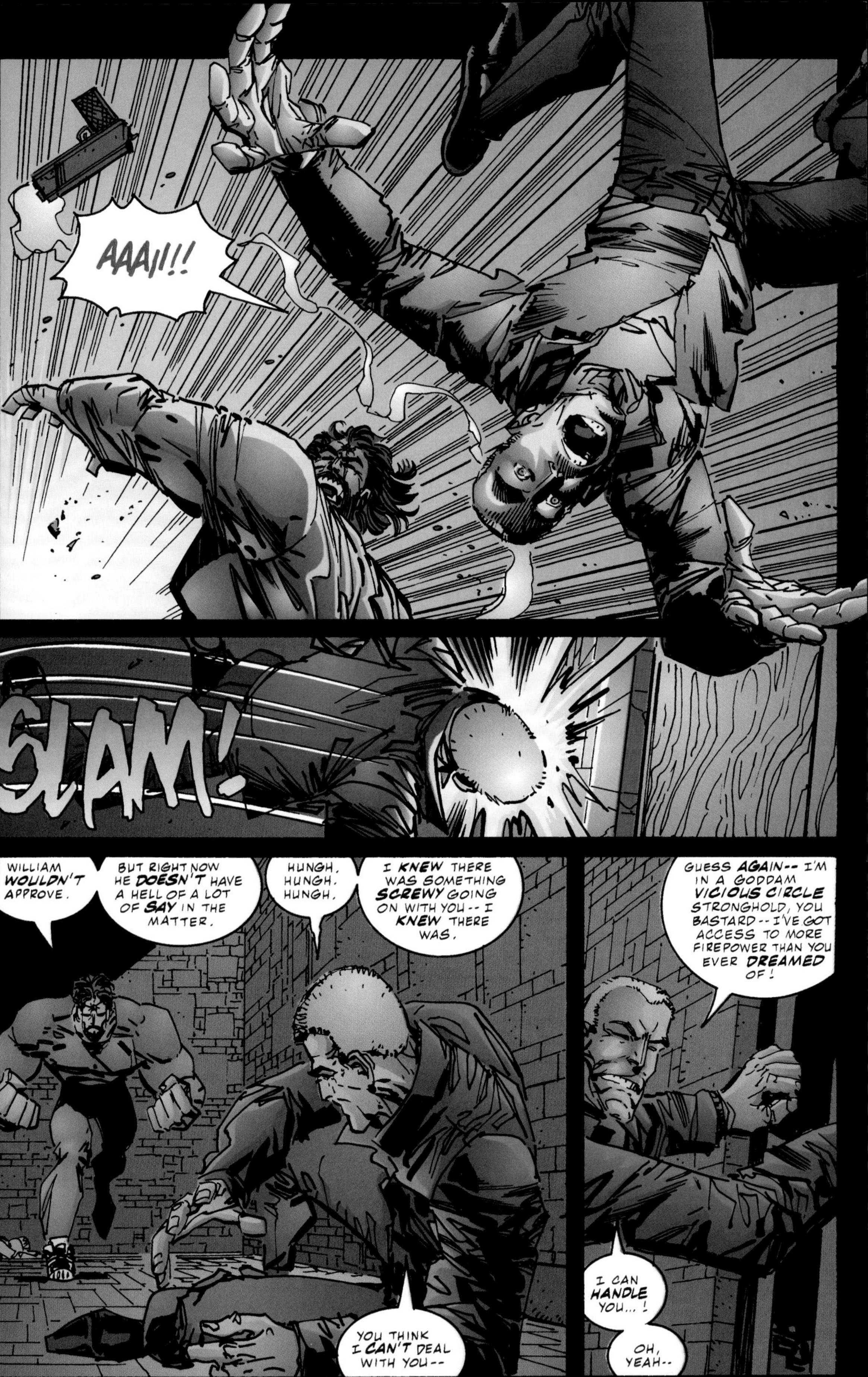

AAAJJ!!
SLAM!
WILLIAM WOULDN'T APPROVE.
BUT RIGHT NOW HE DOESN'T HAVE A HELL OF A LOT OF SAY IN THE MATTER.
HUNGH. HUNGH. HUNGH.
I KNEW THERE WAS SOMETHING SCREWY GOING ON WITH YOU -- I KNEW THERE WAS.
YOU THINK I CAN'T DEAL WITH YOU--
GUESS AGAIN-- I'M IN A GODDAM VICIOUS CIRCLE STRONGHOLD, YOU BASTARD -- I'VE GOT ACCESS TO MORE FIREPOWER THAN YOU EVER DREAMED OF!
I CAN HANDLE YOU... !
OH, YEAH--

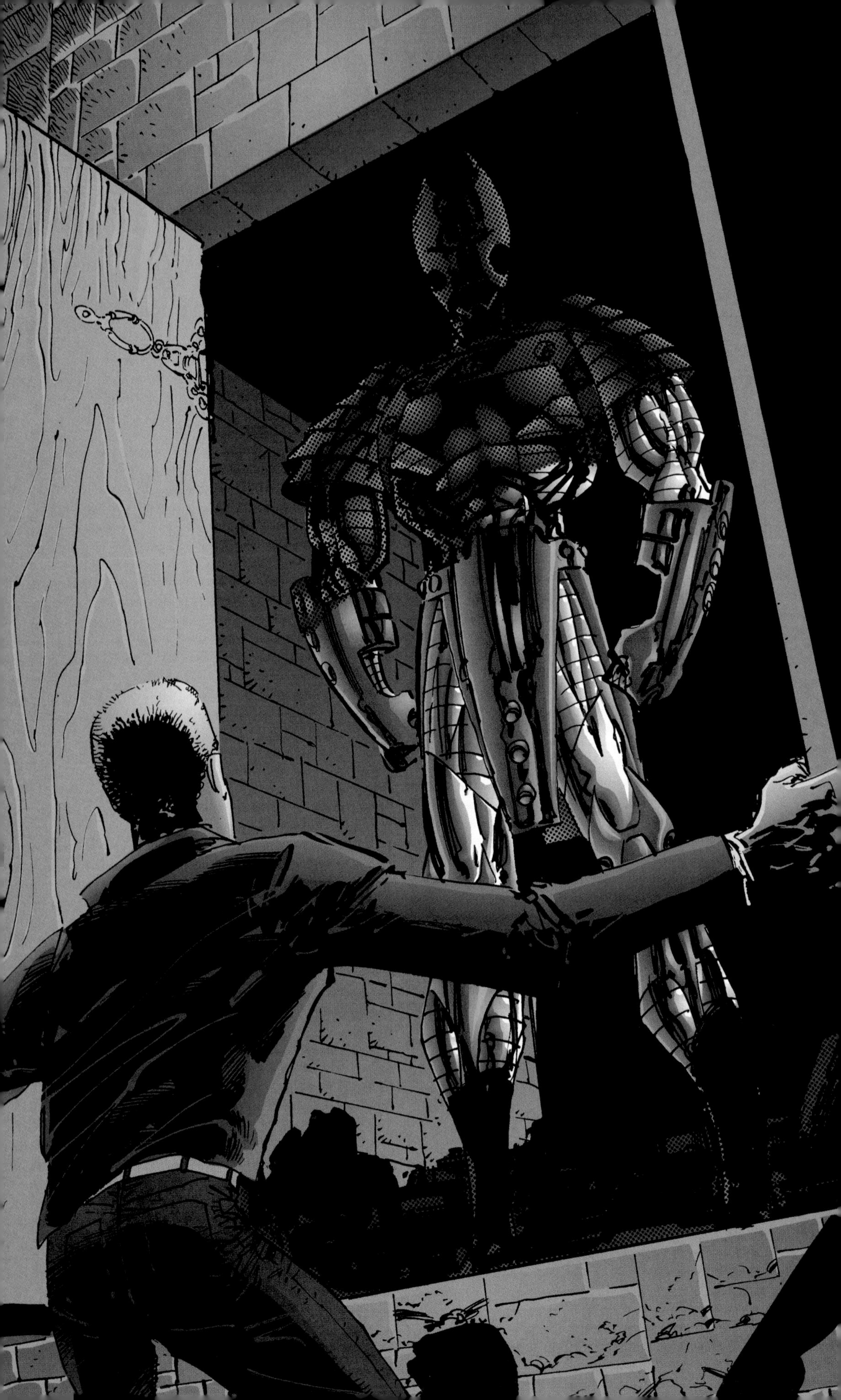

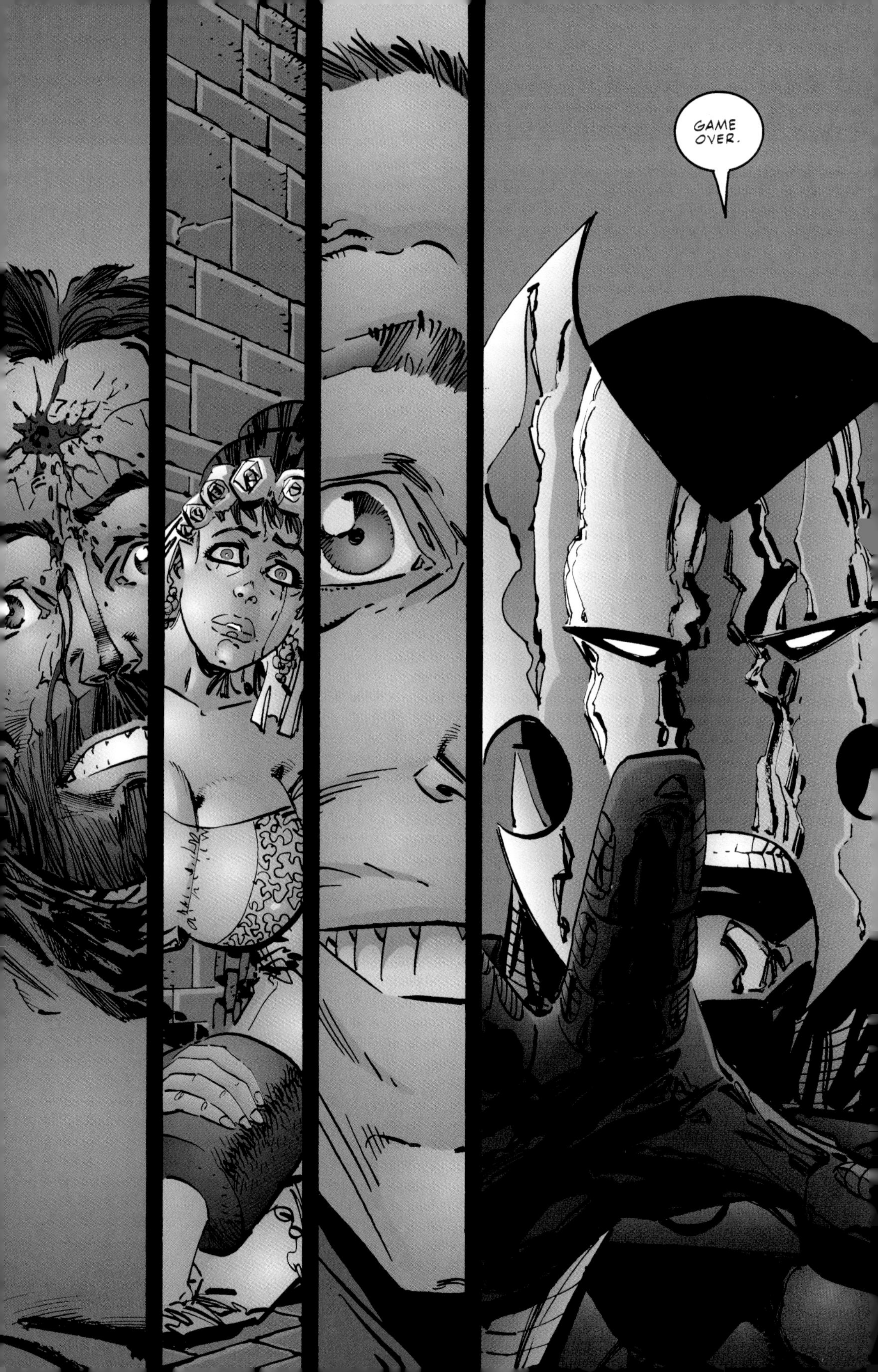
GAME OVER.

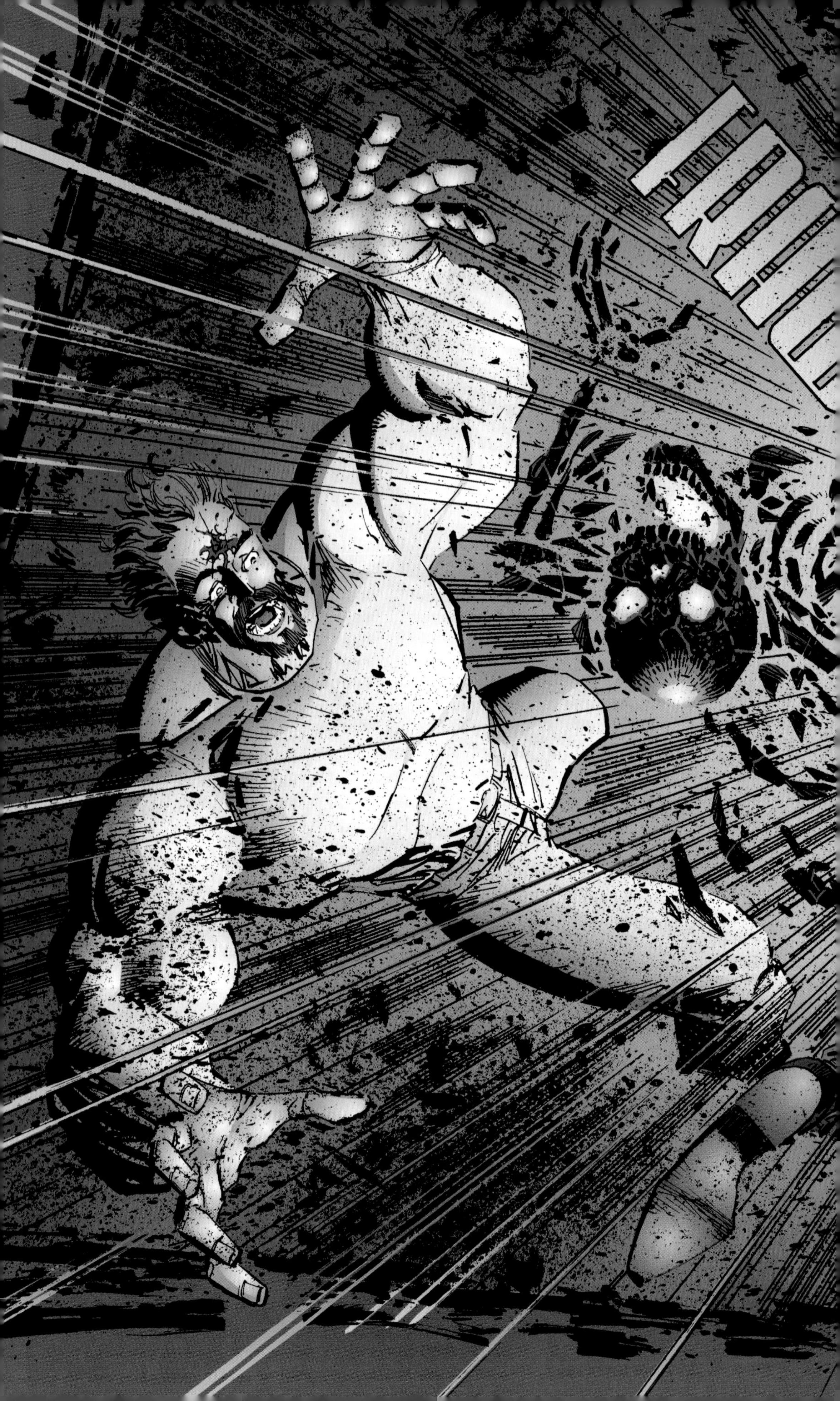

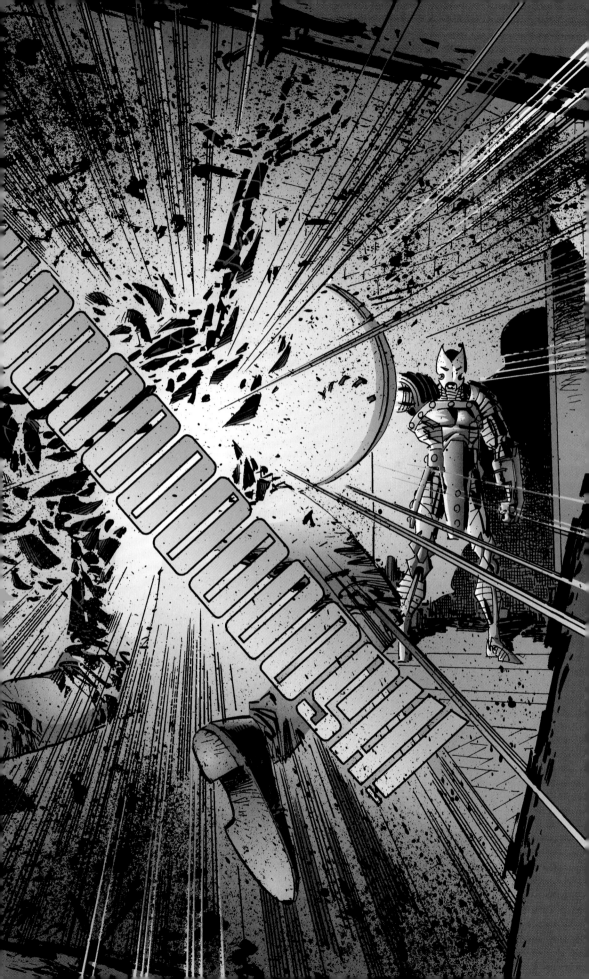

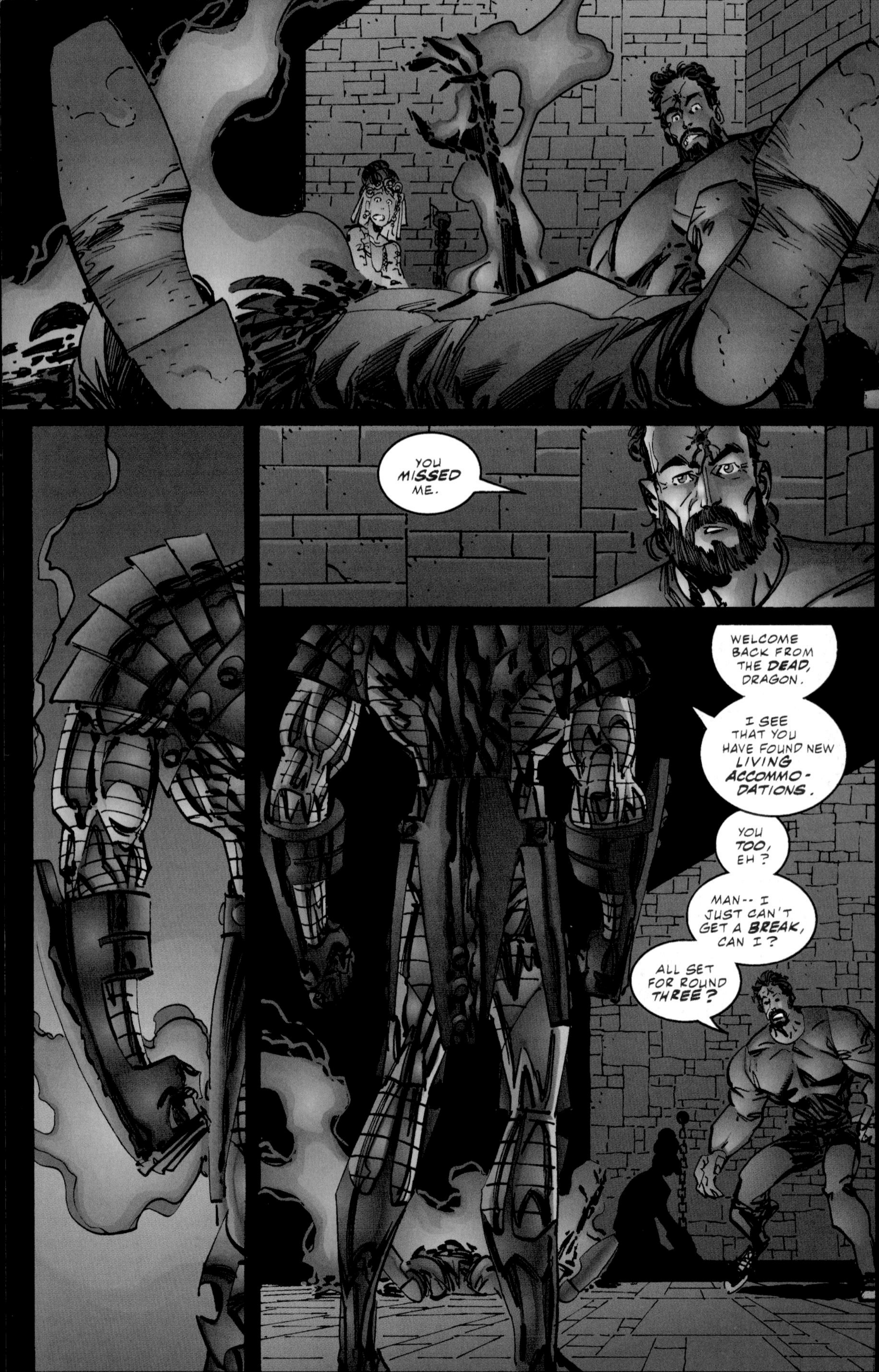
YOU MISSED ME.
WELCOME BACK FROM THE DEAD, DRAGON.
I SEE THAT YOU HAVE FOUND NEW LIVING ACCOMMO-DATIONS.
YOU TOO, EH?
MAN-- I JUST CAN'T GET A BREAK, CAN I?
ALL SET FOR ROUND THREE?

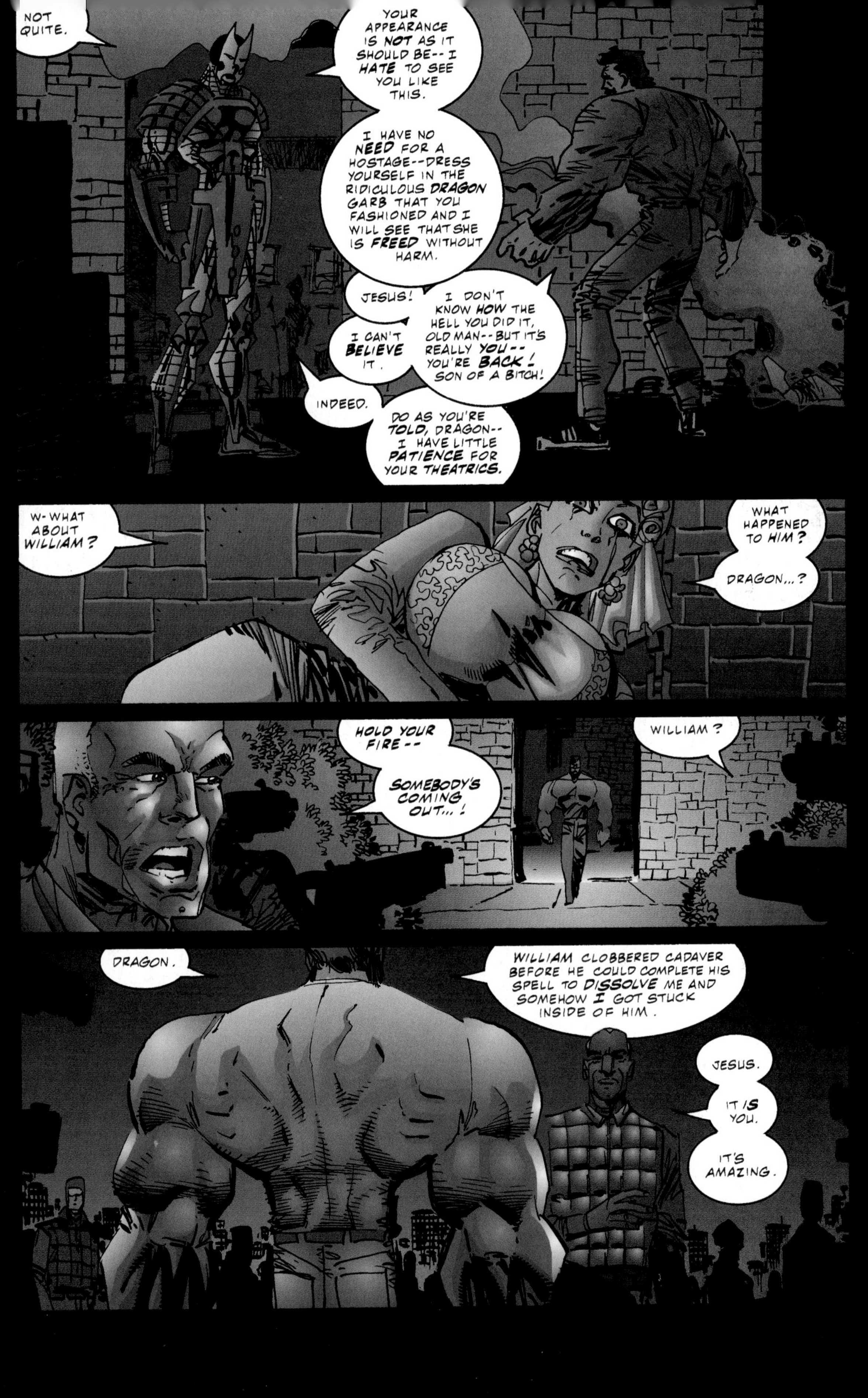
NOT QUITE.
YOUR APPEARANCE IS NOT AS IT SHOULD BE-- I HATE TO SEE YOU LIKE THIS.
I HAVE NO NEED FOR A HOSTAGE--DRESS YOURSELF IN THE RIDICULOUS DRAGON GARB THAT YOU FASHIONED AND I WILL SEE THAT SHE IS FREED WITHOUT HARM.
JESUS!
I CAN'T BELIEVE IT.
I DON'T KNOW HOW THE HELL YOU DID IT, OLD MAN--BUT IT'S REALLY YOU--YOU'RE BACK! SON OF A BITCH!
INDEED.
DO AS YOU'RE TOLD, DRAGON-- I HAVE LITTLE PATIENCE FOR YOUR THEATRICS.
W-WHAT ABOUT WILLIAM?
WHAT HAPPENED TO HIM?
DRAGON...?
HOLD YOUR FIRE--
SOMEBODY'S COMING OUT...!
WILLIAM?
DRAGON.
WILLIAM CLOBBERED CADAVER BEFORE HE COULD COMPLETE HIS SPELL TO DISSOLVE ME AND SOMEHOW I GOT STUCK INSIDE OF HIM.
JESUS.
IT IS YOU.
IT'S AMAZING.

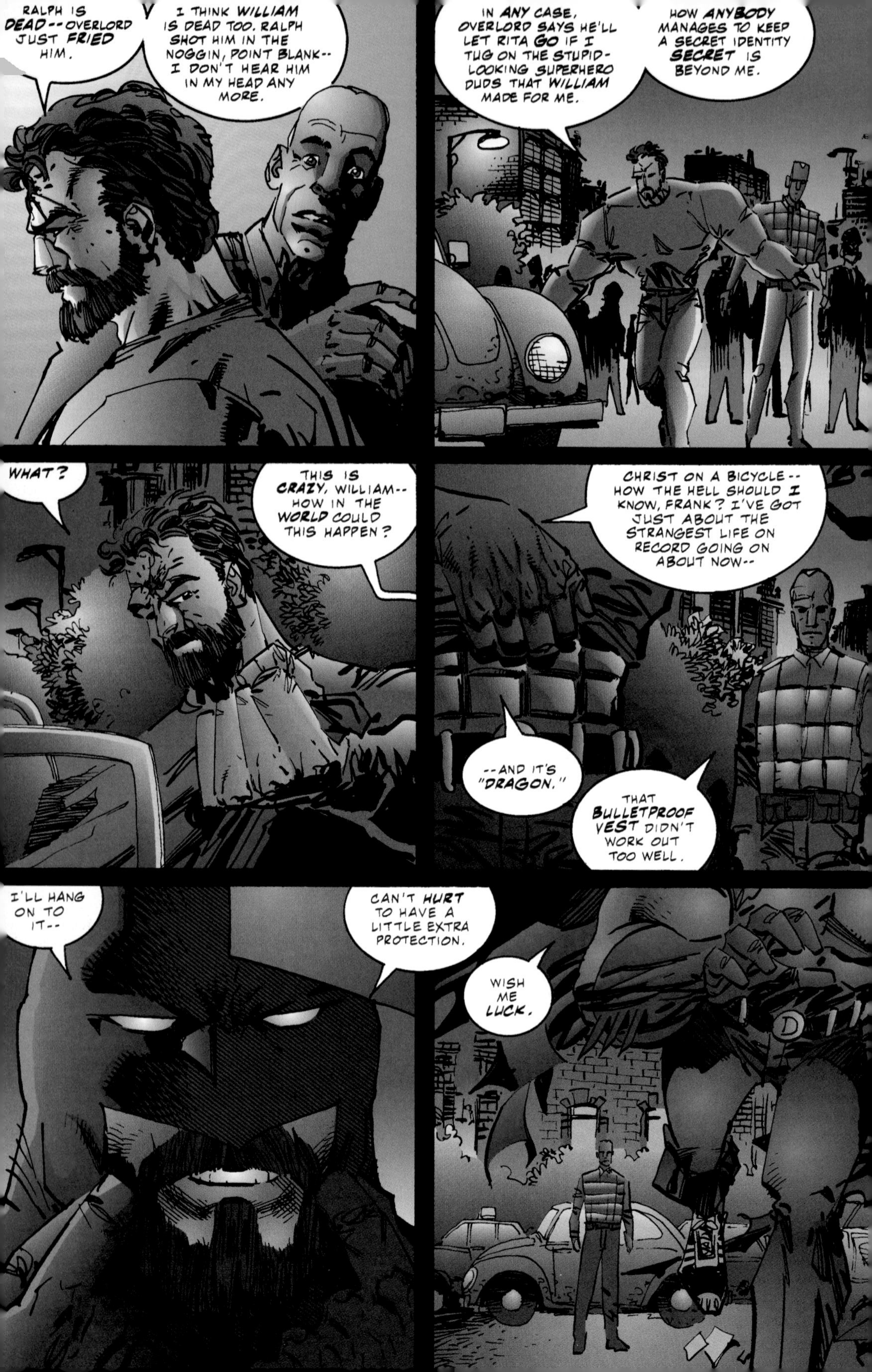
RALPH IS DEAD--OVERLORD JUST FRIED HIM.
I THINK WILLIAM IS DEAD TOO. RALPH SHOT HIM IN THE NOGGIN, POINT BLANK-- I DON'T HEAR HIM IN MY HEAD ANY MORE.
IN ANY CASE, OVERLORD SAYS HE'LL LET RITA GO IF I TUG ON THE STUPID-LOOKING SUPERHERO DUDS THAT WILLIAM MADE FOR ME.
HOW ANYBODY MANAGES TO KEEP A SECRET IDENTITY SECRET IS BEYOND ME.
WHAT?
THIS IS CRAZY, WILLIAM-- HOW IN THE WORLD COULD THIS HAPPEN?
CHRIST ON A BICYCLE-- HOW THE HELL SHOULD I KNOW, FRANK? I'VE GOT JUST ABOUT THE STRANGEST LIFE ON RECORD GOING ON ABOUT NOW--
--AND IT'S "DRAGON."
THAT BULLETPROOF VEST DIDN'T WORK OUT TOO WELL.
I'LL HANG ON TO IT--
CAN'T HURT TO HAVE A LITTLE EXTRA PROTECTION.
WISH ME LUCK.
D

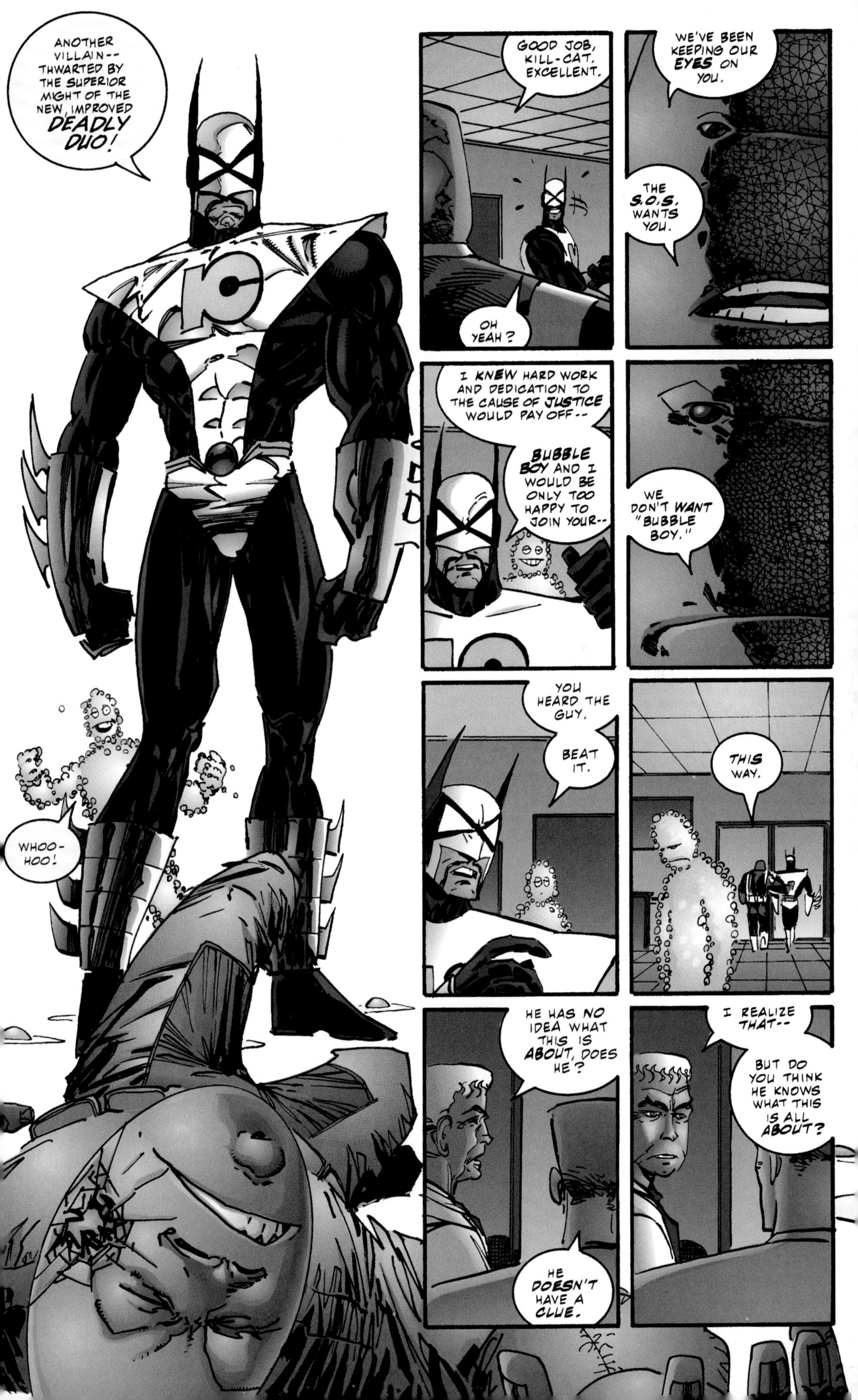
ANOTHER VILLAIN-- THWARTED BY THE SUPERIOR MIGHT OF THE NEW, IMPROVED DEADLY DUO!
WHOO-HOO!
GOOD JOB, KILL-CAT. EXCELLENT.
OH YEAH?
WE'VE BEEN KEEPING OUR EYES ON YOU.
THE S.O.S. WANTS YOU.
I KNEW HARD WORK AND DEDICATION TO THE CAUSE OF JUSTICE WOULD PAY OFF--
BUBBLE BOY AND I WOULD BE ONLY TOO HAPPY TO JOIN YOUR--
WE DON'T WANT "BUBBLE BOY."
YOU HEARD THE GUY.
BEAT IT.
THIS WAY.
HE HAS NO IDEA WHAT THIS IS ABOUT, DOES HE?
HE DOESN'T HAVE A CLUE.
I REALIZE THAT--
BUT DO YOU THINK HE KNOWS WHAT THIS IS ALL ABOUT?

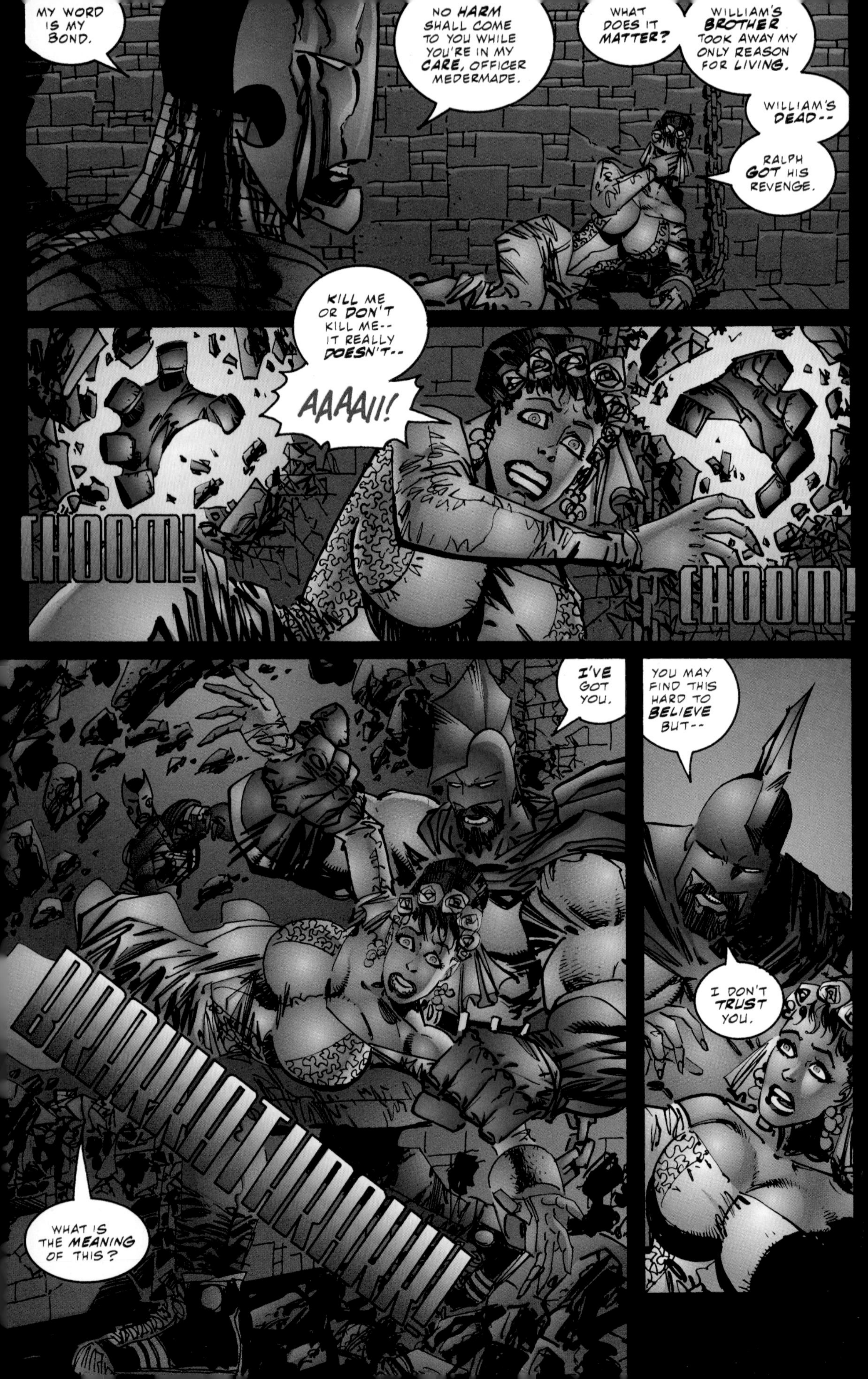

MY WORD IS MY BOND.
NO HARM SHALL COME TO YOU WHILE YOU'RE IN MY CARE, OFFICER MEDERMADE.
WHAT DOES IT MATTER?
WILLIAM'S BROTHER TOOK AWAY MY ONLY REASON FOR LIVING.
WILLIAM'S DEAD--
RALPH GOT HIS REVENGE.
KILL ME OR DON'T KILL ME-- IT REALLY DOESN'T--
AAAAII!
CHOOM!
CHOOM!
I'VE GOT YOU.
YOU MAY FIND THIS HARD TO BELIEVE BUT--
I DON'T TRUST YOU.
WHAT IS THE MEANING OF THIS?

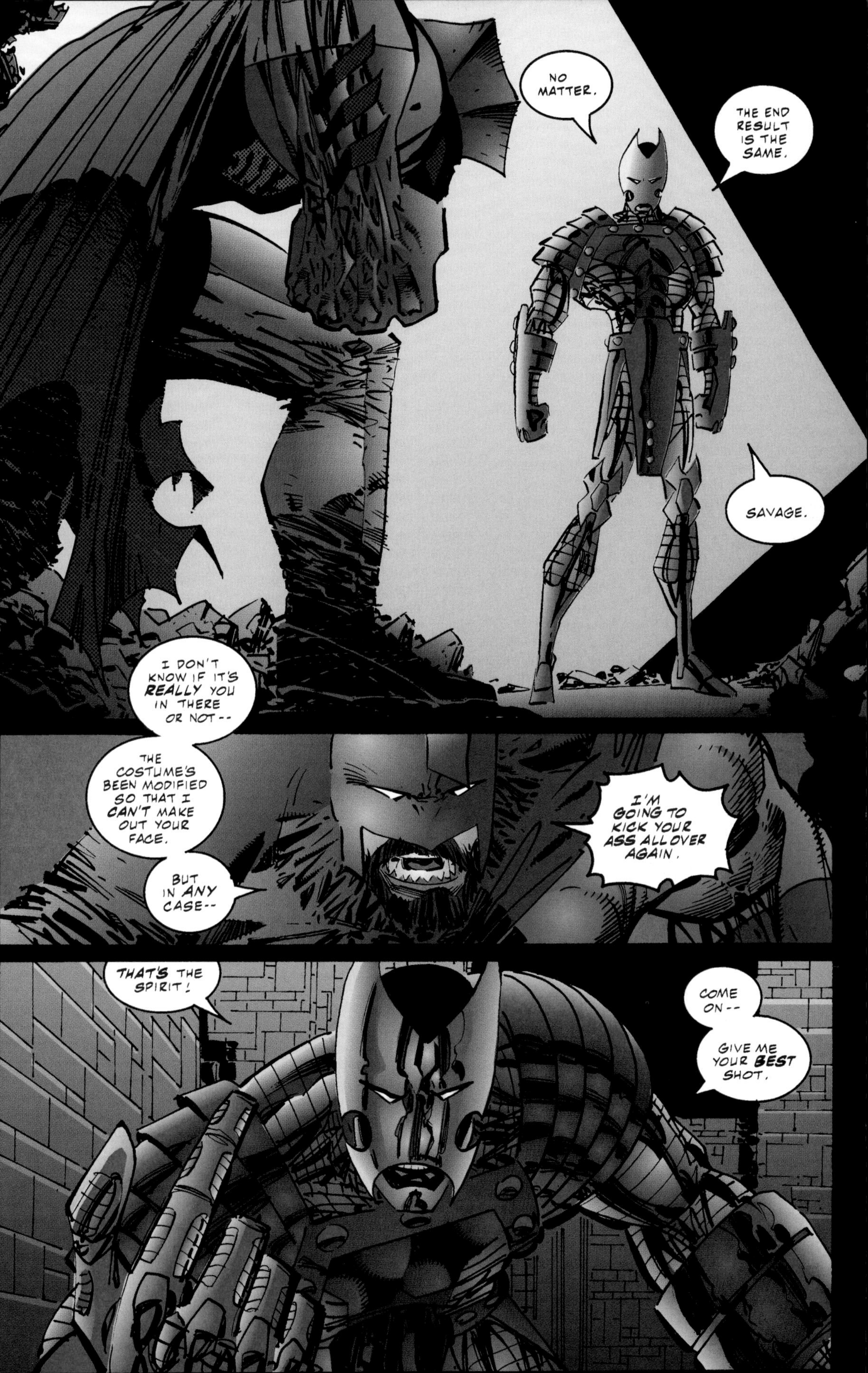
NO MATTER.
THE END RESULT IS THE SAME.
SAVAGE.
I DON'T KNOW IF IT'S **REALLY** YOU IN THERE OR NOT--
THE COSTUME'S BEEN MODIFIED SO THAT I **CAN'T** MAKE OUT YOUR FACE.
BUT IN **ANY** CASE--
I'M GOING TO KICK YOUR **ASS** ALL OVER AGAIN.
THAT'S THE SPIRIT!
COME ON--
GIVE ME YOUR **BEST** SHOT.

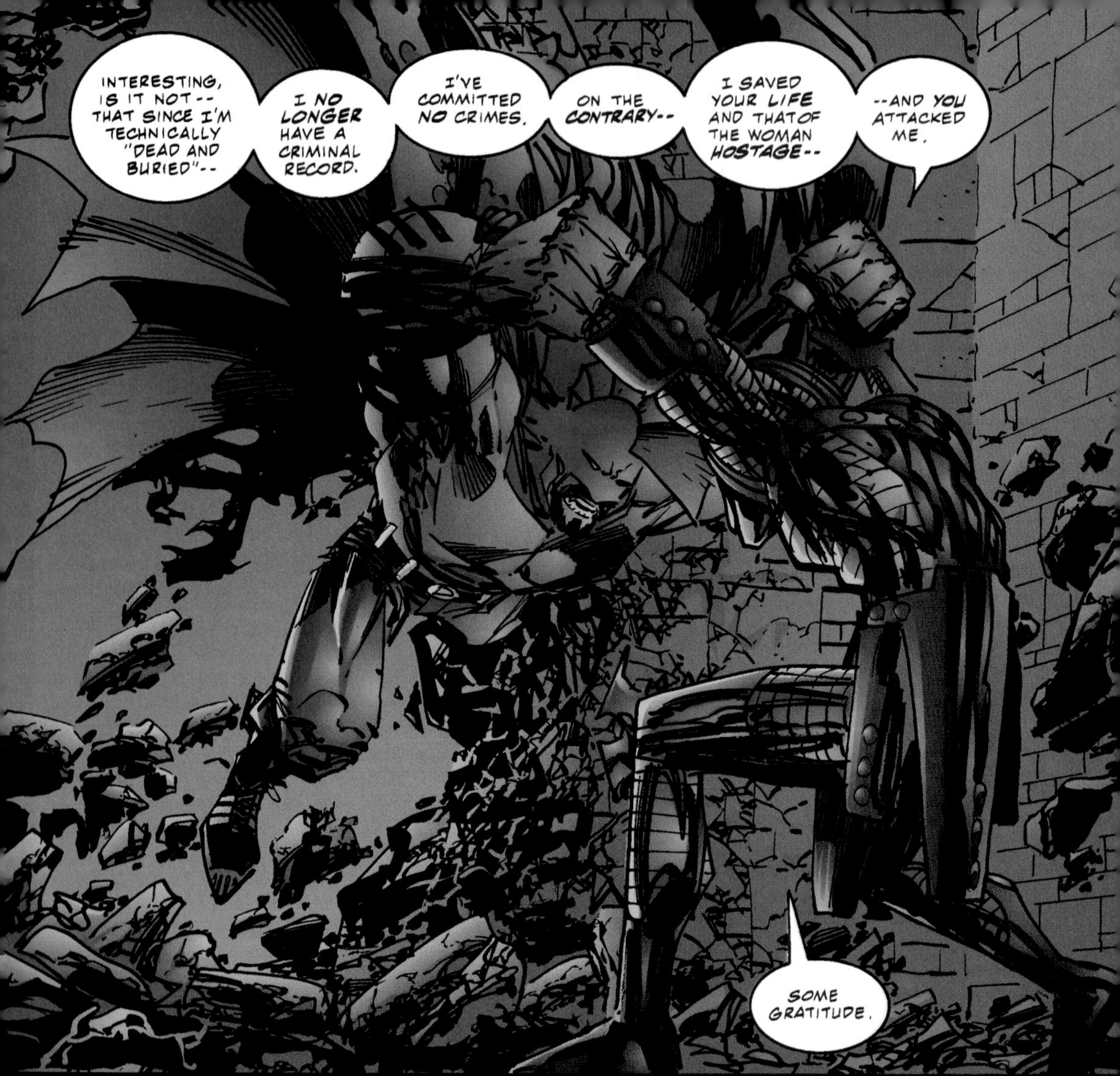
INTERESTING, IS IT NOT-- THAT SINCE I'M TECHNICALLY "DEAD AND BURIED"--
I NO LONGER HAVE A CRIMINAL RECORD.
I'VE COMMITTED NO CRIMES.
ON THE CONTRARY--
I SAVED YOUR LIFE AND THAT OF THE WOMAN HOSTAGE--
--AND YOU ATTACKED ME.
SOME GRATITUDE.

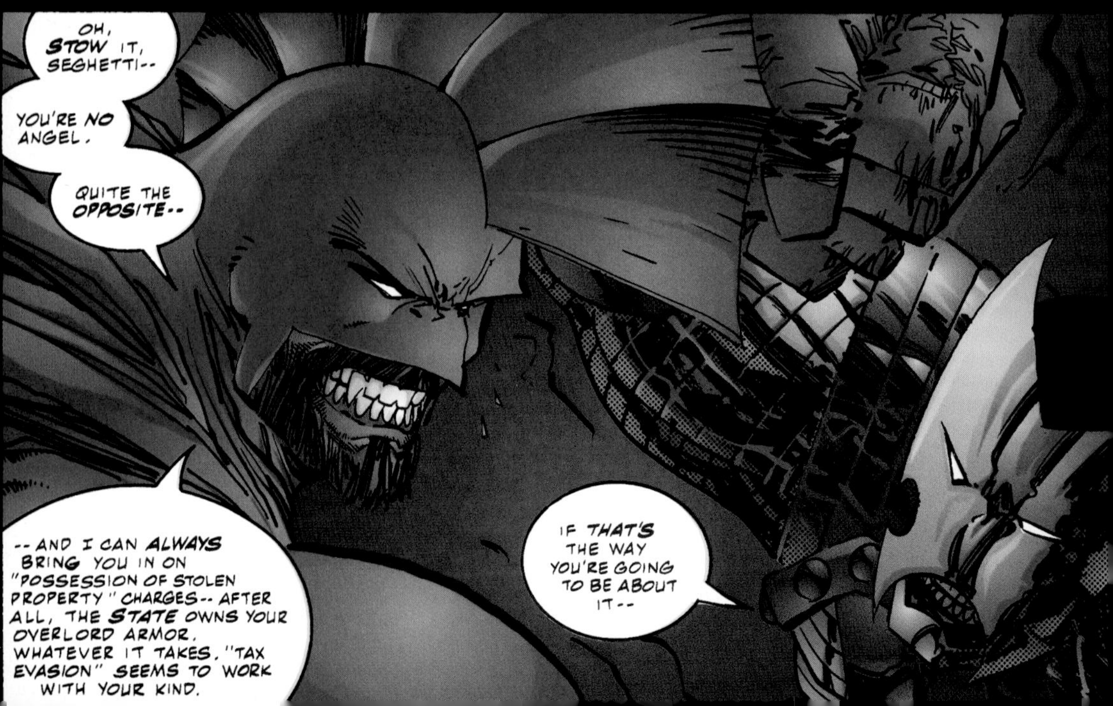
OH, STOW IT, SEGHETTI--
YOU'RE NO ANGEL.
QUITE THE OPPOSITE--
--AND I CAN ALWAYS BRING YOU IN ON "POSSESSION OF STOLEN PROPERTY" CHARGES-- AFTER ALL, THE STATE OWNS YOUR OVERLORD ARMOR. WHATEVER IT TAKES. "TAX EVASION" SEEMS TO WORK WITH YOUR KIND.
IF THAT'S THE WAY YOU'RE GOING TO BE ABOUT IT--

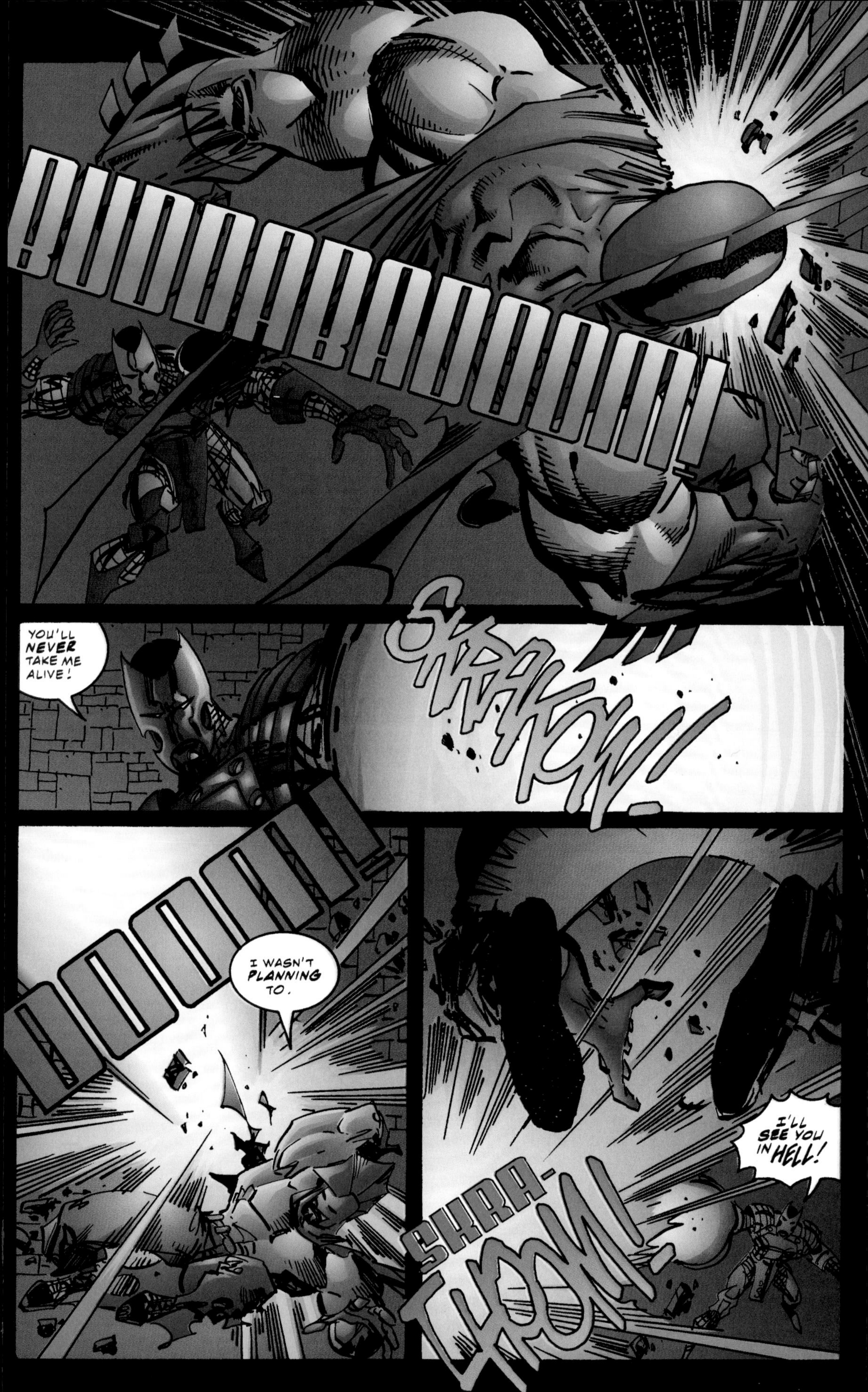
SKRAKOW!
YOU'LL NEVER TAKE ME ALIVE!
BOOOM!
I WASN'T PLANNING TO.
I'LL SEE YOU IN HELL!
SHRA-THOOM!

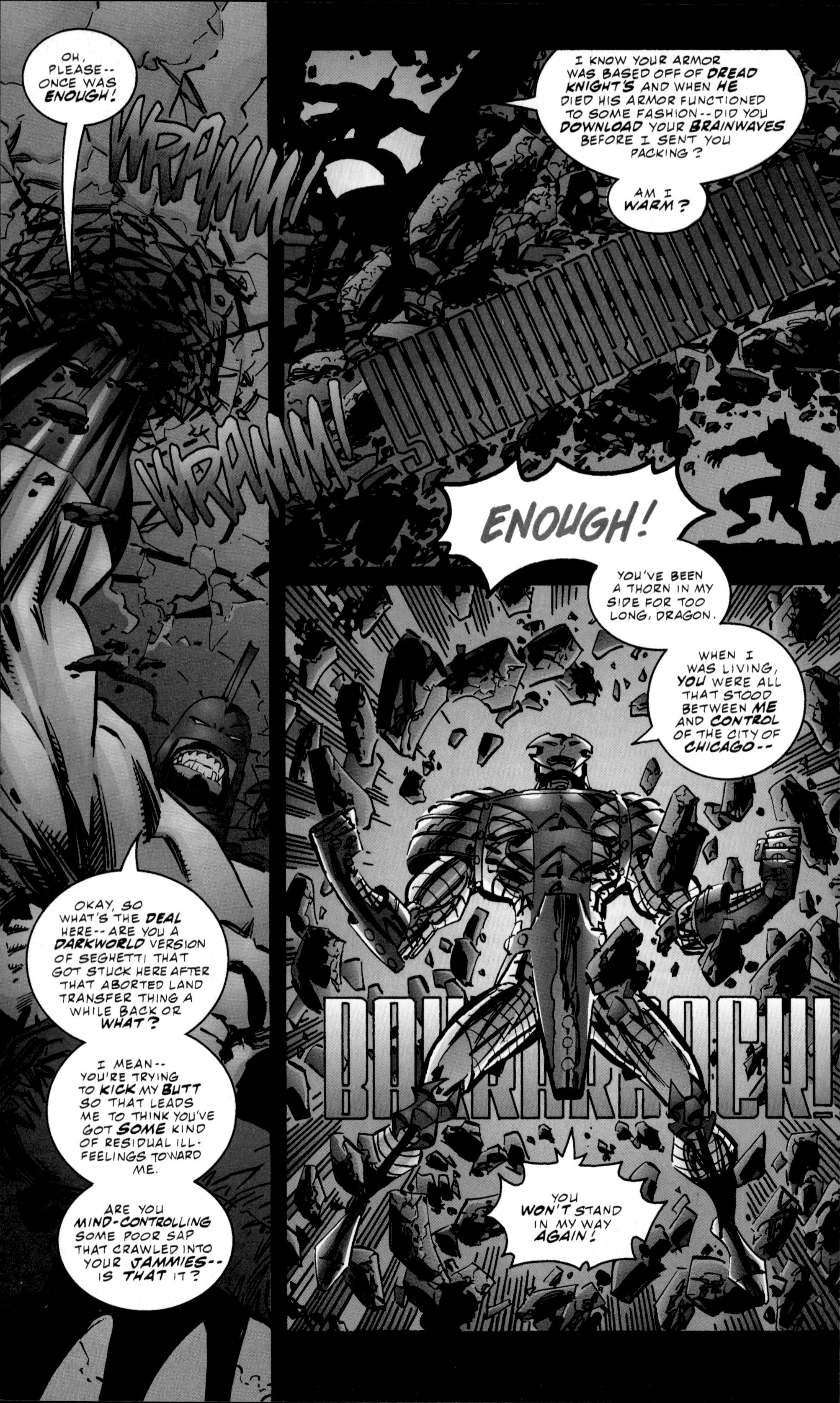

OH, PLEASE-- ONCE WAS ENOUGH!
WRAMM!
WRAMM!
I KNOW YOUR ARMOR WAS BASED OFF OF DREAD KNIGHT'S AND WHEN HE DIED HIS ARMOR FUNCTIONED TO SOME FASHION--DID YOU DOWNLOAD YOUR BRAINWAVES BEFORE I SENT YOU PACKING?
AM I WARM?
ENOUGH!
YOU'VE BEEN A THORN IN MY SIDE FOR TOO LONG, DRAGON.
WHEN I WAS LIVING, YOU WERE ALL THAT STOOD BETWEEN ME AND CONTROL OF THE CITY OF CHICAGO--
OKAY, SO WHAT'S THE DEAL HERE-- ARE YOU A DARKWORLD VERSION OF SEGHETTI THAT GOT STUCK HERE AFTER THAT ABORTED LAND TRANSFER THING A WHILE BACK OR WHAT?
I MEAN-- YOU'RE TRYING TO KICK MY BUTT SO THAT LEADS ME TO THINK YOU'VE GOT SOME KIND OF RESIDUAL ILL-FEELINGS TOWARD ME.
ARE YOU MIND-CONTROLLING SOME POOR SAP THAT CRAWLED INTO YOUR JAMMIES-- IS THAT IT?
YOU WON'T STAND IN MY WAY AGAIN!

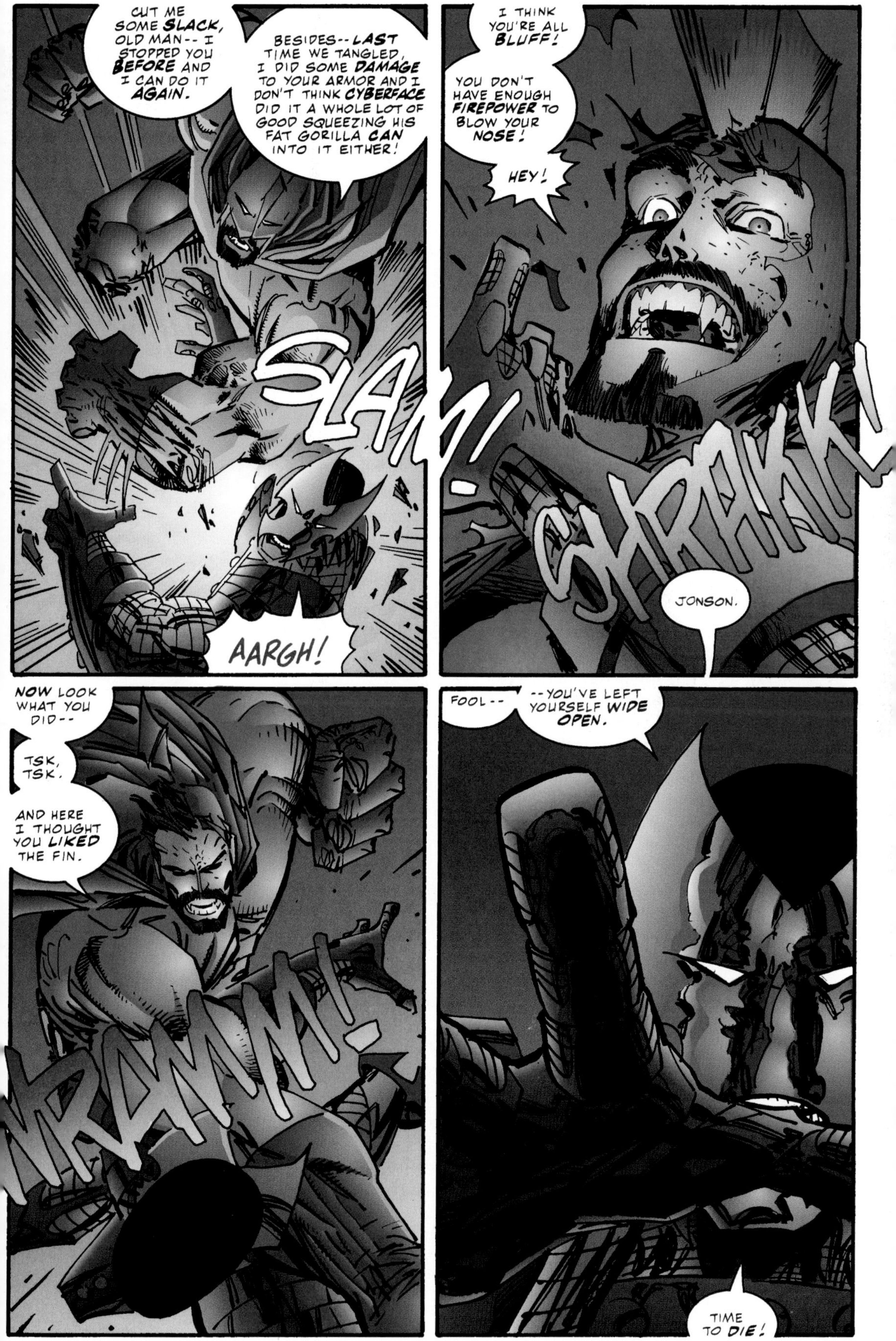

CUT ME SOME SLACK, OLD MAN-- I STOPPED YOU BEFORE AND I CAN DO IT AGAIN.
BESIDES--LAST TIME WE TANGLED, I DID SOME DAMAGE TO YOUR ARMOR AND I DON'T THINK CYBERFACE DID IT A WHOLE LOT OF GOOD SQUEEZING HIS FAT GORILLA CAN INTO IT EITHER!
SLAM!
AARGH!
I THINK YOU'RE ALL BLUFF!
YOU DON'T HAVE ENOUGH FIREPOWER TO BLOW YOUR NOSE!
HEY!
JONSON.
NOW LOOK WHAT YOU DID--
TSK, TSK.
AND HERE I THOUGHT YOU LIKED THE FIN.
FOOL--
--YOU'VE LEFT YOURSELF WIDE OPEN.
TIME TO DIE!

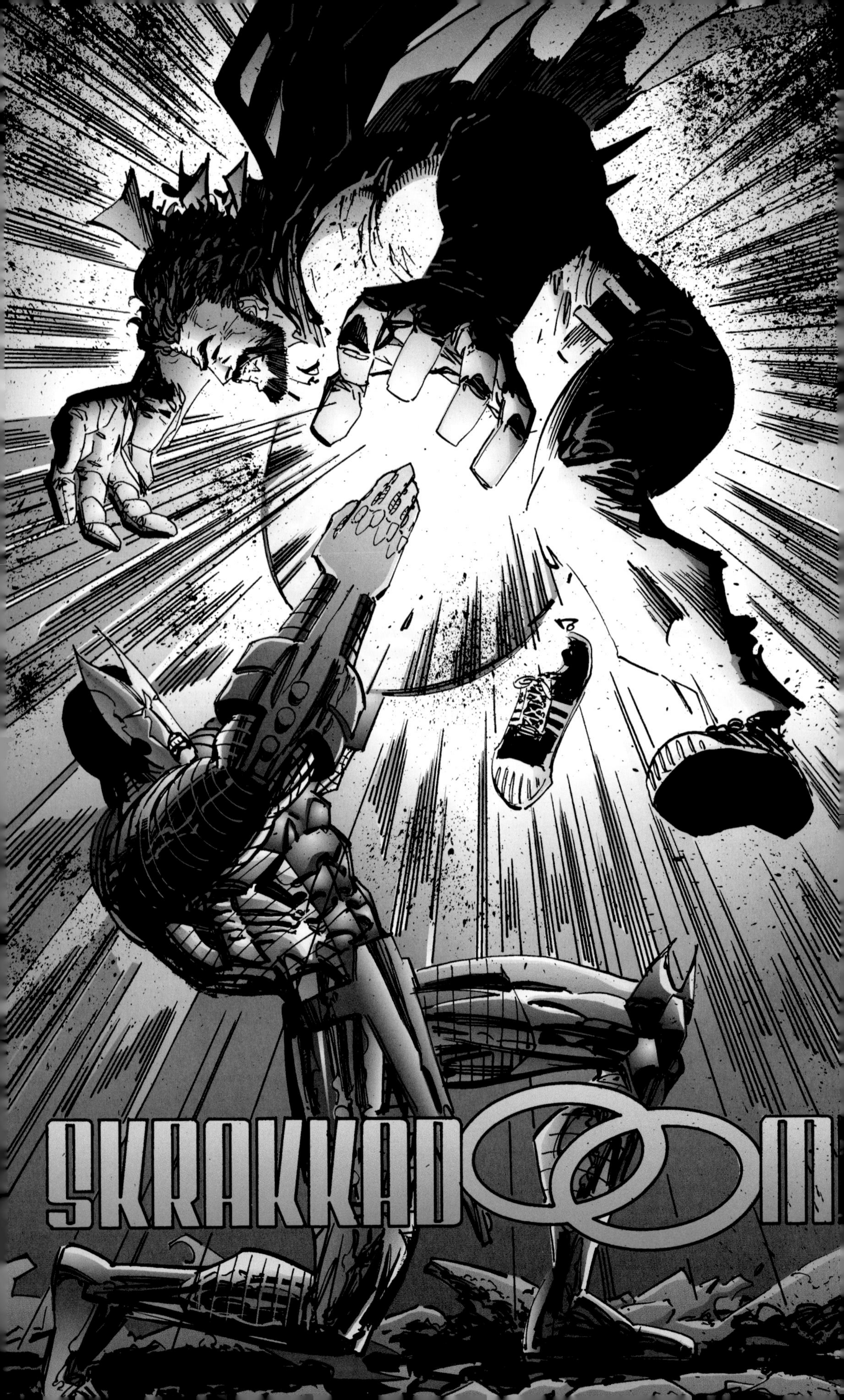
SKRAKKADOOM

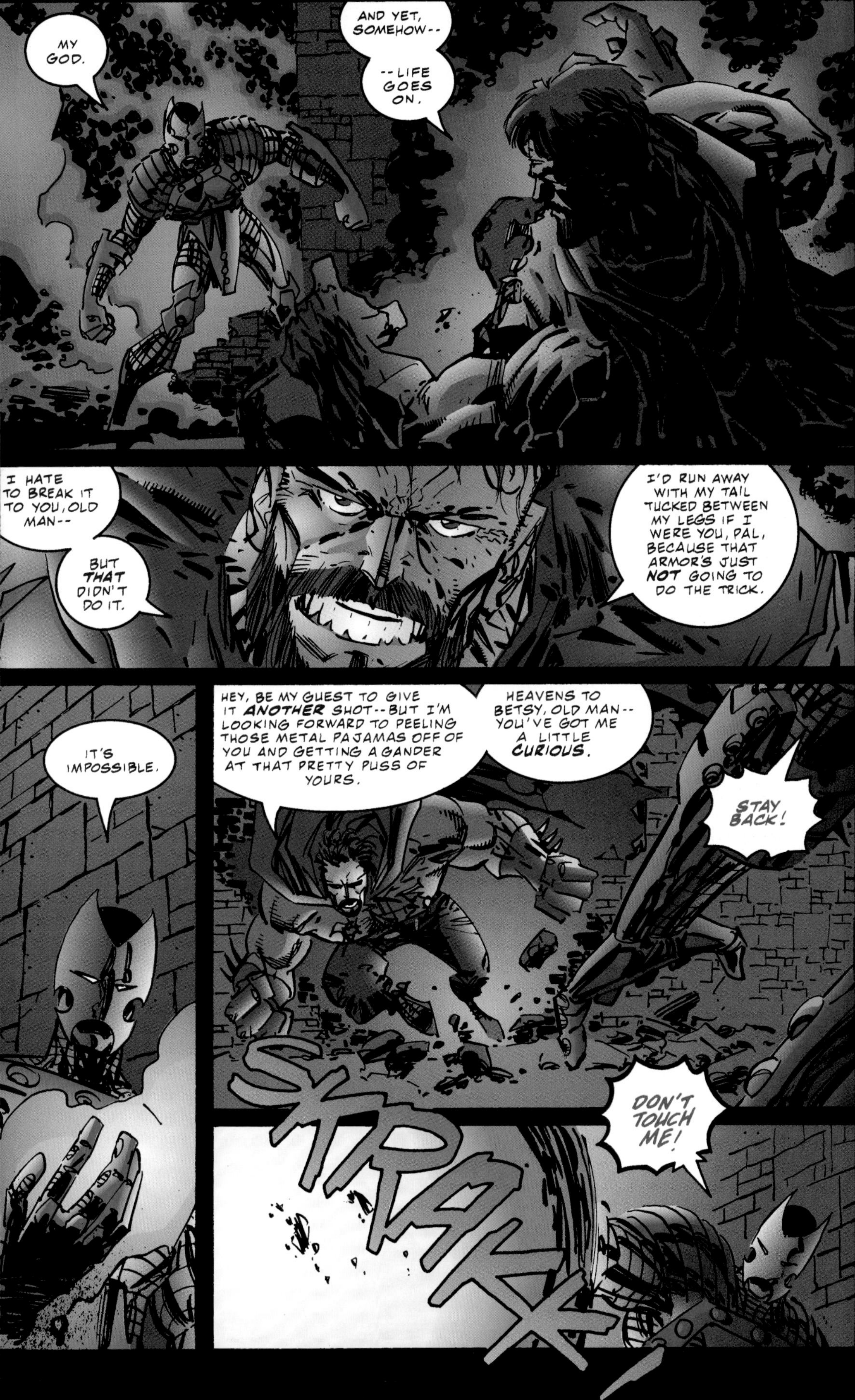
MY GOD.
AND YET, SOMEHOW--
--LIFE GOES ON.
I HATE TO BREAK IT TO YOU, OLD MAN--
BUT **THAT** DIDN'T DO IT.
I'D RUN AWAY WITH MY TAIL TUCKED BETWEEN MY LEGS IF I WERE YOU, PAL, BECAUSE THAT ARMOR'S JUST **NOT** GOING TO DO THE TRICK.
IT'S IMPOSSIBLE.
HEY, BE MY GUEST TO GIVE IT **ANOTHER** SHOT--BUT I'M LOOKING FORWARD TO PEELING THOSE METAL PAJAMAS OFF OF YOU AND GETTING A GANDER AT THAT PRETTY PUSS OF YOURS.
HEAVENS TO BETSY, OLD MAN--YOU'VE GOT ME A LITTLE **CURIOUS**.
STAY BACK!
DON'T TOUCH ME!
SKRAK

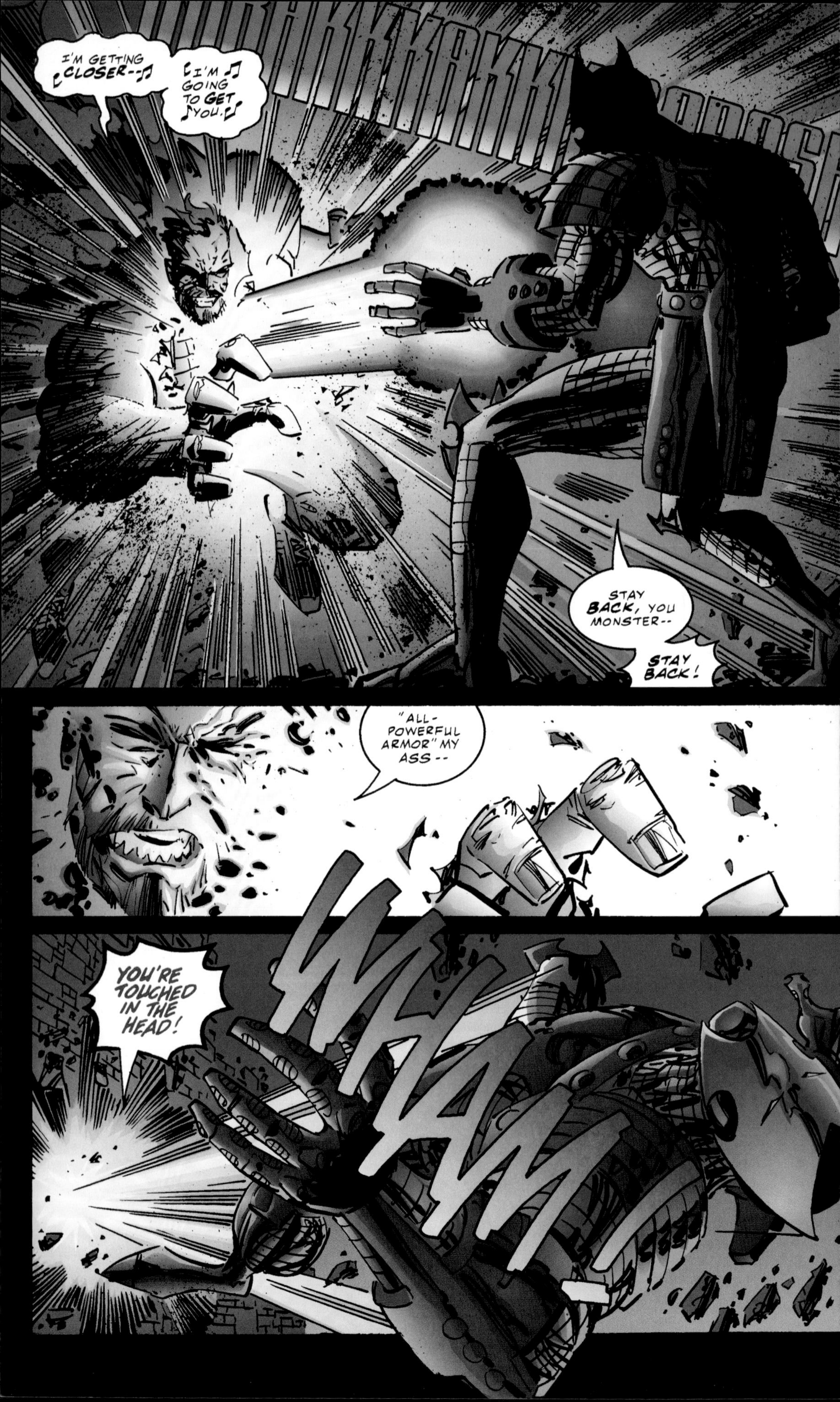
I'M GETTING CLOSER--♫
♫I'M GOING TO GET YOU.♫
STAY BACK, YOU MONSTER--
STAY BACK!
"ALL-POWERFUL ARMOR" MY ASS--
WHAM
YOU'RE TOUCHED IN THE HEAD!

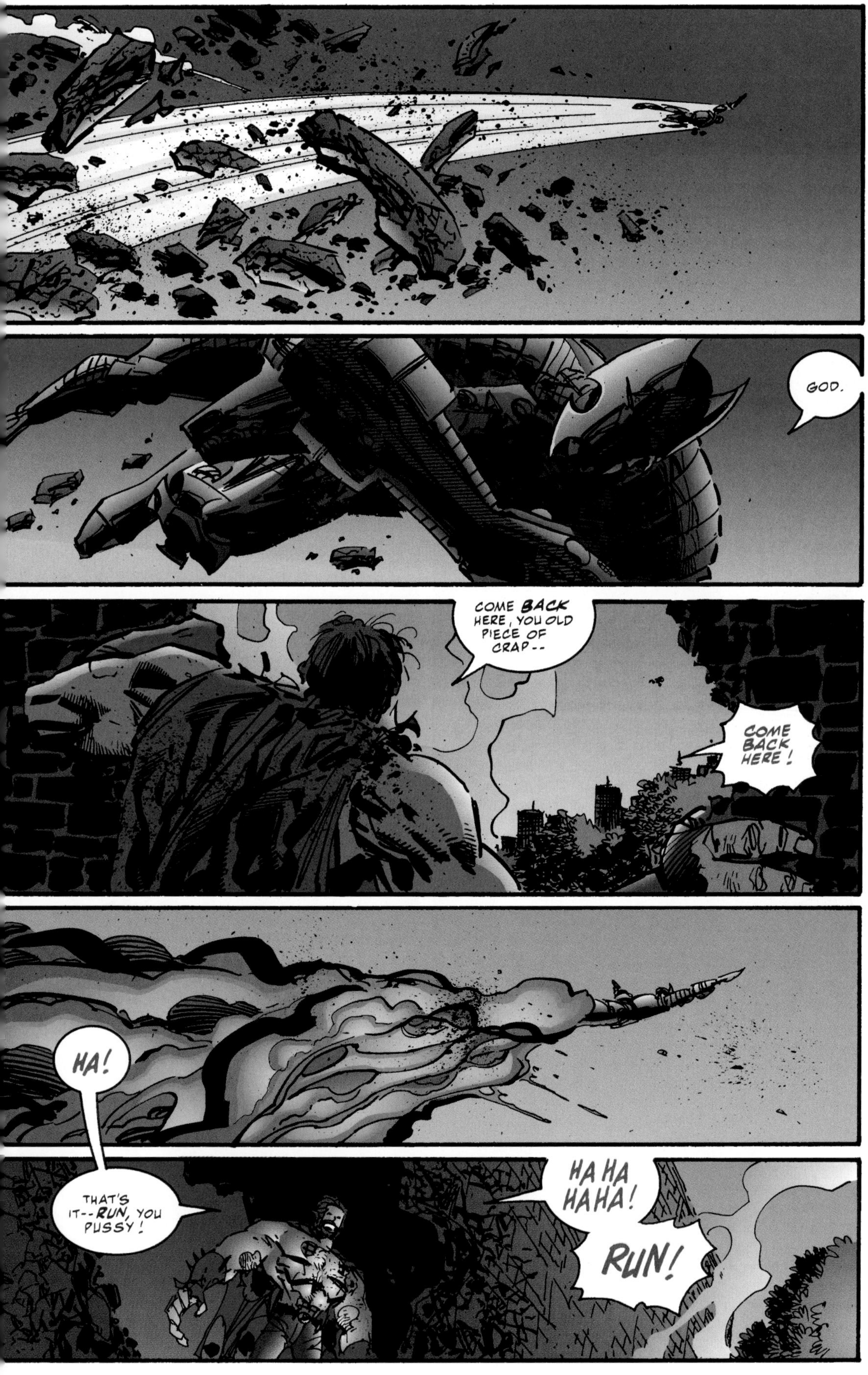
GOD.
COME BACK HERE, YOU OLD PIECE OF CRAP--
COME BACK HERE!
HA!
THAT'S IT--RUN, YOU PUSSY!
HA HA HAHA!
RUN!

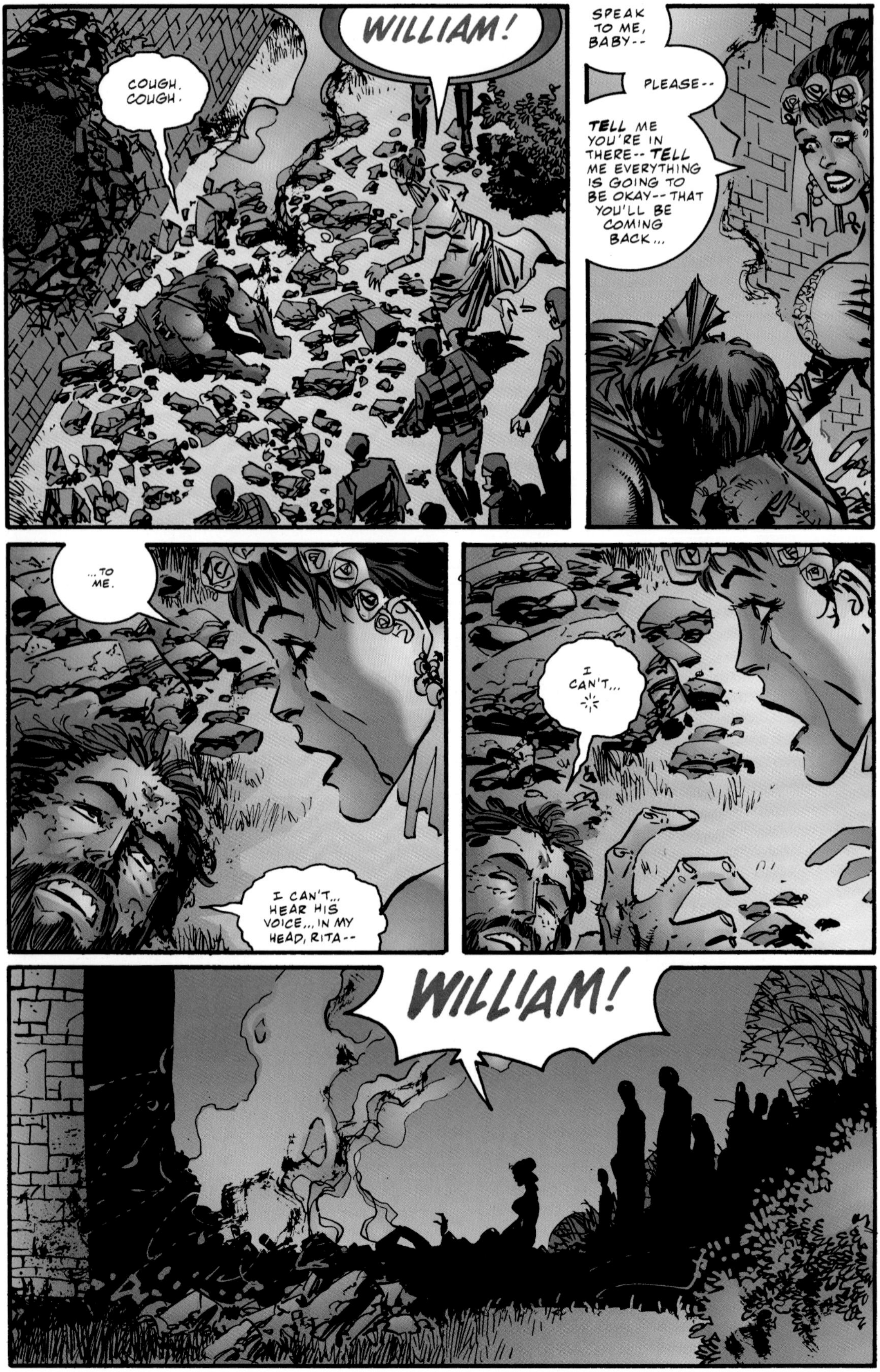
WILLIAM!
COUGH. COUGH.
SPEAK TO ME, BABY--
PLEASE--
TELL ME YOU'RE IN THERE-- TELL ME EVERYTHING IS GOING TO BE OKAY-- THAT YOU'LL BE COMING BACK...
...TO ME.
I CAN'T... HEAR HIS VOICE... IN MY HEAD, RITA--
I CAN'T...
WILLIAM!

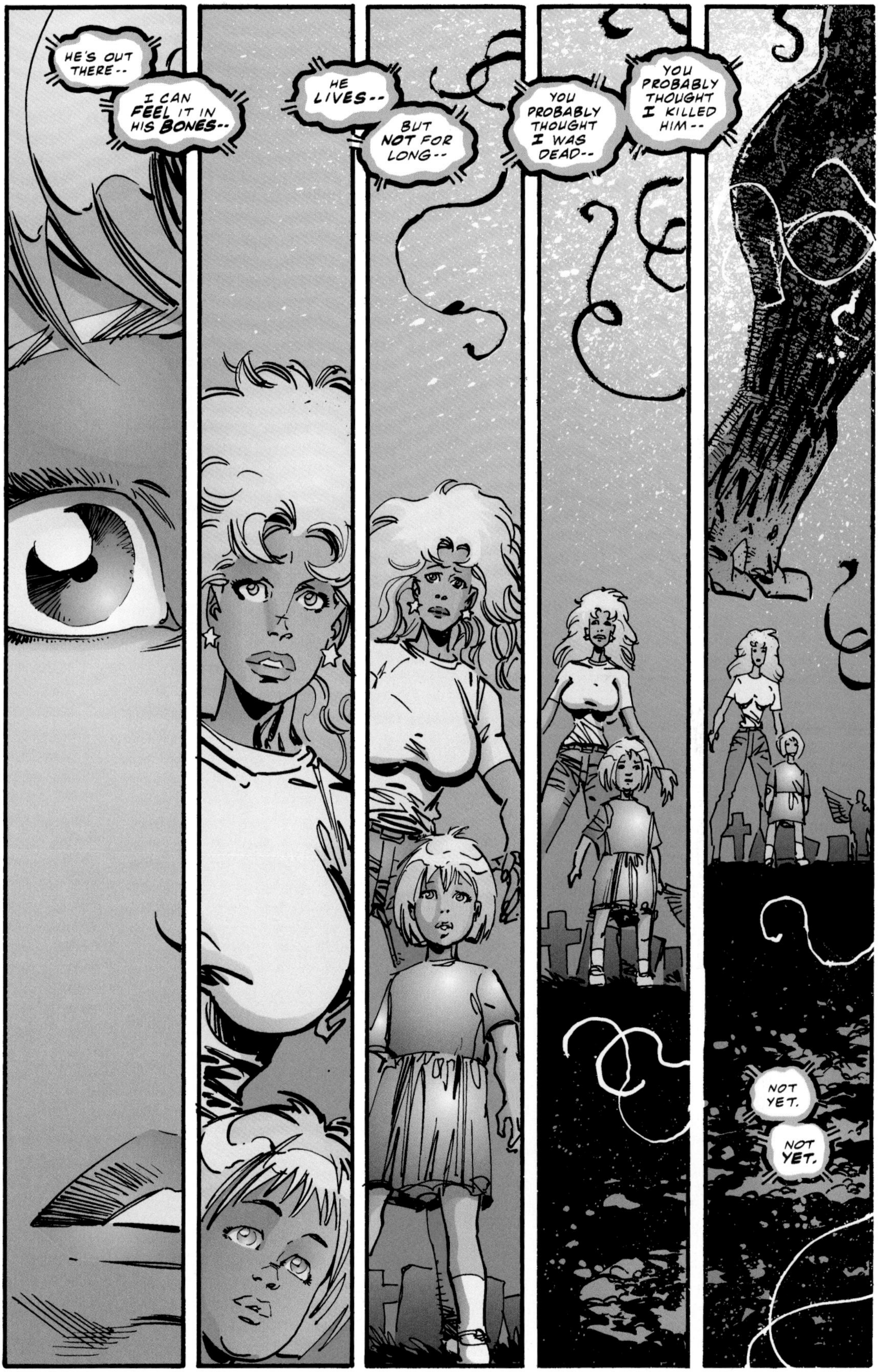
HE'S OUT THERE--
I CAN FEEL IT IN HIS BONES--
HE LIVES--
BUT NOT FOR LONG--
YOU PROBABLY THOUGHT I WAS DEAD--
YOU PROBABLY THOUGHT I KILLED HIM--
NOT YET.
NOT YET.

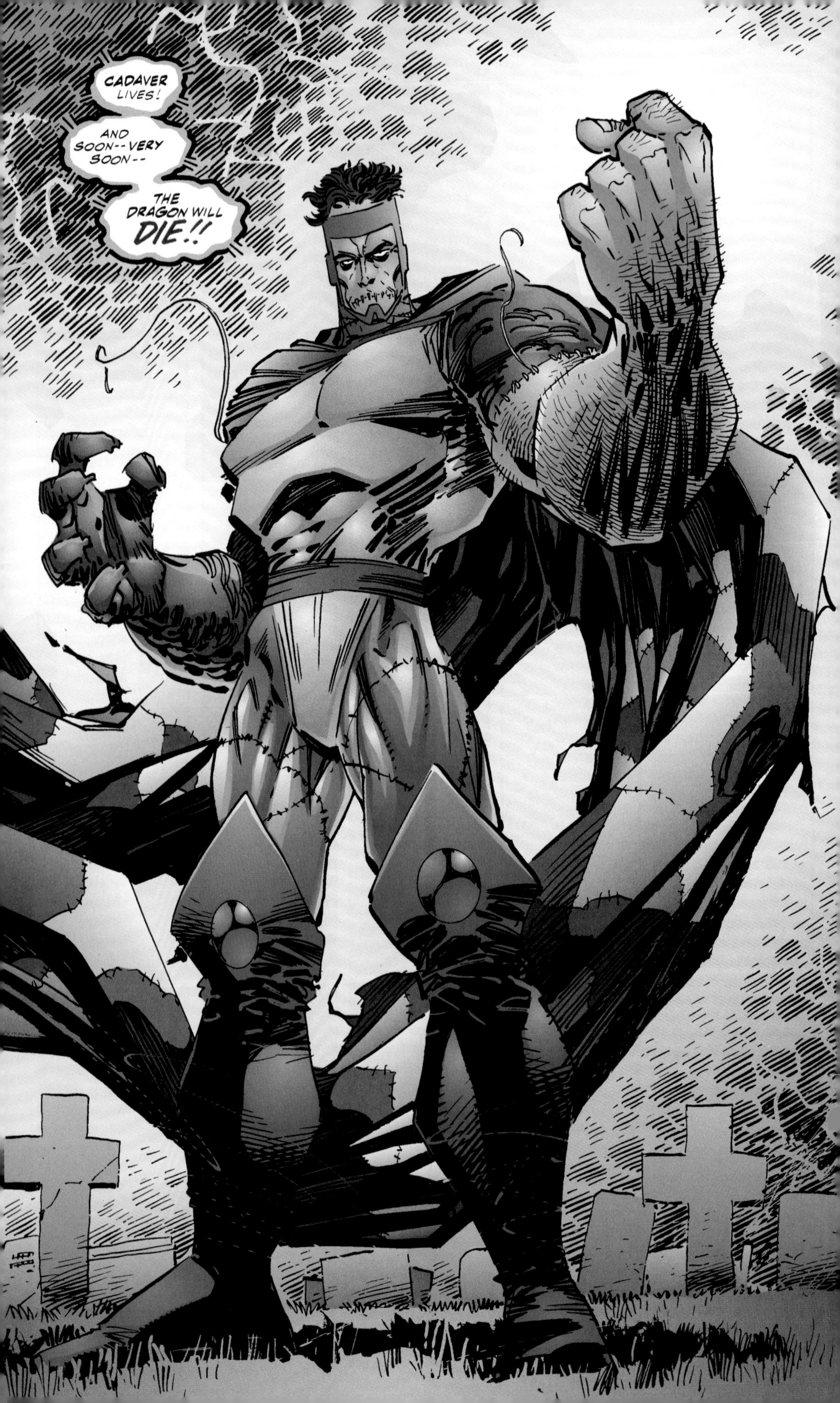
CADAVER LIVES!
AND SOON--VERY SOON--
THE DRAGON WILL DIE!!

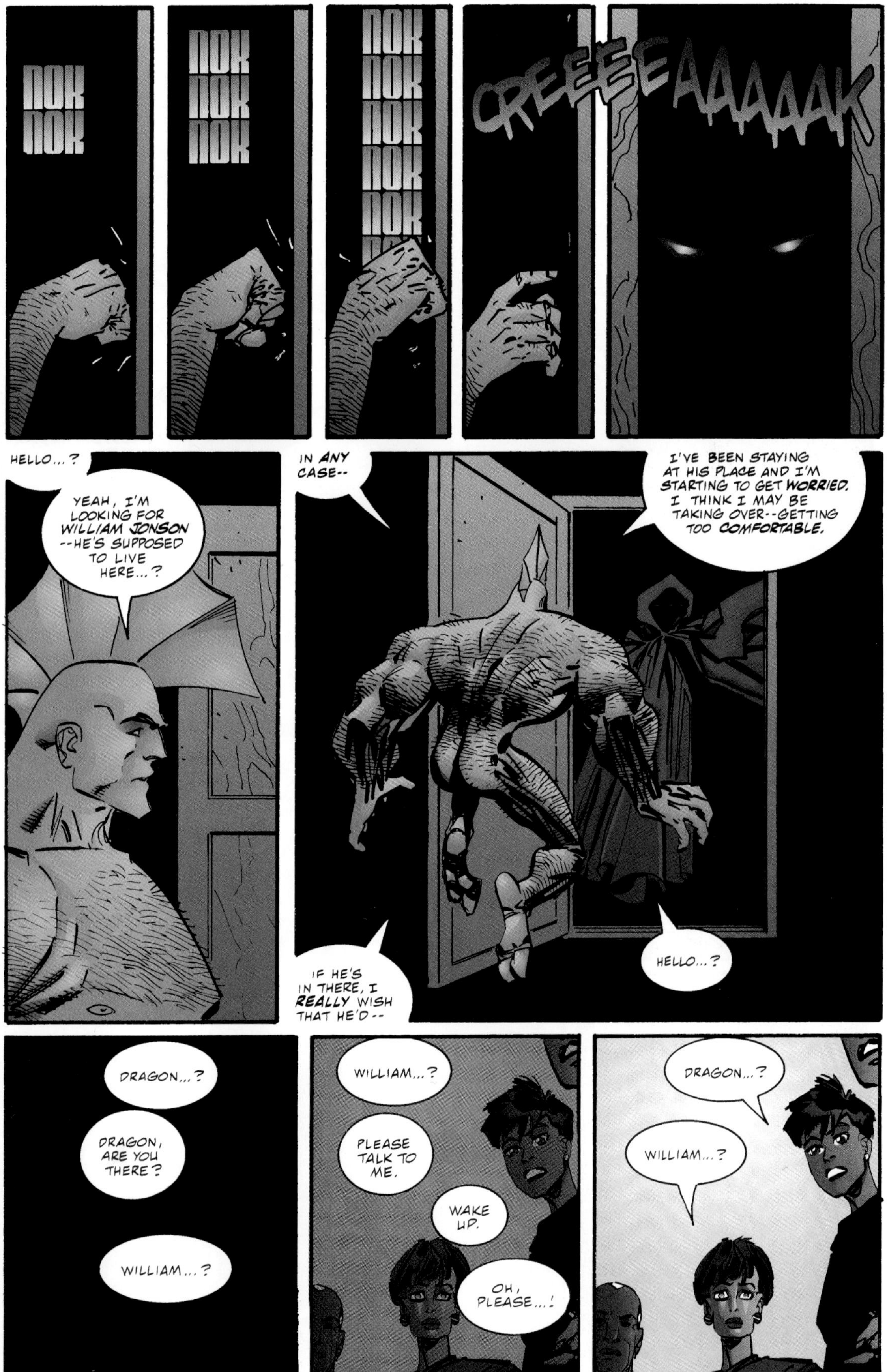

NOK
NOK
NOK
NOK
NOK
NOK
NOK
NOK
NOK
NOK
NOK
CREEEEAAAAAK
HELLO...?
YEAH, I'M LOOKING FOR WILLIAM JONSON --HE'S SUPPOSED TO LIVE HERE...?
IN ANY CASE--
I'VE BEEN STAYING AT HIS PLACE AND I'M STARTING TO GET WORRIED. I THINK I MAY BE TAKING OVER--GETTING TOO COMFORTABLE.
IF HE'S IN THERE, I REALLY WISH THAT HE'D--
HELLO...?
DRAGON...?
DRAGON, ARE YOU THERE?
WILLIAM...?
WILLIAM...?
PLEASE TALK TO ME.
WAKE UP.
OH, PLEASE...!
DRAGON...?
WILLIAM...?

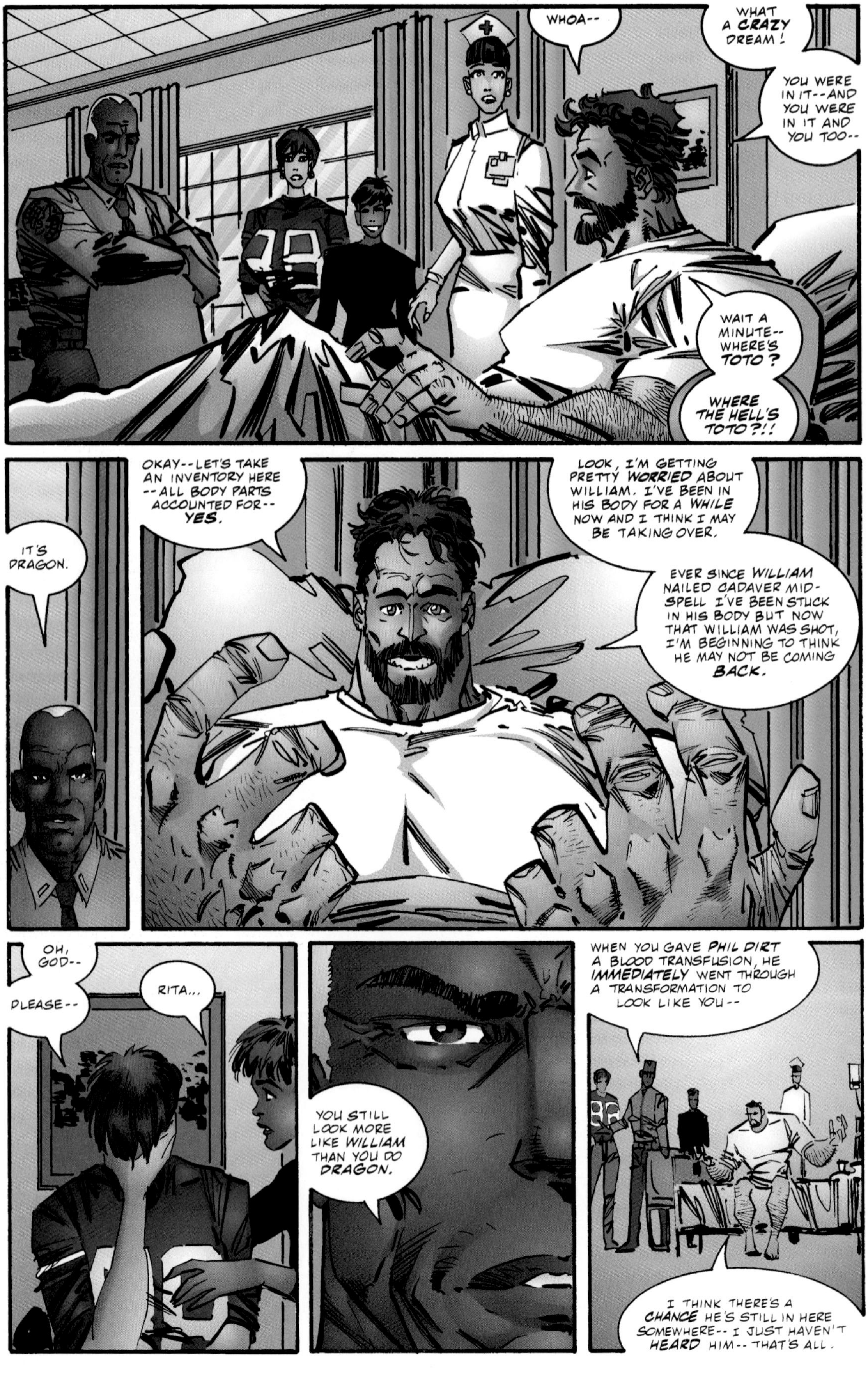

WHOA--
WHAT A CRAZY DREAM!
YOU WERE IN IT--AND YOU WERE IN IT AND YOU TOO--
WAIT A MINUTE-- WHERE'S TOTO?
WHERE THE HELL'S TOTO?!!
IT'S DRAGON.
OKAY--LET'S TAKE AN INVENTORY HERE --ALL BODY PARTS ACCOUNTED FOR-- YES.
LOOK, I'M GETTING PRETTY WORRIED ABOUT WILLIAM. I'VE BEEN IN HIS BODY FOR A WHILE NOW AND I THINK I MAY BE TAKING OVER.
EVER SINCE WILLIAM NAILED CADAVER MID-SPELL I'VE BEEN STUCK IN HIS BODY BUT NOW THAT WILLIAM WAS SHOT, I'M BEGINNING TO THINK HE MAY NOT BE COMING BACK.
OH, GOD--
PLEASE--
RITA...
YOU STILL LOOK MORE LIKE WILLIAM THAN YOU DO DRAGON.
WHEN YOU GAVE PHIL DIRT A BLOOD TRANSFUSION, HE IMMEDIATELY WENT THROUGH A TRANSFORMATION TO LOOK LIKE YOU--
I THINK THERE'S A CHANCE HE'S STILL IN HERE SOMEWHERE-- I JUST HAVEN'T HEARD HIM-- THAT'S ALL.

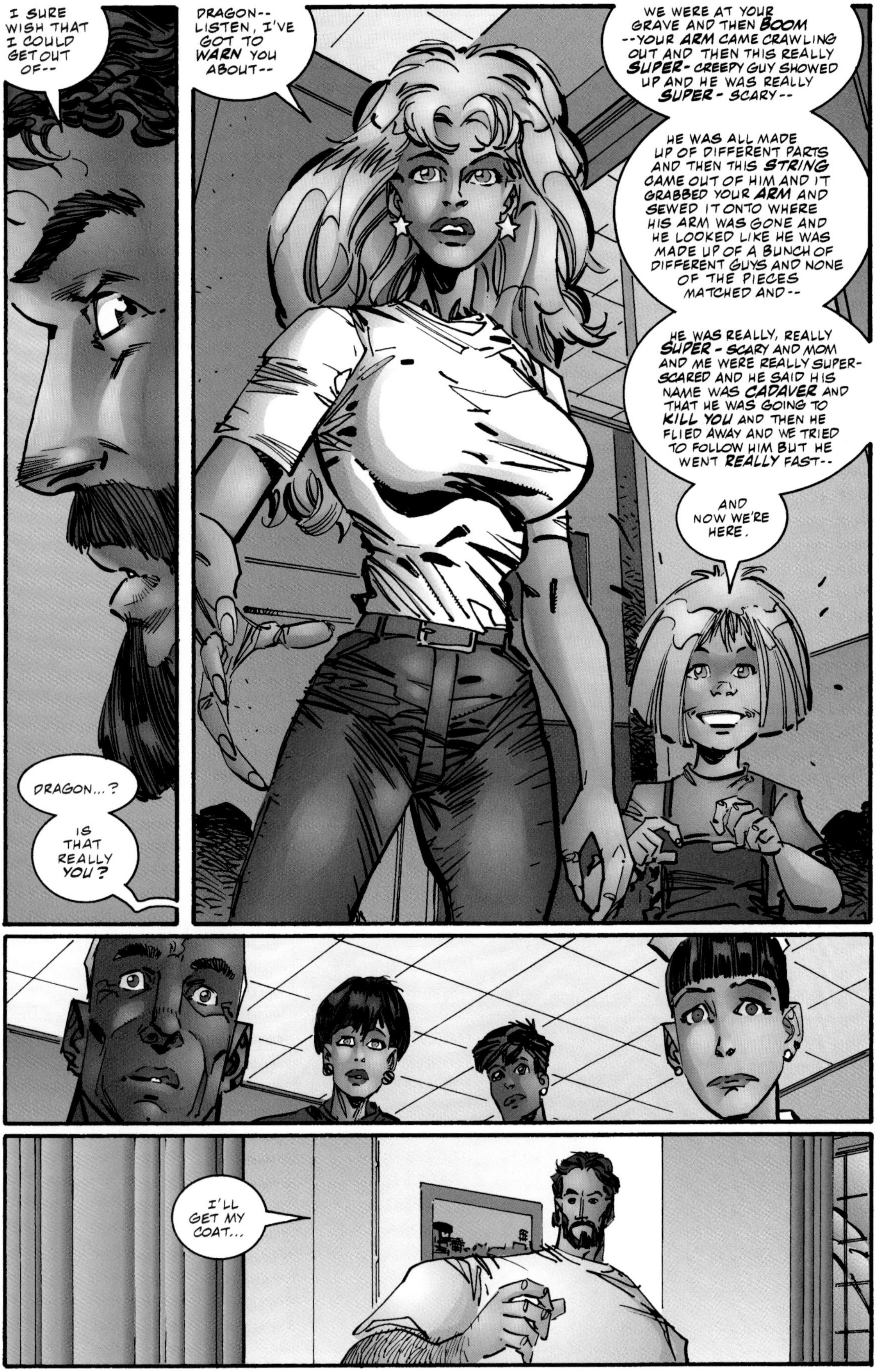
I SURE WISH THAT I COULD GET OUT OF--
DRAGON-- LISTEN, I'VE GOT TO WARN YOU ABOUT--
WE WERE AT YOUR GRAVE AND THEN BOOM --YOUR ARM CAME CRAWLING OUT AND THEN THIS REALLY SUPER-CREEPY GUY SHOWED UP AND HE WAS REALLY SUPER-SCARY--
HE WAS ALL MADE UP OF DIFFERENT PARTS AND THEN THIS STRING CAME OUT OF HIM AND IT GRABBED YOUR ARM AND SEWED IT ONTO WHERE HIS ARM WAS GONE AND HE LOOKED LIKE HE WAS MADE UP OF A BUNCH OF DIFFERENT GUYS AND NONE OF THE PIECES MATCHED AND--
HE WAS REALLY, REALLY SUPER-SCARY AND MOM AND ME WERE REALLY SUPER-SCARED AND HE SAID HIS NAME WAS CADAVER AND THAT HE WAS GOING TO KILL YOU AND THEN HE FLIED AWAY AND WE TRIED TO FOLLOW HIM BUT HE WENT REALLY FAST--
AND NOW WE'RE HERE.
DRAGON...?
IS THAT REALLY YOU?
I'LL GET MY COAT...

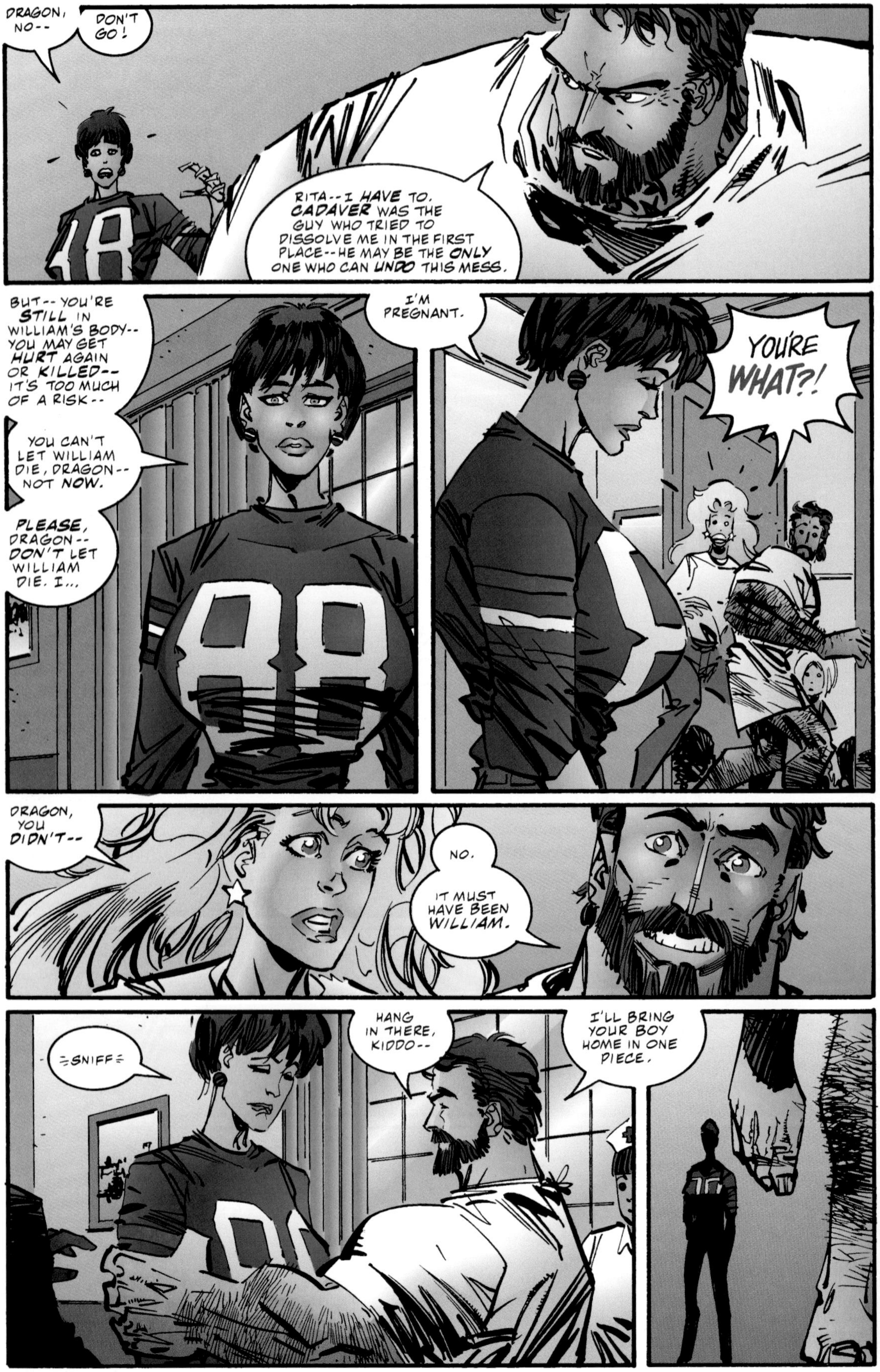
DRAGON, NO--
DON'T GO!
RITA--I HAVE TO. CADAVER WAS THE GUY WHO TRIED TO DISSOLVE ME IN THE FIRST PLACE--HE MAY BE THE ONLY ONE WHO CAN UNDO THIS MESS.
BUT--YOU'RE STILL IN WILLIAM'S BODY--YOU MAY GET HURT AGAIN OR KILLED--IT'S TOO MUCH OF A RISK--
YOU CAN'T LET WILLIAM DIE, DRAGON--NOT NOW.
PLEASE, DRAGON--DON'T LET WILLIAM DIE. I...
I'M PREGNANT.
YOU'RE WHAT?!
DRAGON, YOU DIDN'T--
NO.
IT MUST HAVE BEEN WILLIAM.
=SNIFF=
HANG IN THERE, KIDDO--
I'LL BRING YOUR BOY HOME IN ONE PIECE.

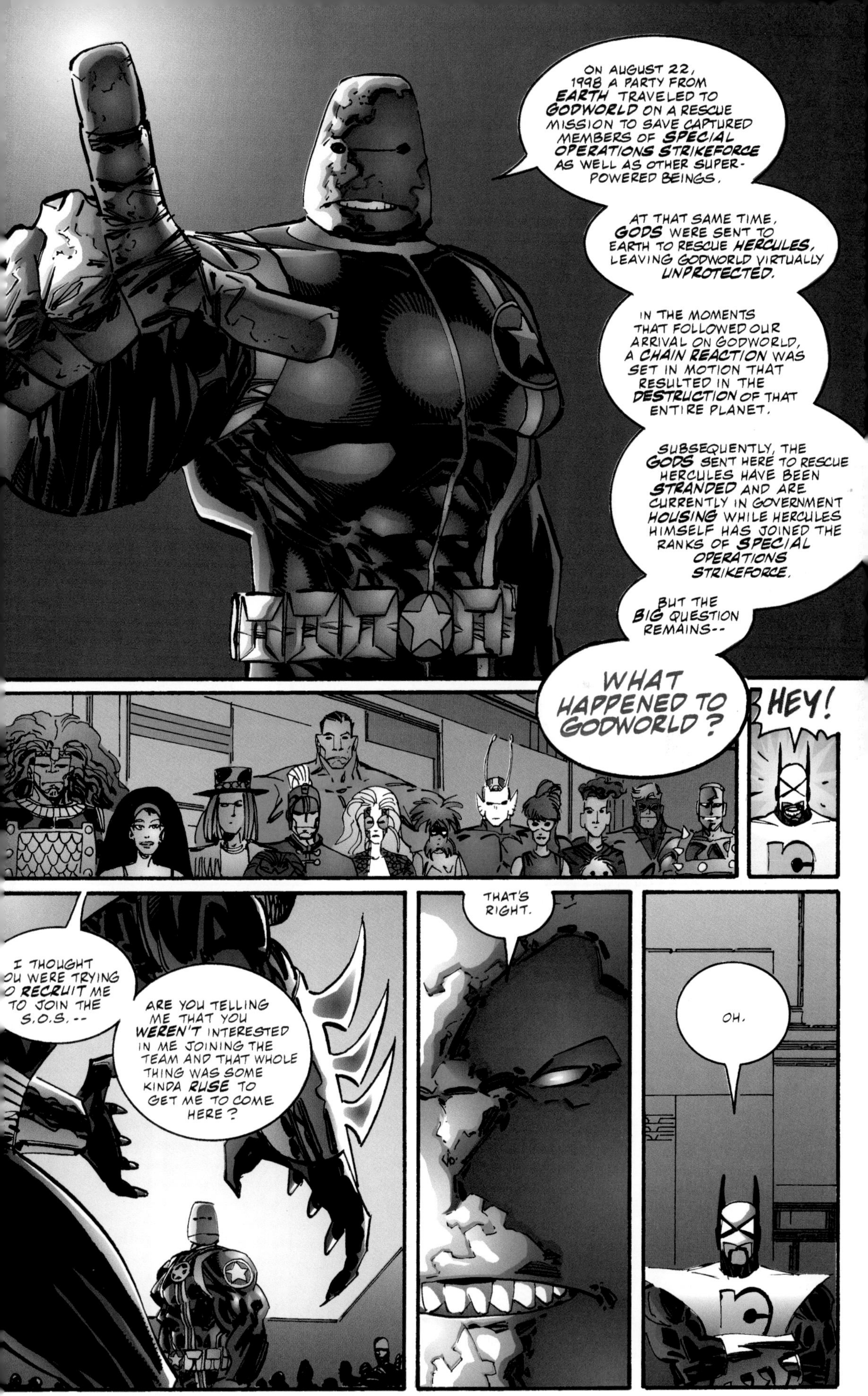

ON AUGUST 22, 1998 A PARTY FROM EARTH TRAVELED TO GODWORLD ON A RESCUE MISSION TO SAVE CAPTURED MEMBERS OF SPECIAL OPERATIONS STRIKEFORCE AS WELL AS OTHER SUPER-POWERED BEINGS.
AT THAT SAME TIME, GODS WERE SENT TO EARTH TO RESCUE HERCULES, LEAVING GODWORLD VIRTUALLY UNPROTECTED.
IN THE MOMENTS THAT FOLLOWED OUR ARRIVAL ON GODWORLD, A CHAIN REACTION WAS SET IN MOTION THAT RESULTED IN THE DESTRUCTION OF THAT ENTIRE PLANET.
SUBSEQUENTLY, THE GODS SENT HERE TO RESCUE HERCULES HAVE BEEN STRANDED AND ARE CURRENTLY IN GOVERNMENT HOUSING WHILE HERCULES HIMSELF HAS JOINED THE RANKS OF SPECIAL OPERATIONS STRIKEFORCE.
BUT THE BIG QUESTION REMAINS--
WHAT HAPPENED TO GODWORLD?
HEY!
I THOUGHT OU WERE TRYING O RECRUIT ME TO JOIN THE S.O.S.--
ARE YOU TELLING ME THAT YOU WEREN'T INTERESTED IN ME JOINING THE TEAM AND THAT WHOLE THING WAS SOME KINDA RUSE TO GET ME TO COME HERE?
THAT'S RIGHT.
OH.

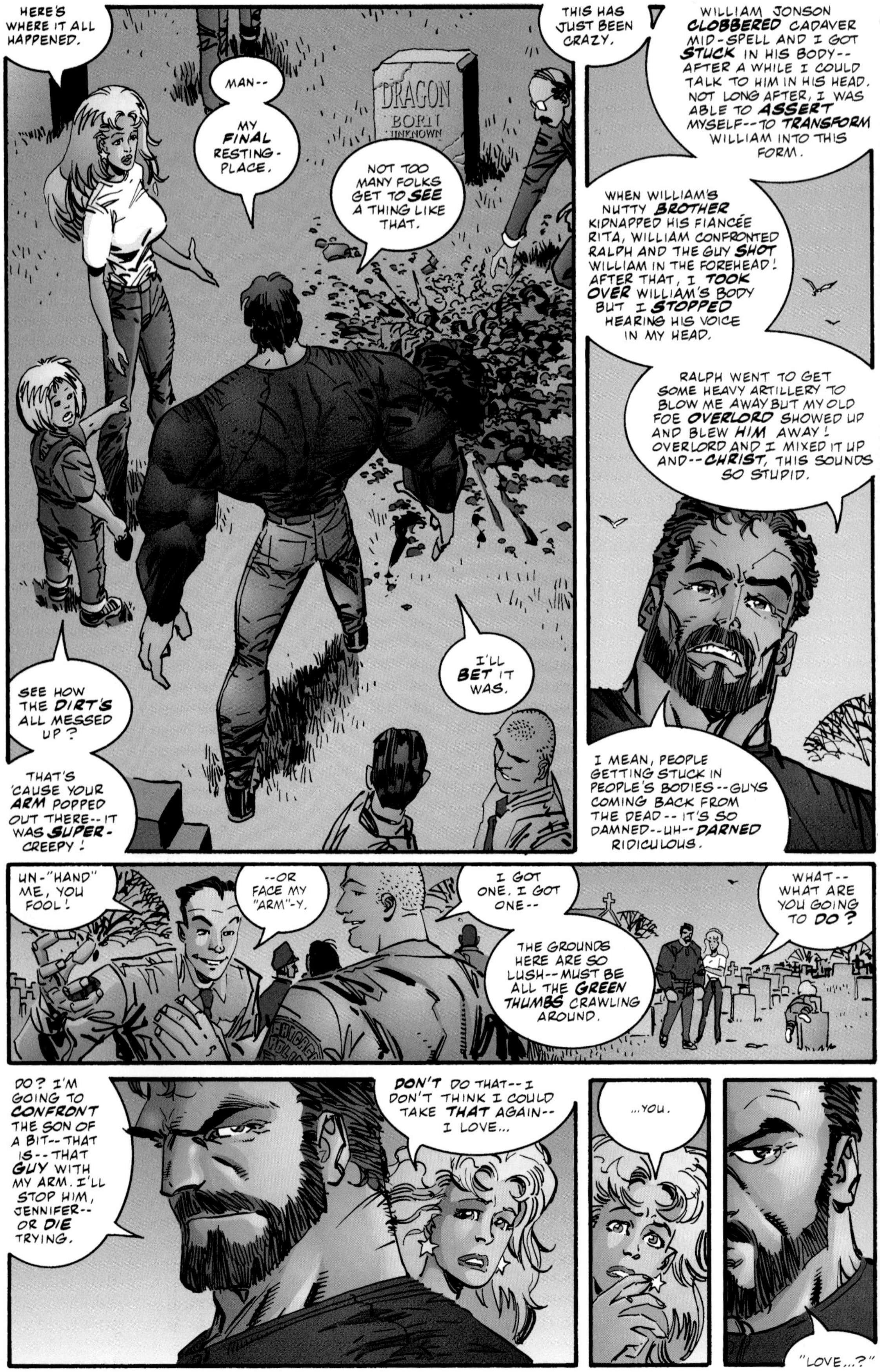
HERE'S WHERE IT ALL HAPPENED.
MAN--
MY FINAL RESTING-PLACE.
NOT TOO MANY FOLKS GET TO SEE A THING LIKE THAT.
DRAGON BORN UNKNOWN
SEE HOW THE DIRT'S ALL MESSED UP?
THAT'S 'CAUSE YOUR ARM POPPED OUT THERE-- IT WAS SUPER-CREEPY!
I'LL BET IT WAS.
THIS HAS JUST BEEN CRAZY.
WILLIAM JONSON CLOBBERED CADAVER MID-SPELL AND I GOT STUCK IN HIS BODY-- AFTER A WHILE I COULD TALK TO HIM IN HIS HEAD. NOT LONG AFTER, I WAS ABLE TO ASSERT MYSELF--TO TRANSFORM WILLIAM INTO THIS FORM.
WHEN WILLIAM'S NUTTY BROTHER KIDNAPPED HIS FIANCÉE RITA, WILLIAM CONFRONTED RALPH AND THE GUY SHOT WILLIAM IN THE FOREHEAD! AFTER THAT, I TOOK OVER WILLIAM'S BODY BUT I STOPPED HEARING HIS VOICE IN MY HEAD.
RALPH WENT TO GET SOME HEAVY ARTILLERY TO BLOW ME AWAY BUT MY OLD FOE OVERLORD SHOWED UP AND BLEW HIM AWAY! OVERLORD AND I MIXED IT UP AND--CHRIST, THIS SOUNDS SO STUPID.
I MEAN, PEOPLE GETTING STUCK IN PEOPLE'S BODIES--GUYS COMING BACK FROM THE DEAD-- IT'S SO DAMNED--UH--DARNED RIDICULOUS.
UN-"HAND" ME, YOU FOOL!
--OR FACE MY "ARM"-Y.
I GOT ONE. I GOT ONE--
THE GROUNDS HERE ARE SO LUSH--MUST BE ALL THE GREEN THUMBS CRAWLING AROUND.
WHAT-- WHAT ARE YOU GOING TO DO?
DO? I'M GOING TO CONFRONT THE SON OF A BIT--THAT IS--THAT GUY WITH MY ARM. I'LL STOP HIM, JENNIFER-- OR DIE TRYING.
DON'T DO THAT-- I DON'T THINK I COULD TAKE THAT AGAIN-- I LOVE...
...YOU.
"LOVE...?"

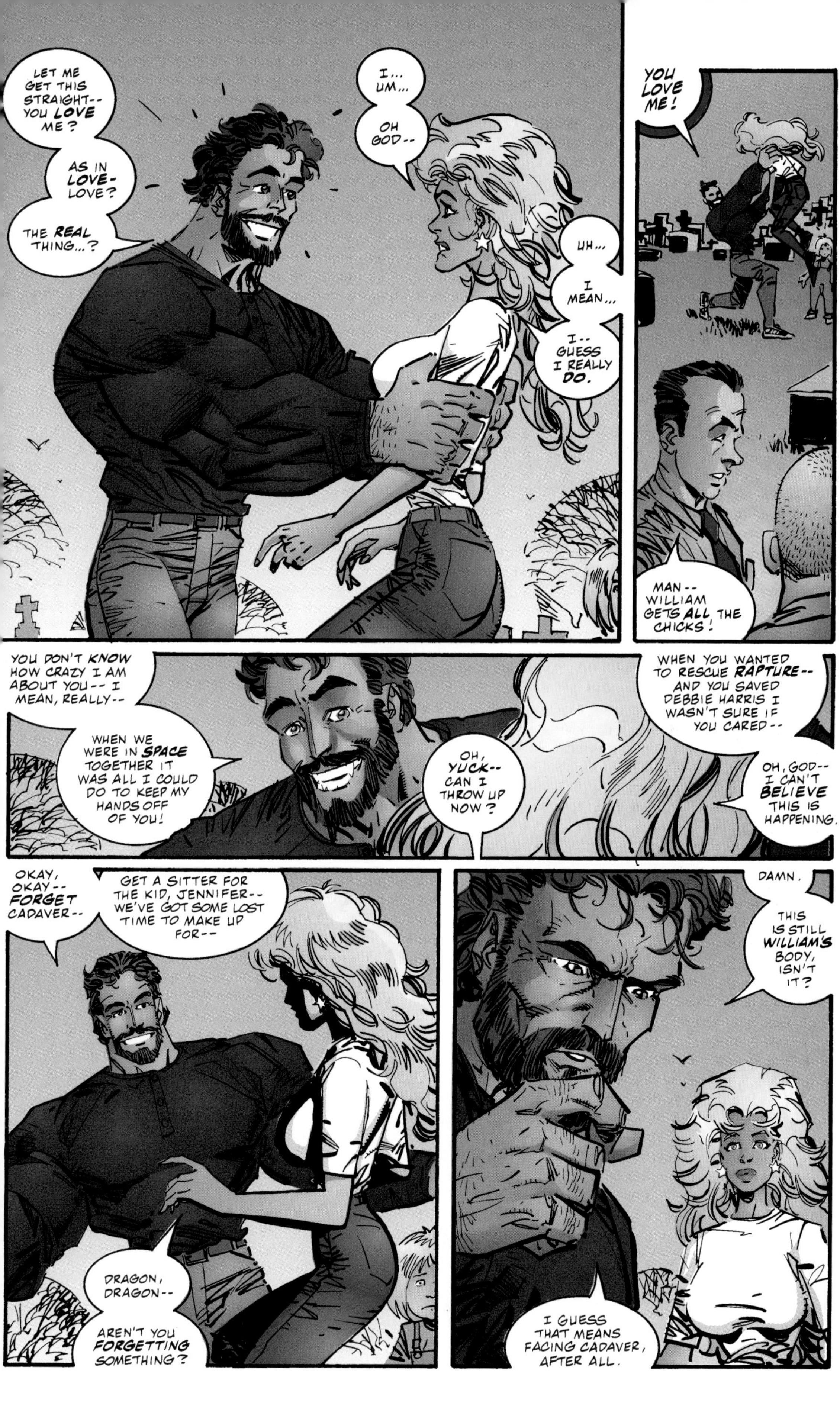
LET ME GET THIS STRAIGHT-- YOU LOVE ME?
AS IN LOVE-LOVE?
THE REAL THING...?
I... UM...
OH GOD--
UH...
I MEAN...
I-- GUESS I REALLY DO.
YOU LOVE ME!
MAN-- WILLIAM GETS ALL THE CHICKS!
YOU DON'T KNOW HOW CRAZY I AM ABOUT YOU-- I MEAN, REALLY--
WHEN WE WERE IN SPACE TOGETHER IT WAS ALL I COULD DO TO KEEP MY HANDS OFF OF YOU!
OH, YUCK-- CAN I THROW UP NOW?
WHEN YOU WANTED TO RESCUE RAPTURE-- AND YOU SAVED DEBBIE HARRIS I WASN'T SURE IF YOU CARED--
OH, GOD-- I CAN'T BELIEVE THIS IS HAPPENING.
OKAY, OKAY-- FORGET CADAVER--
GET A SITTER FOR THE KID, JENNIFER-- WE'VE GOT SOME LOST TIME TO MAKE UP FOR--
DRAGON, DRAGON--
AREN'T YOU FORGETTING SOMETHING?
DAMN.
THIS IS STILL WILLIAM'S BODY, ISN'T IT?
I GUESS THAT MEANS FACING CADAVER, AFTER ALL.

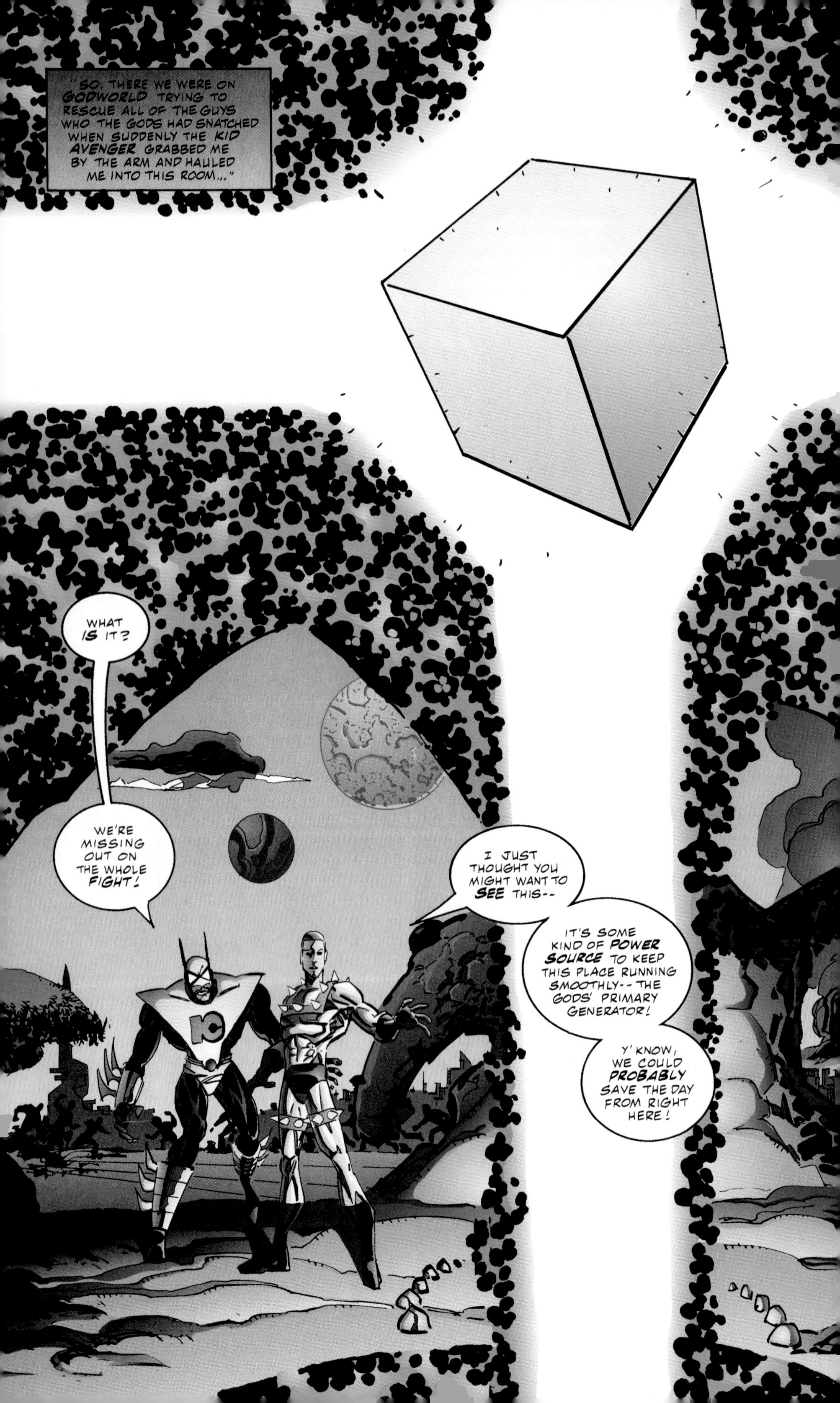
"SO, THERE WE WERE ON GODWORLD TRYING TO RESCUE ALL OF THE GUYS WHO THE GODS HAD SNATCHED WHEN SUDDENLY THE KID AVENGER GRABBED ME BY THE ARM AND HAULED ME INTO THIS ROOM..."
WHAT IS IT?
WE'RE MISSING OUT ON THE WHOLE FIGHT!
I JUST THOUGHT YOU MIGHT WANT TO SEE THIS--
IT'S SOME KIND OF POWER SOURCE TO KEEP THIS PLACE RUNNING SMOOTHLY--THE GODS' PRIMARY GENERATOR!
Y'KNOW, WE COULD PROBABLY SAVE THE DAY FROM RIGHT HERE!

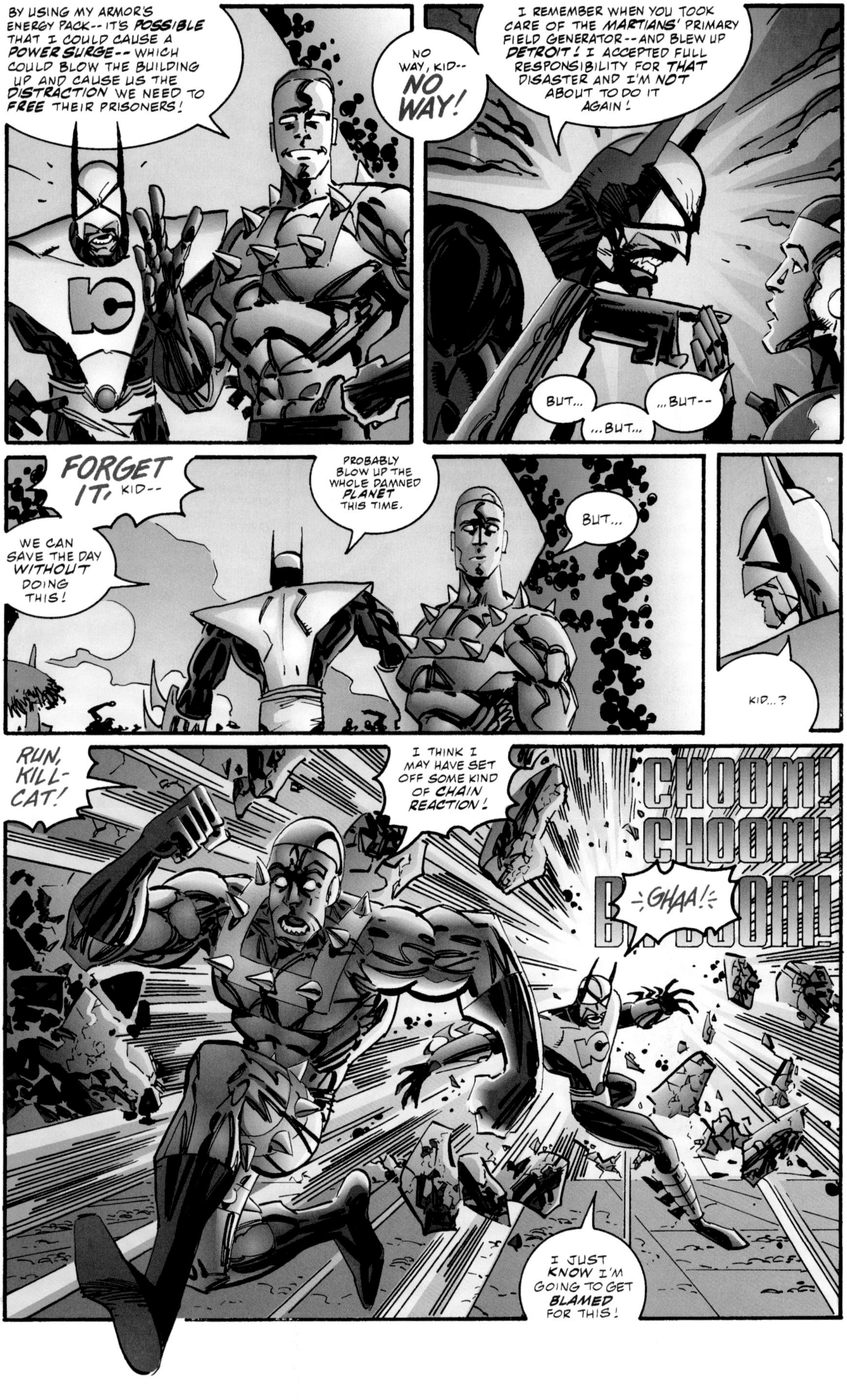

BY USING MY ARMOR'S ENERGY PACK-- IT'S POSSIBLE THAT I COULD CAUSE A POWER SURGE-- WHICH COULD BLOW THE BUILDING UP AND CAUSE US THE DISTRACTION WE NEED TO FREE THEIR PRISONERS!
NO WAY, KID-- NO WAY!
I REMEMBER WHEN YOU TOOK CARE OF THE MARTIANS' PRIMARY FIELD GENERATOR--AND BLEW UP DETROIT! I ACCEPTED FULL RESPONSIBILITY FOR THAT DISASTER AND I'M NOT ABOUT TO DO IT AGAIN!
BUT...
...BUT...
...BUT--
FORGET IT, KID--
WE CAN SAVE THE DAY WITHOUT DOING THIS!
PROBABLY BLOW UP THE WHOLE DAMNED PLANET THIS TIME.
BUT...
KID...?
RUN, KILL-CAT!
I THINK I MAY HAVE SET OFF SOME KIND OF CHAIN REACTION!
CHOOM! CHOOM!
GHAA!
I JUST KNOW I'M GOING TO GET BLAMED FOR THIS!

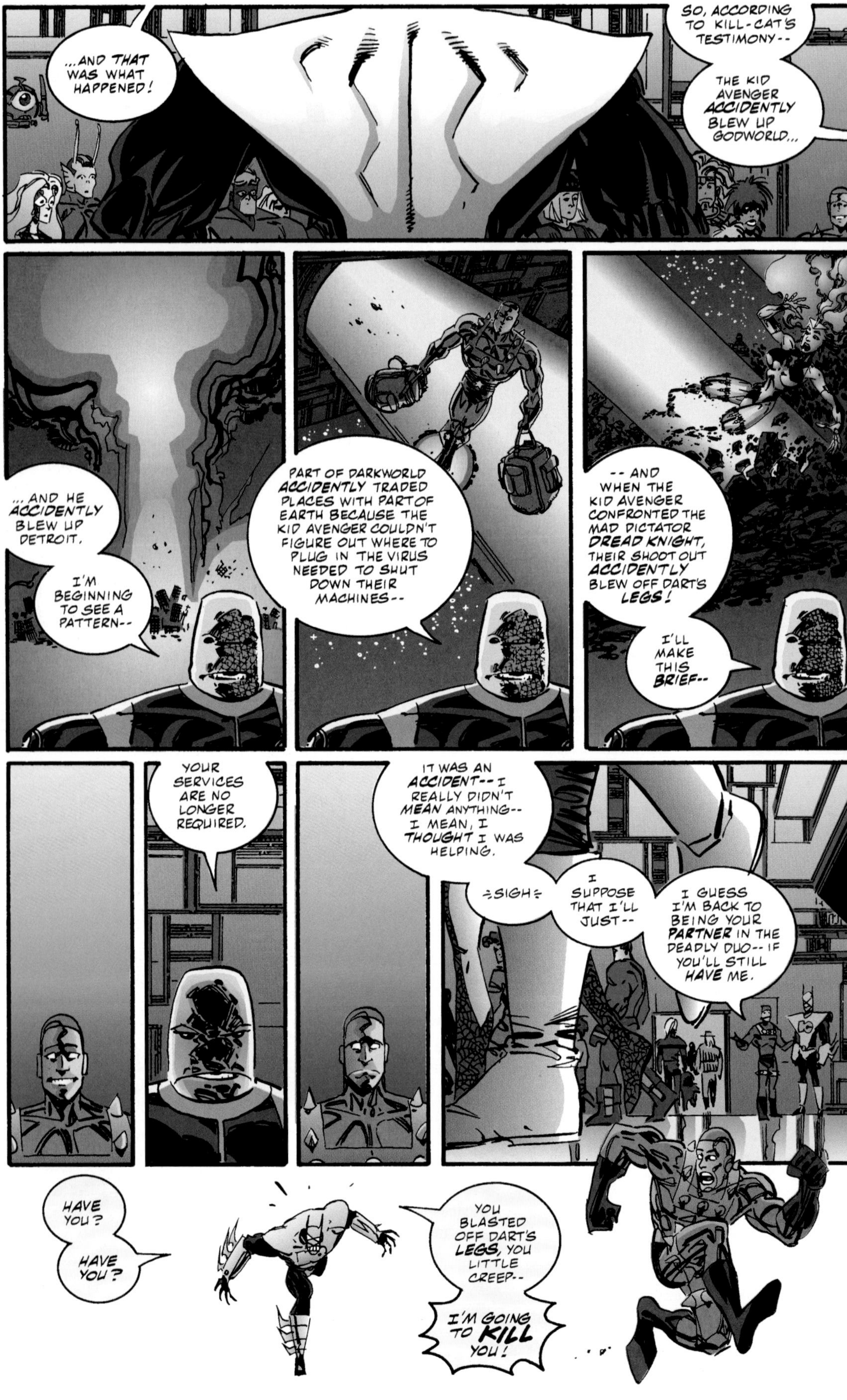

...AND THAT WAS WHAT HAPPENED!
SO, ACCORDING TO KILL-CAT'S TESTIMONY--
THE KID AVENGER ACCIDENTLY BLEW UP GODWORLD...
...AND HE ACCIDENTLY BLEW UP DETROIT.
I'M BEGINNING TO SEE A PATTERN--
PART OF DARKWORLD ACCIDENTLY TRADED PLACES WITH PART OF EARTH BECAUSE THE KID AVENGER COULDN'T FIGURE OUT WHERE TO PLUG IN THE VIRUS NEEDED TO SHUT DOWN THEIR MACHINES--
-- AND WHEN THE KID AVENGER CONFRONTED THE MAD DICTATOR DREAD KNIGHT, THEIR SHOOT OUT ACCIDENTLY BLEW OFF DART'S LEGS!
I'LL MAKE THIS BRIEF--
YOUR SERVICES ARE NO LONGER REQUIRED.
IT WAS AN ACCIDENT-- I REALLY DIDN'T MEAN ANYTHING-- I MEAN, I THOUGHT I WAS HELPING.
=SIGH=
I SUPPOSE THAT I'LL JUST--
I GUESS I'M BACK TO BEING YOUR PARTNER IN THE DEADLY DUO-- IF YOU'LL STILL HAVE ME.
HAVE YOU?
HAVE YOU?
YOU BLASTED OFF DART'S LEGS, YOU LITTLE CREEP--
I'M GOING TO KILL YOU!

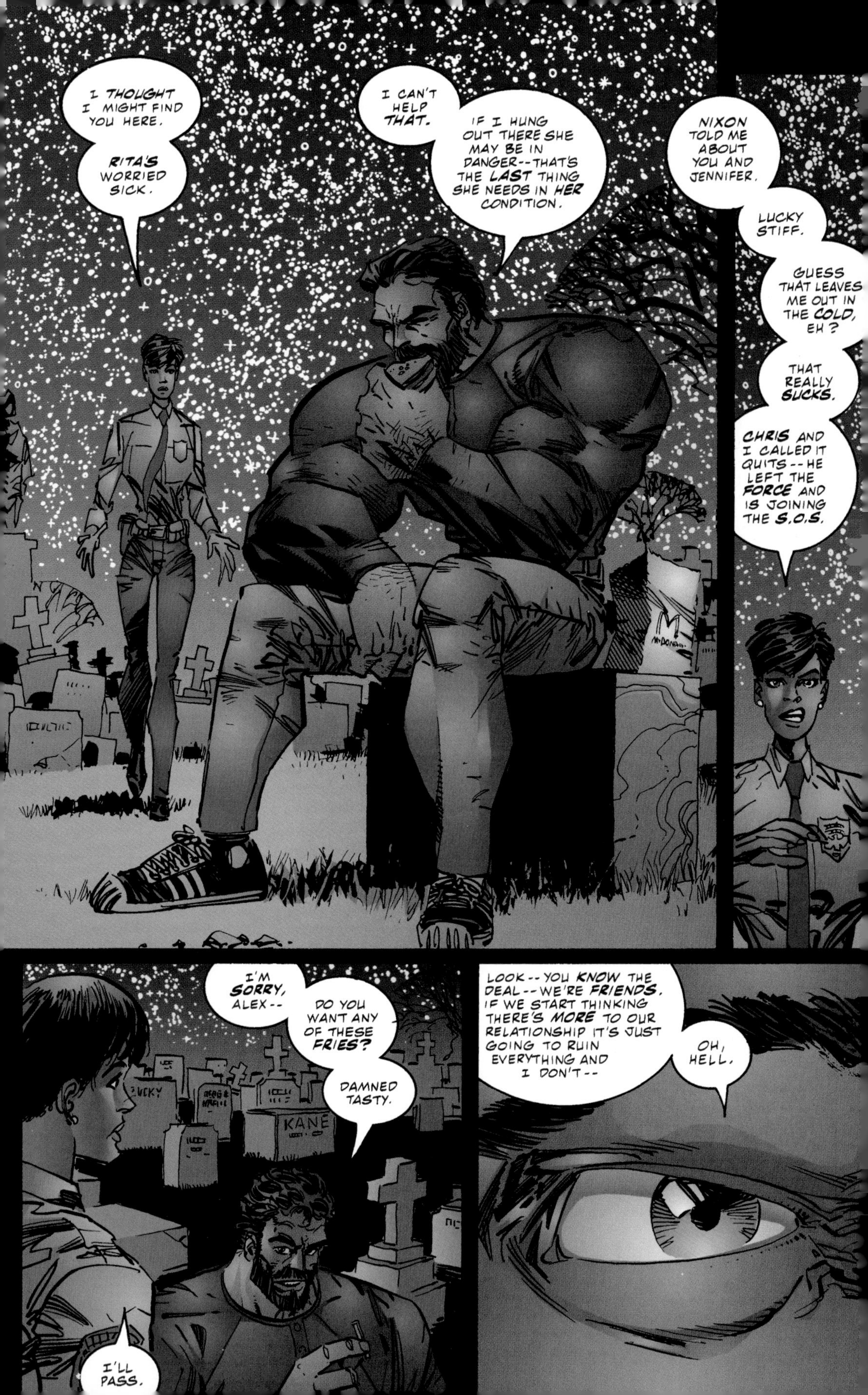
I THOUGHT I MIGHT FIND YOU HERE.
RITA'S WORRIED SICK.
I CAN'T HELP THAT.
IF I HUNG OUT THERE SHE MAY BE IN DANGER--THAT'S THE LAST THING SHE NEEDS IN HER CONDITION.
NIXON TOLD ME ABOUT YOU AND JENNIFER.
LUCKY STIFF.
GUESS THAT LEAVES ME OUT IN THE COLD, EH?
THAT REALLY SUCKS.
CHRIS AND I CALLED IT QUITS--HE LEFT THE FORCE AND IS JOINING THE S.O.S.
I'M SORRY, ALEX--
DO YOU WANT ANY OF THESE FRIES?
DAMNED TASTY.
I'LL PASS.
KANE
LOOK--YOU KNOW THE DEAL--WE'RE FRIENDS. IF WE START THINKING THERE'S MORE TO OUR RELATIONSHIP IT'S JUST GOING TO RUIN EVERYTHING AND I DON'T--
OH, HELL.

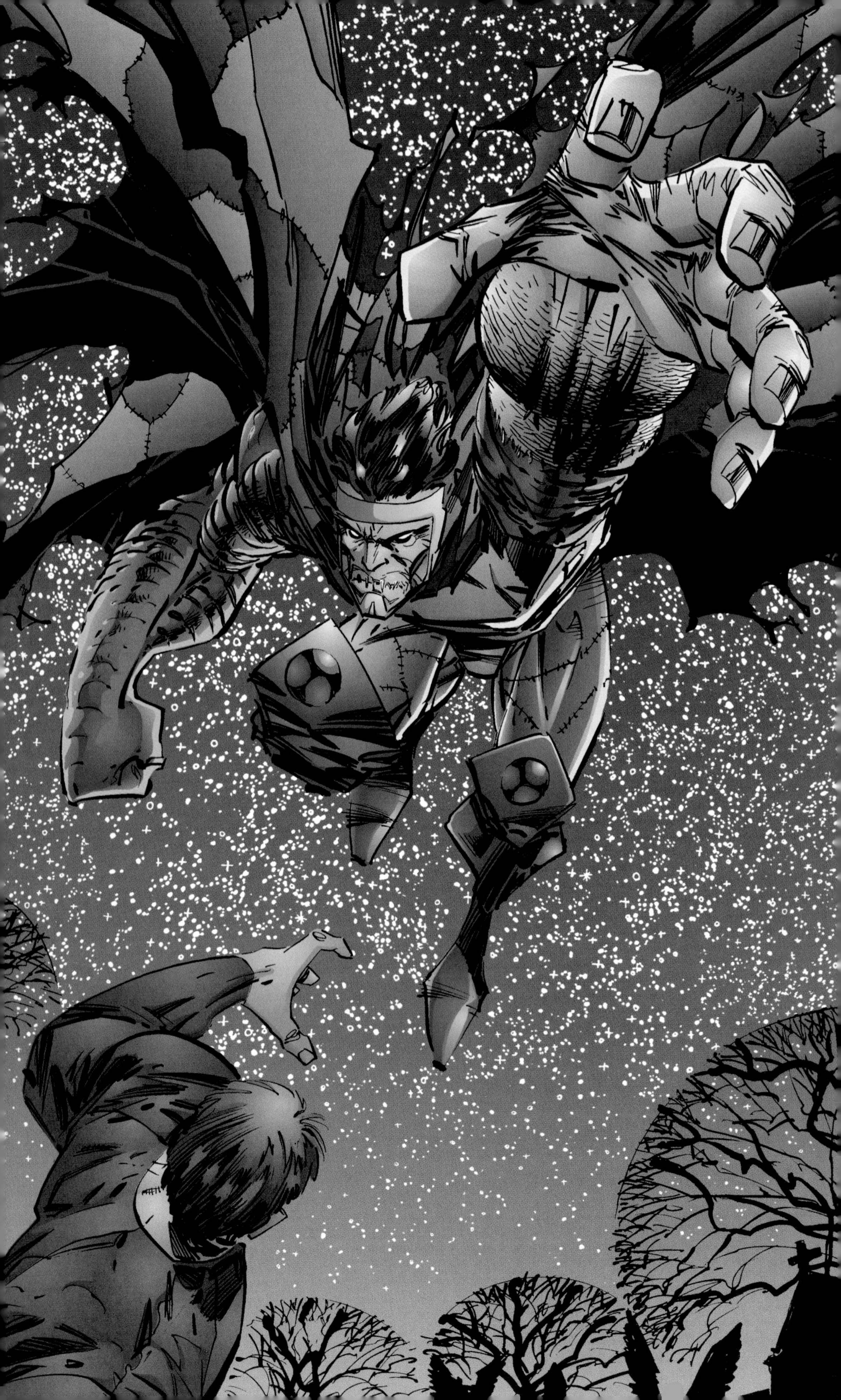

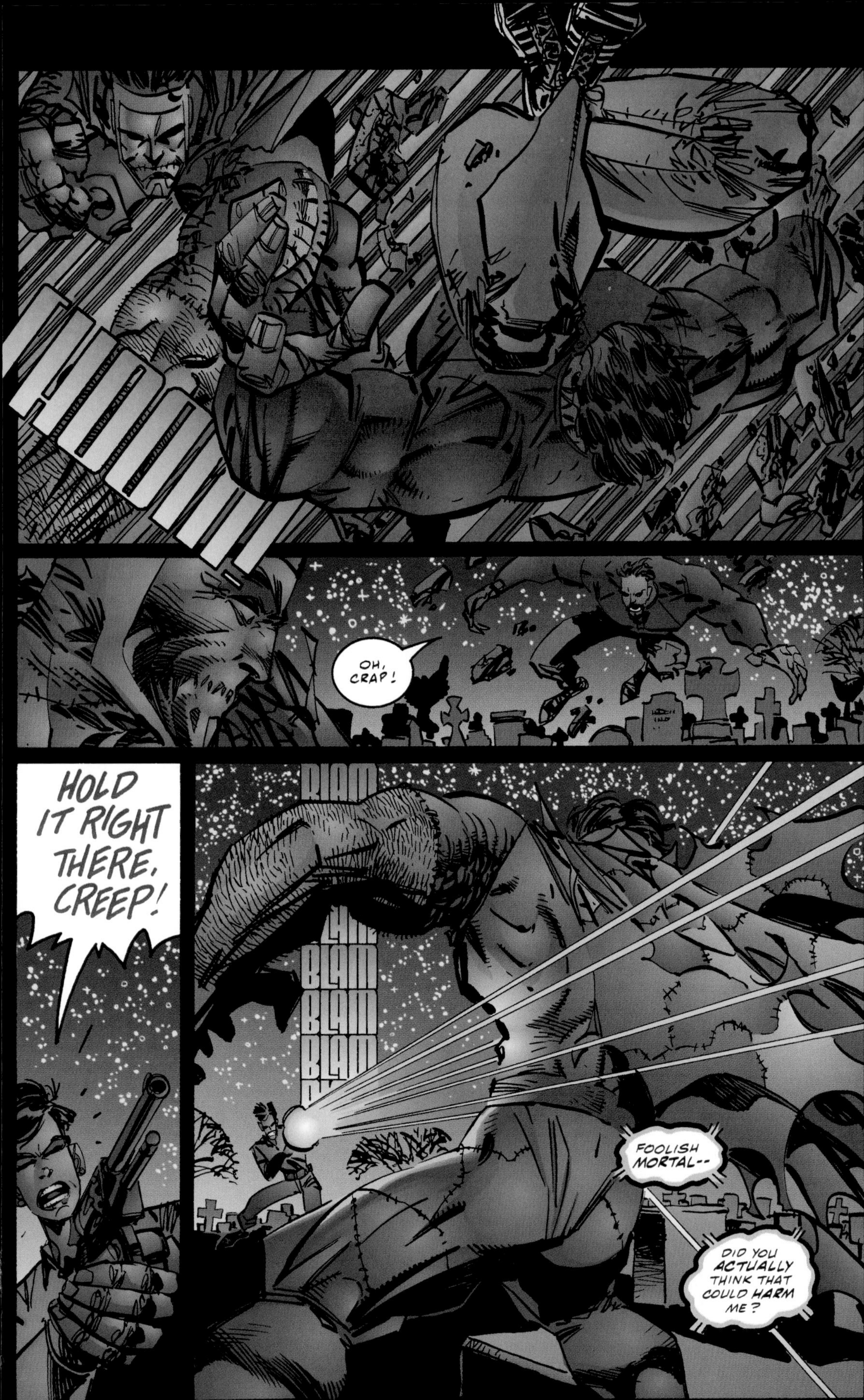
OH, CRAP!
HOLD IT RIGHT THERE, CREEP!
BLAM
BLAM
BLAM
FOOLISH MORTAL--
DID YOU ACTUALLY THINK THAT COULD HARM ME?

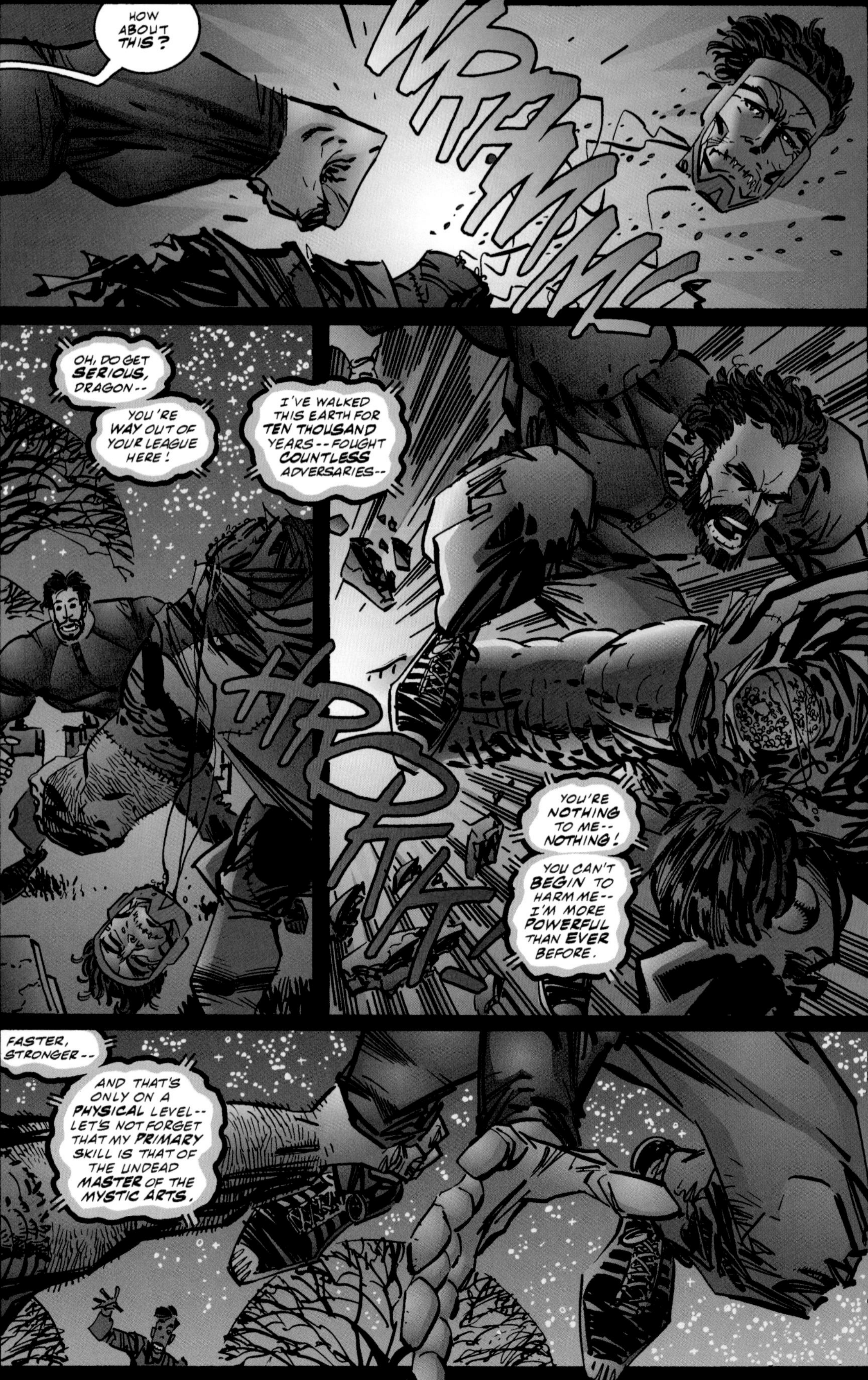
HOW ABOUT THIS?
WHAMM!
OH, DO GET SERIOUS, DRAGON--
YOU'RE WAY OUT OF YOUR LEAGUE HERE!
I'VE WALKED THIS EARTH FOR TEN THOUSAND YEARS--FOUGHT COUNTLESS ADVERSARIES--
HRRAKK
YOU'RE NOTHING TO ME--NOTHING!
YOU CAN'T BEGIN TO HARM ME--I'M MORE POWERFUL THAN EVER BEFORE.
FASTER, STRONGER--
AND THAT'S ONLY ON A PHYSICAL LEVEL--LET'S NOT FORGET THAT MY PRIMARY SKILL IS THAT OF THE UNDEAD MASTER OF THE MYSTIC ARTS.

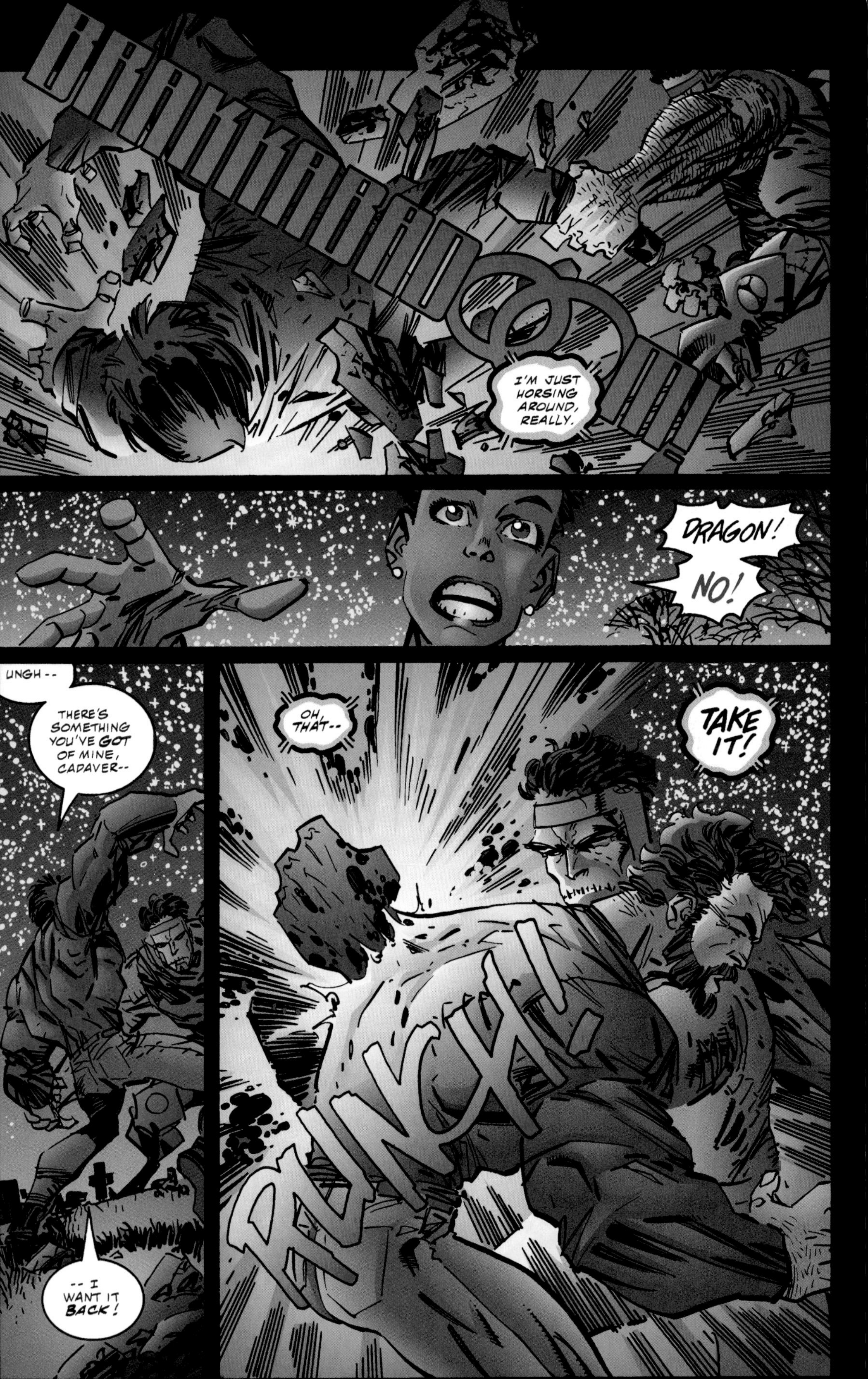
I'M JUST HORSING AROUND, REALLY.
DRAGON!
NO!
UNGH --
THERE'S SOMETHING YOU'VE GOT OF MINE, CADAVER--
-- I WANT IT BACK!
OH, THAT--
TAKE IT!

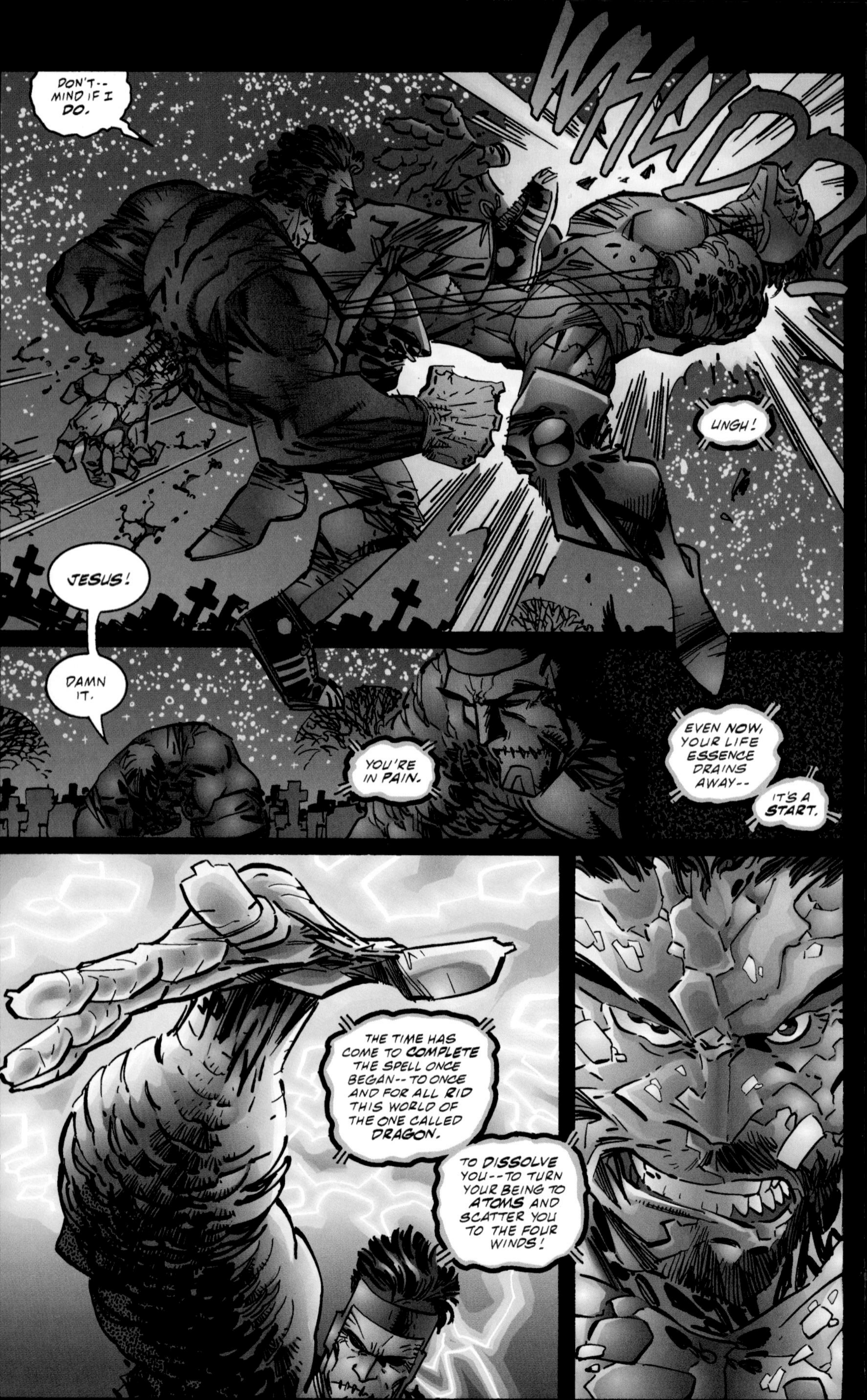
DON'T-- MIND IF I DO.
WHUD
UNGH!
JESUS!
DAMN IT.
YOU'RE IN PAIN.
EVEN NOW, YOUR LIFE ESSENCE DRAINS AWAY--
IT'S A START.
THE TIME HAS COME TO COMPLETE THE SPELL ONCE BEGAN--TO ONCE AND FOR ALL RID THIS WORLD OF THE ONE CALLED DRAGON.
TO DISSOLVE YOU--TO TURN YOUR BEING TO ATOMS AND SCATTER YOU TO THE FOUR WINDS!

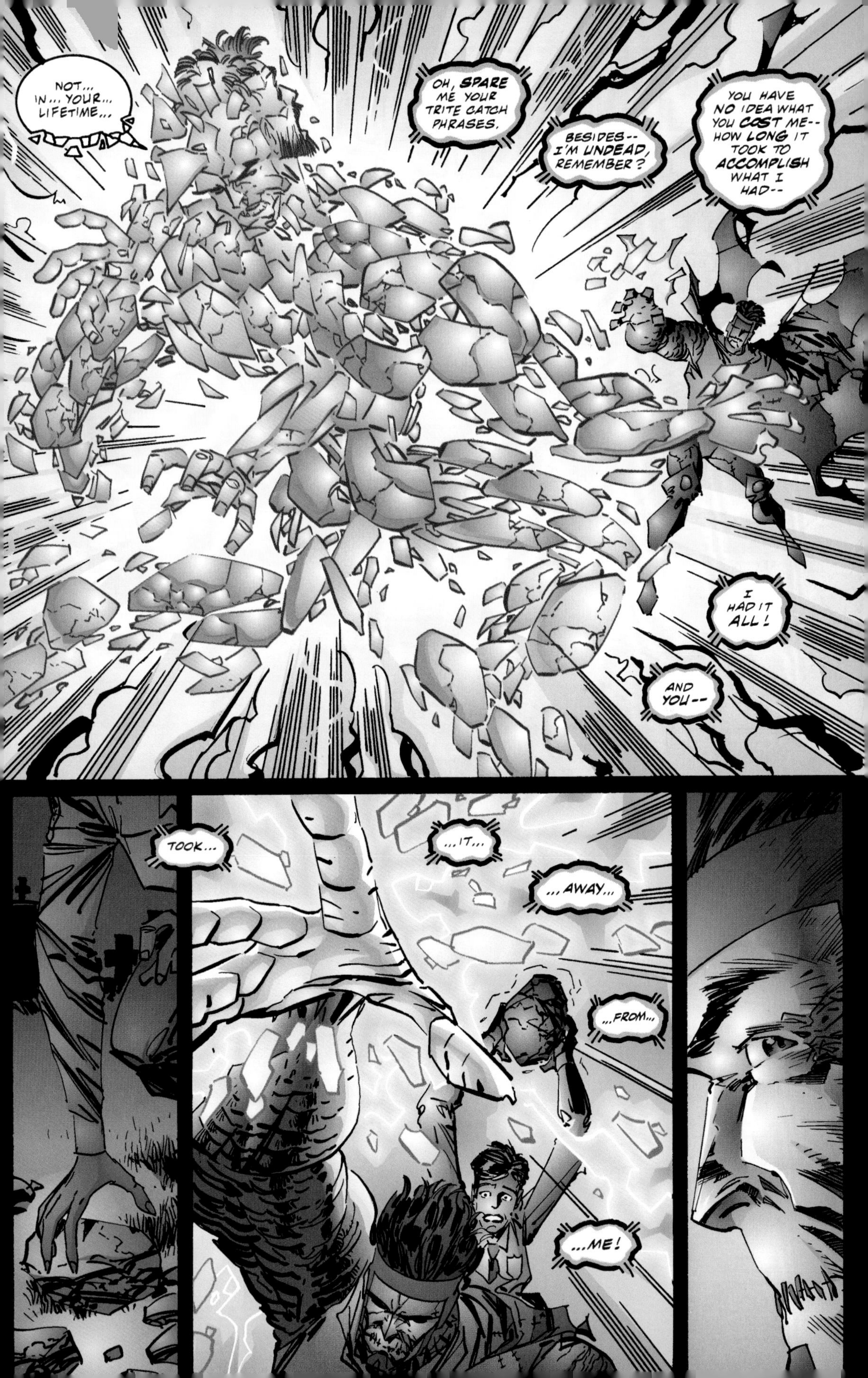
NOT... IN... YOUR... LIFETIME...
OH, SPARE ME YOUR TRITE CATCH PHRASES.
BESIDES-- I'M UNDEAD, REMEMBER?
YOU HAVE NO IDEA WHAT YOU COST ME-- HOW LONG IT TOOK TO ACCOMPLISH WHAT I HAD--
I HAD IT ALL!
AND YOU--
TOOK...
...IT...
...AWAY...
...FROM...
...ME!

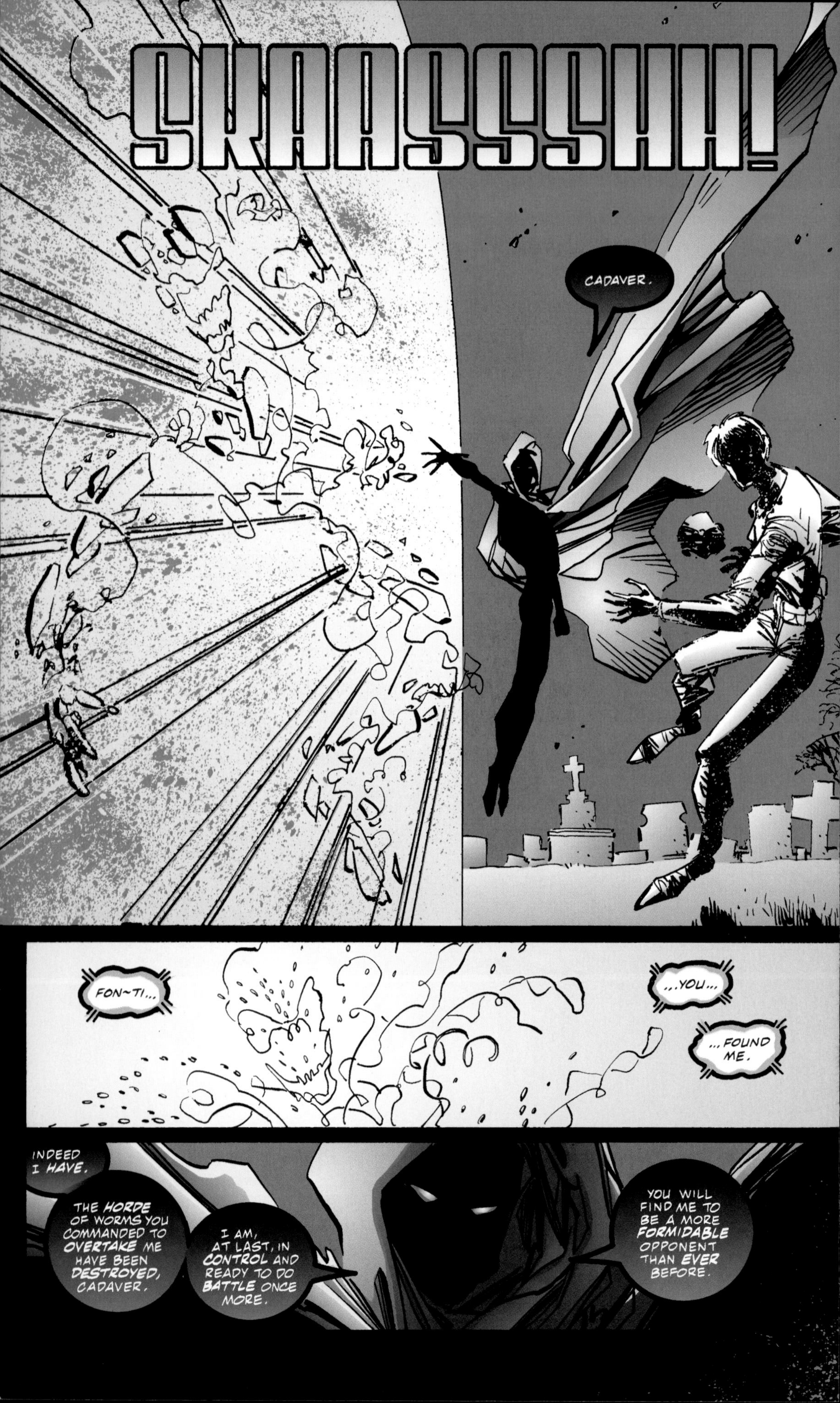
SKAASSSHH!
CADAVER.
FON~TI...
...YOU...
...FOUND ME.
INDEED I HAVE.
THE HORDE OF WORMS YOU COMMANDED TO OVERTAKE ME HAVE BEEN DESTROYED, CADAVER.
I AM, AT LAST, IN CONTROL AND READY TO DO BATTLE ONCE MORE.
YOU WILL FIND ME TO BE A MORE FORMIDABLE OPPONENT THAN EVER BEFORE.

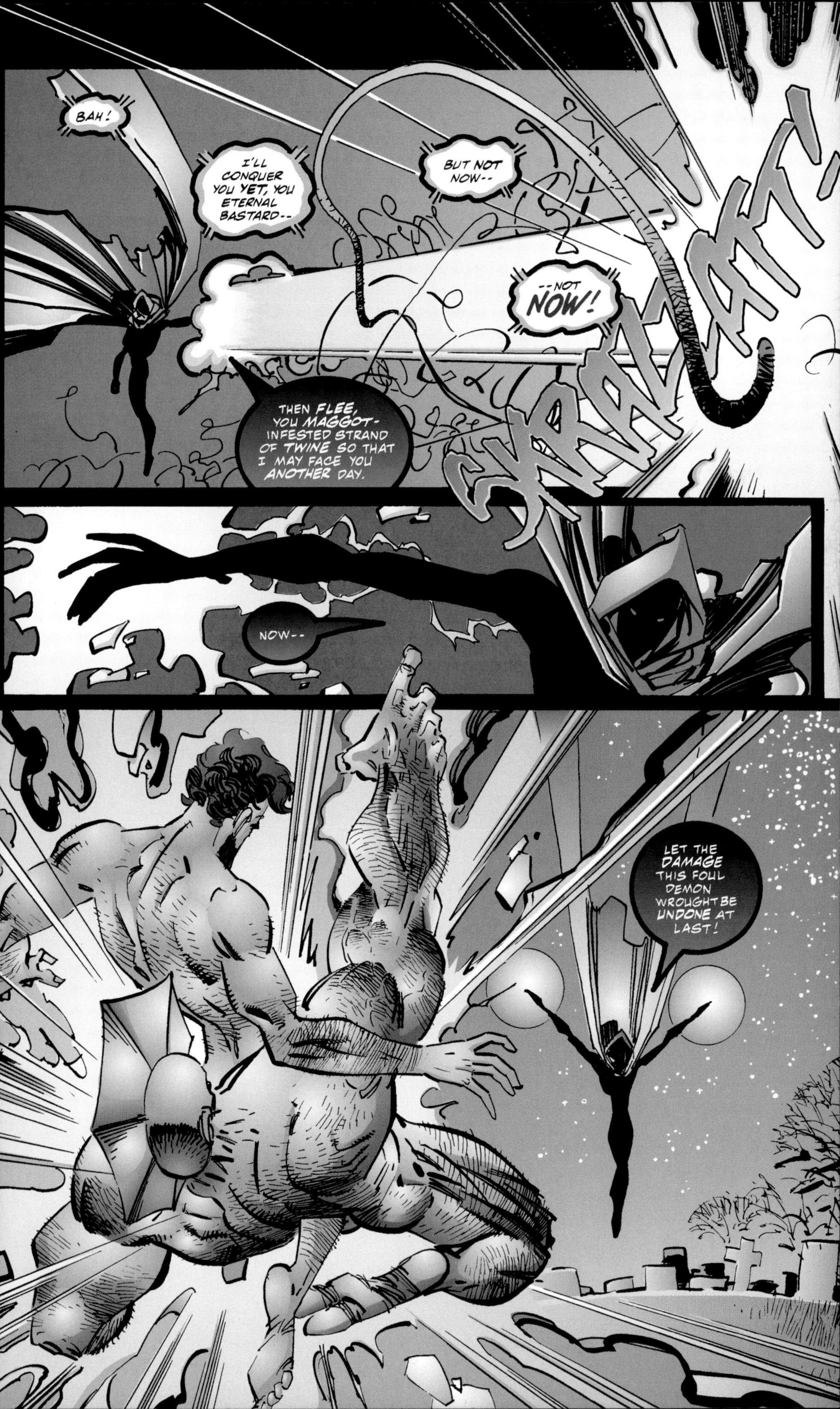
BAH!
I'LL CONQUER YOU YET, YOU ETERNAL BASTARD--
BUT NOT NOW--
--NOT NOW!
THEN FLEE, YOU MAGGOT-INFESTED STRAND OF TWINE SO THAT I MAY FACE YOU ANOTHER DAY.
SKRAKATT!
NOW--
LET THE DAMAGE THIS FOUL DEMON WROUGHT BE UNDONE AT LAST!

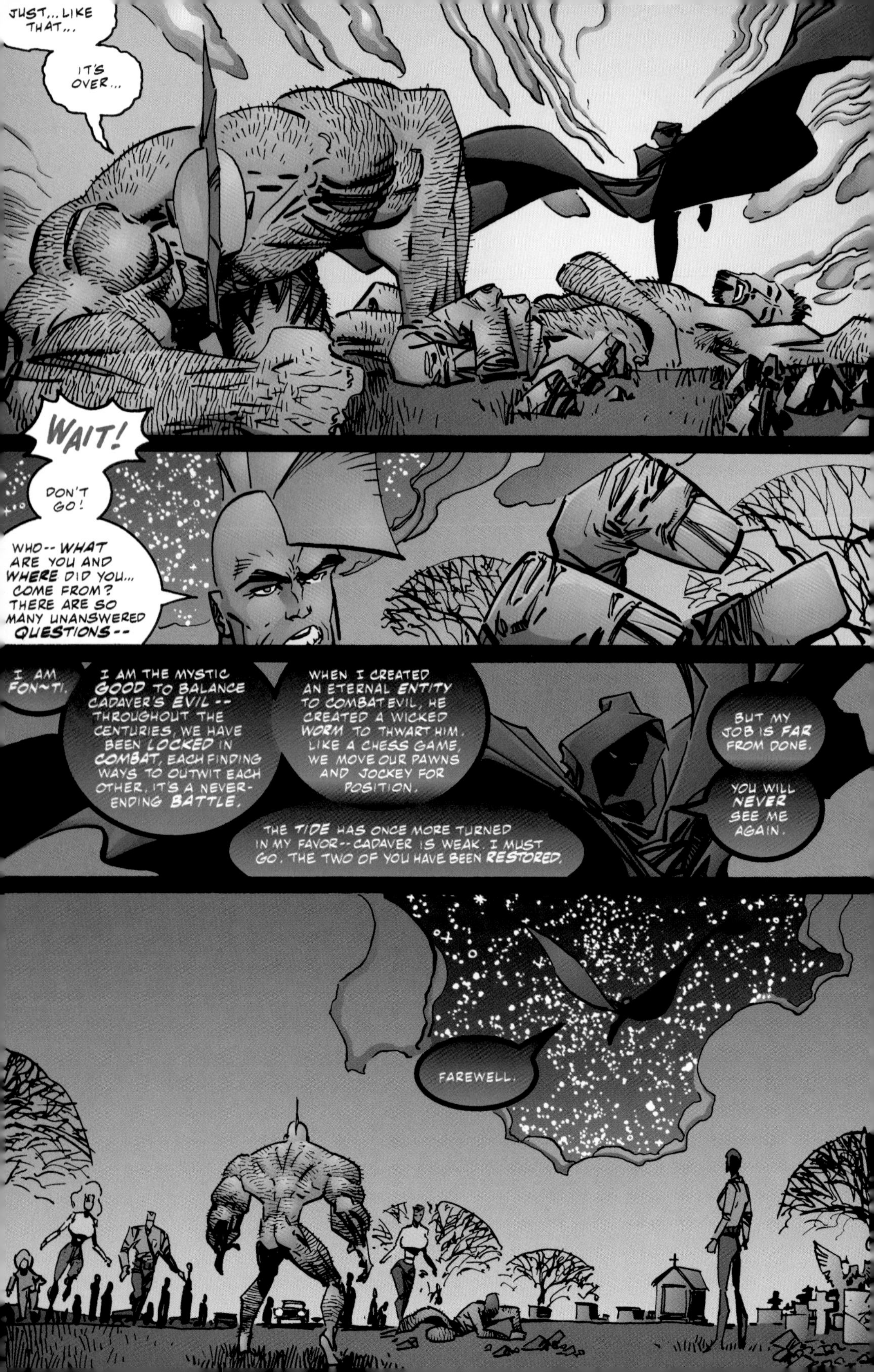

JUST... LIKE THAT...
IT'S OVER...
WAIT!
DON'T GO!
WHO-- WHAT ARE YOU AND WHERE DID YOU... COME FROM? THERE ARE SO MANY UNANSWERED QUESTIONS--
I AM FON~TI.
I AM THE MYSTIC GOOD TO BALANCE CADAVER'S EVIL-- THROUGHOUT THE CENTURIES, WE HAVE BEEN LOCKED IN COMBAT, EACH FINDING WAYS TO OUTWIT EACH OTHER. IT'S A NEVER-ENDING BATTLE.
WHEN I CREATED AN ETERNAL ENTITY TO COMBAT EVIL, HE CREATED A WICKED WORM TO THWART HIM. LIKE A CHESS GAME, WE MOVE OUR PAWNS AND JOCKEY FOR POSITION.
THE TIDE HAS ONCE MORE TURNED IN MY FAVOR-- CADAVER IS WEAK. I MUST GO. THE TWO OF YOU HAVE BEEN RESTORED.
BUT MY JOB IS FAR FROM DONE.
YOU WILL NEVER SEE ME AGAIN.
FAREWELL.

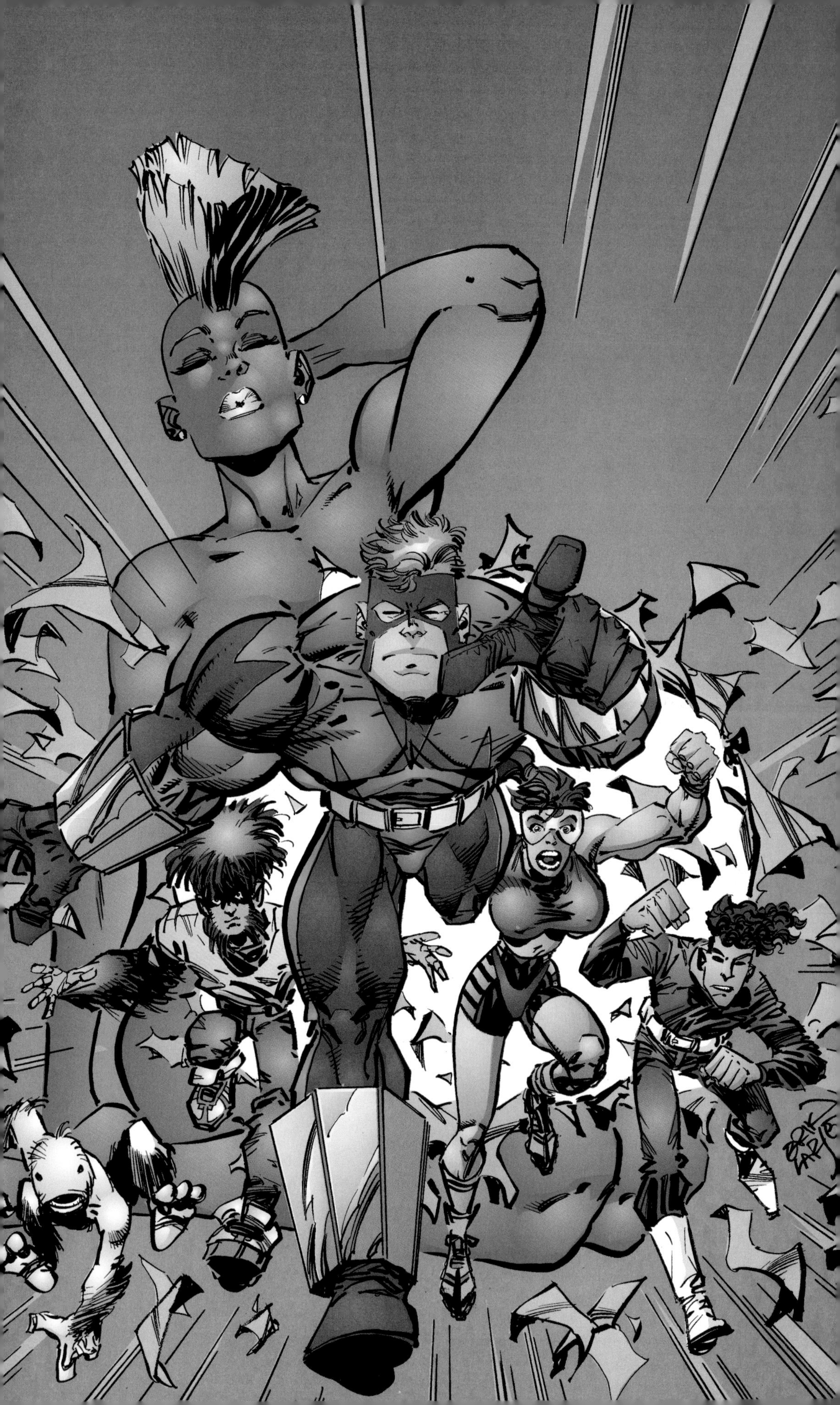

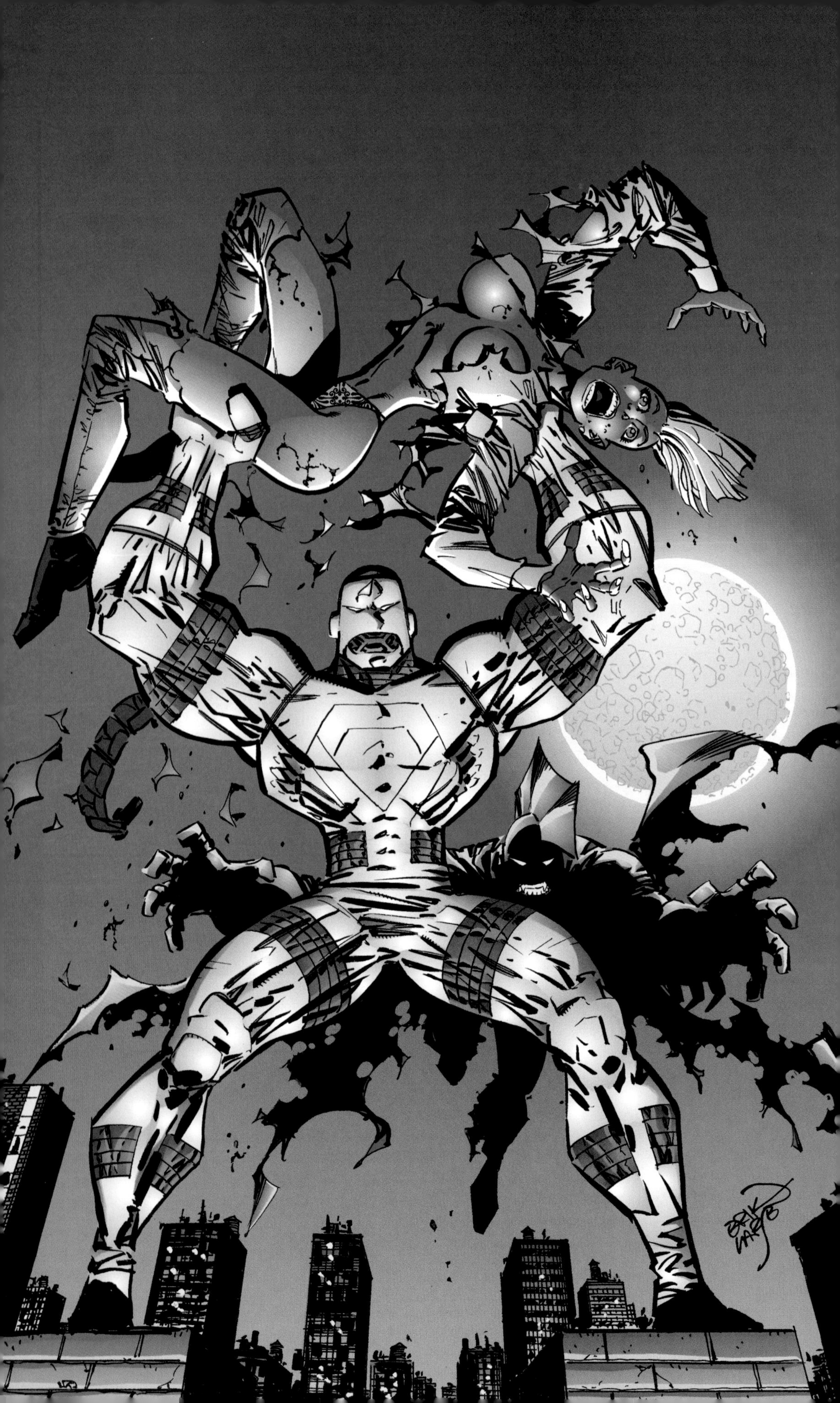

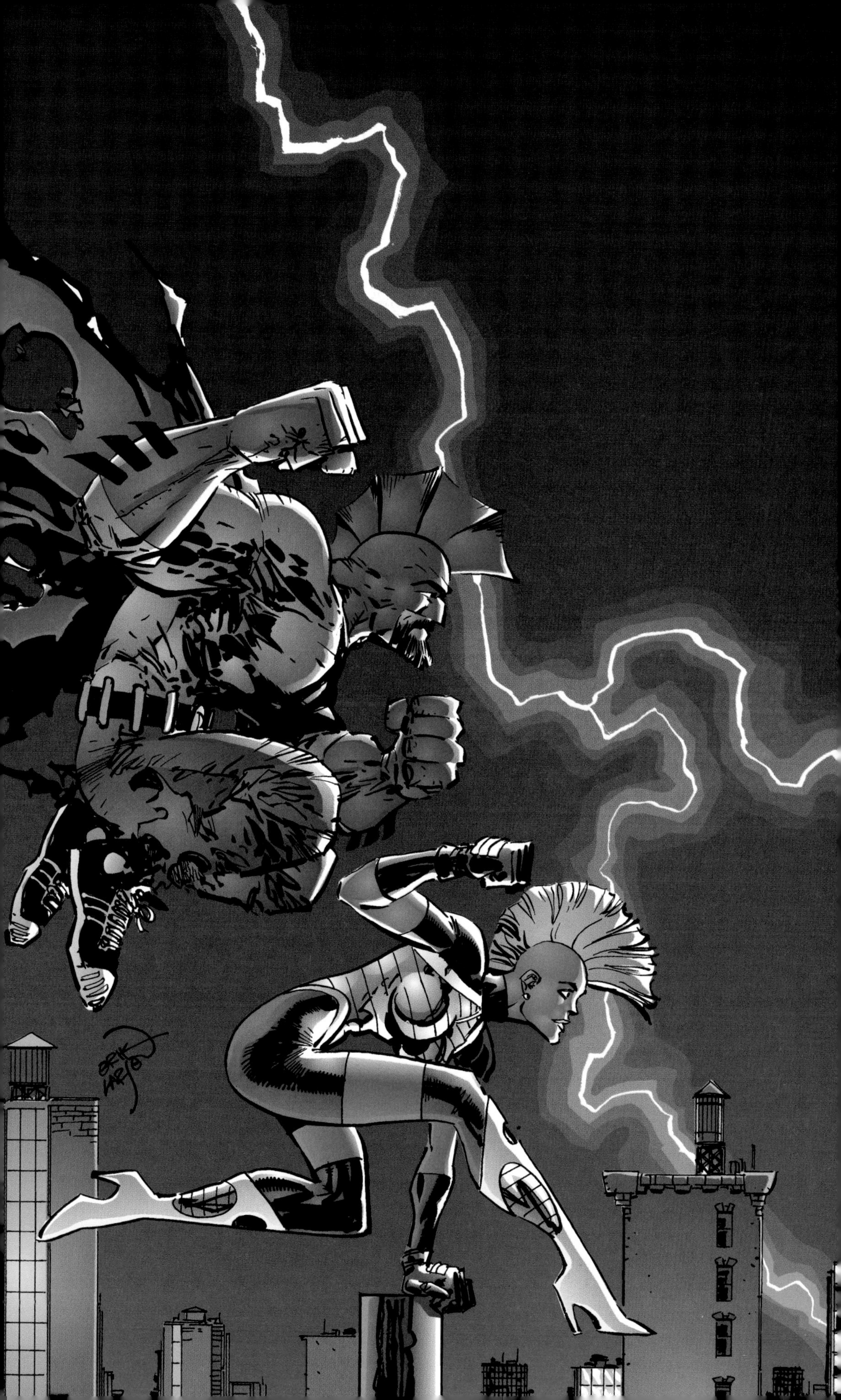

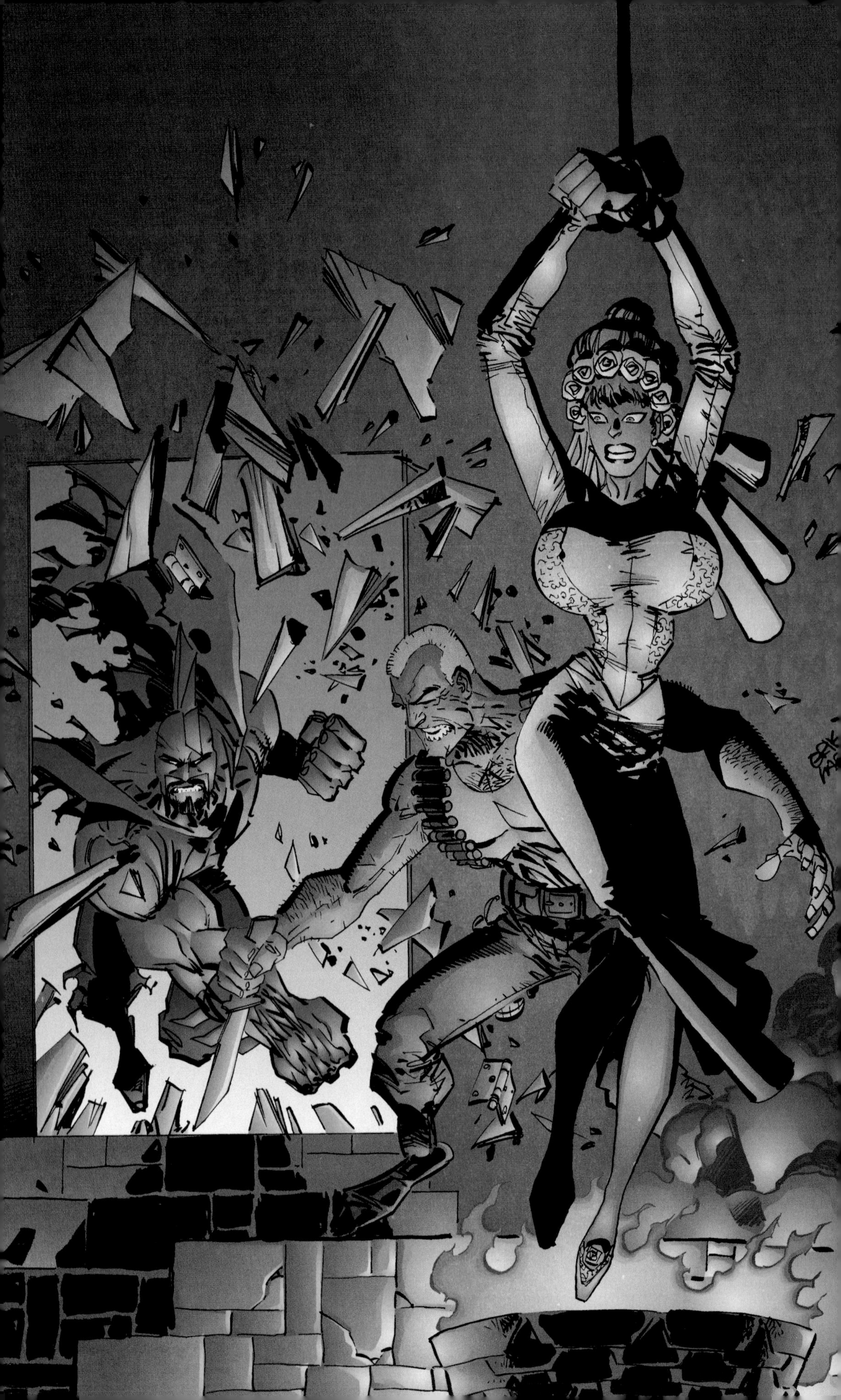

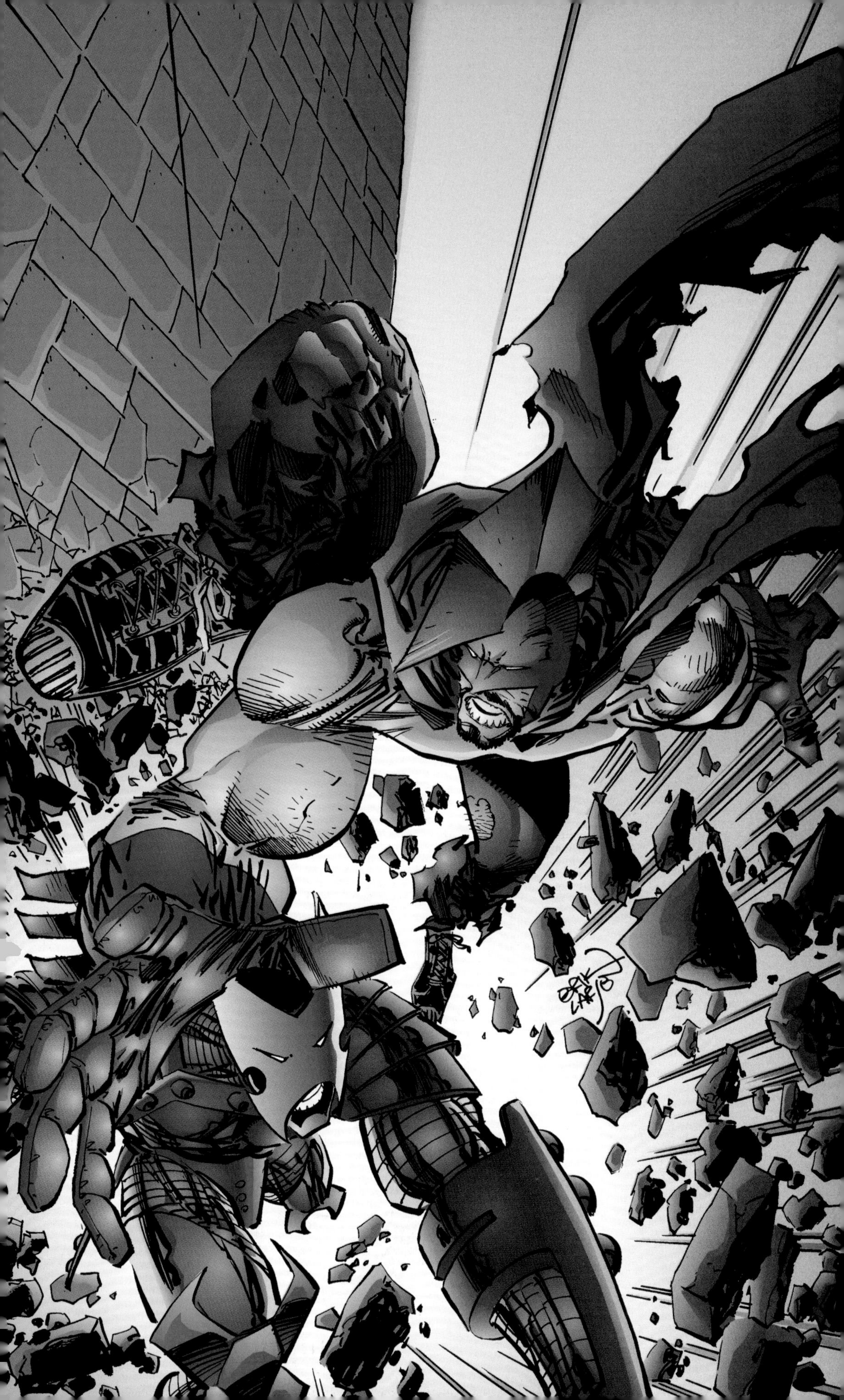

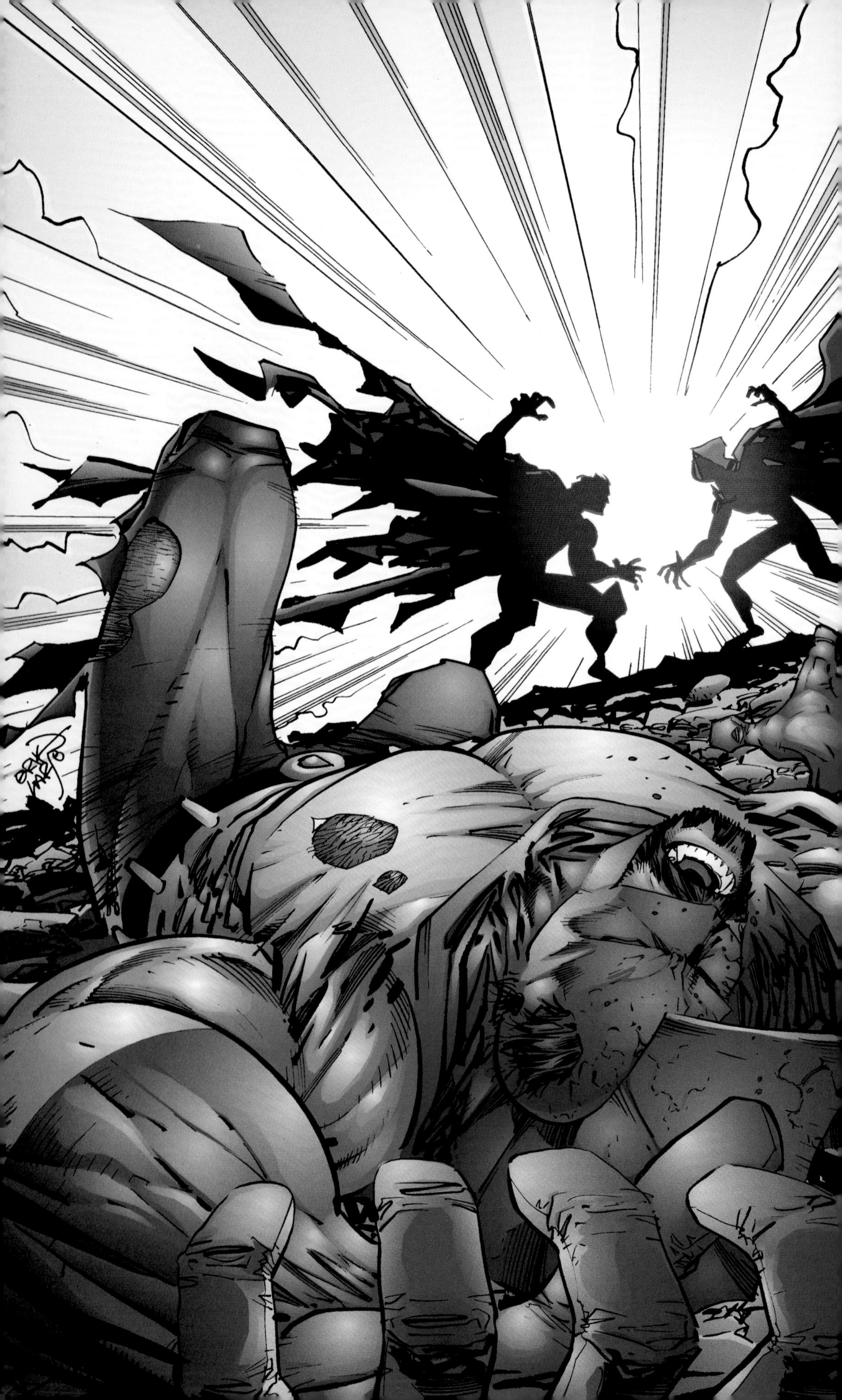

SAVAGE DRAGON SKETCHBOOK

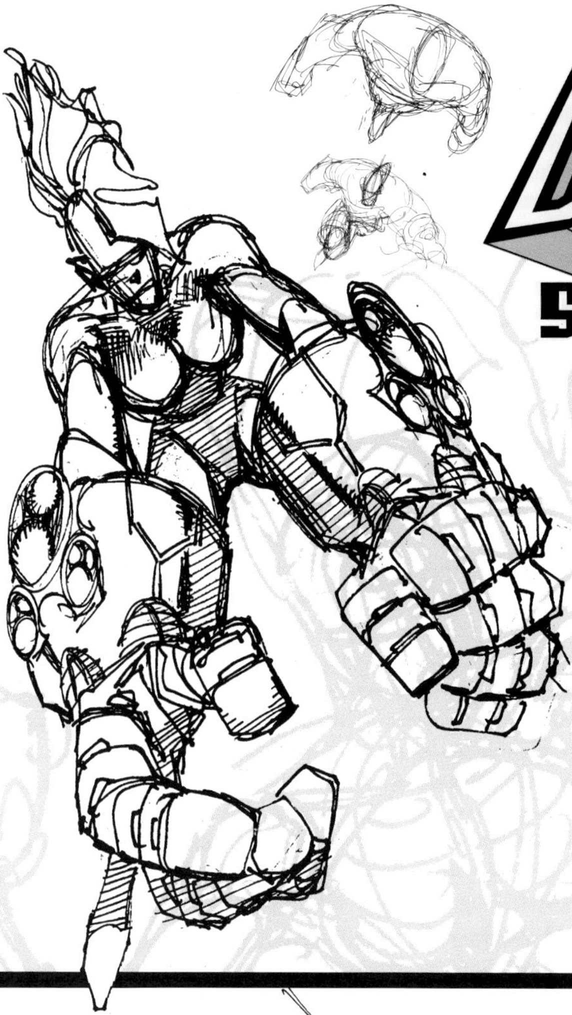

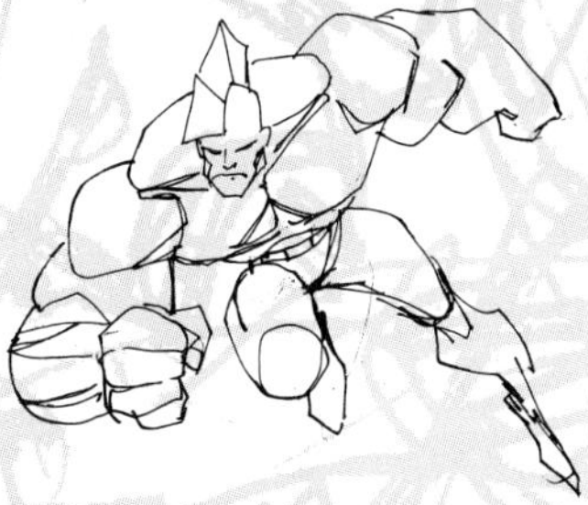

By this point in the game I wasn't doing a lot of preliminary sketching. Just a few roughs for covers here and there. All other effort was going directly into the book itself.

Below left was a rough sketch for a cover from the Star miniseries. Below right was a sketch for issue #54 that I didn't use. I wanted something where Dragon was a silhouette so that the big reveal could be inside the pages of the comic itself, but it wasn't working.

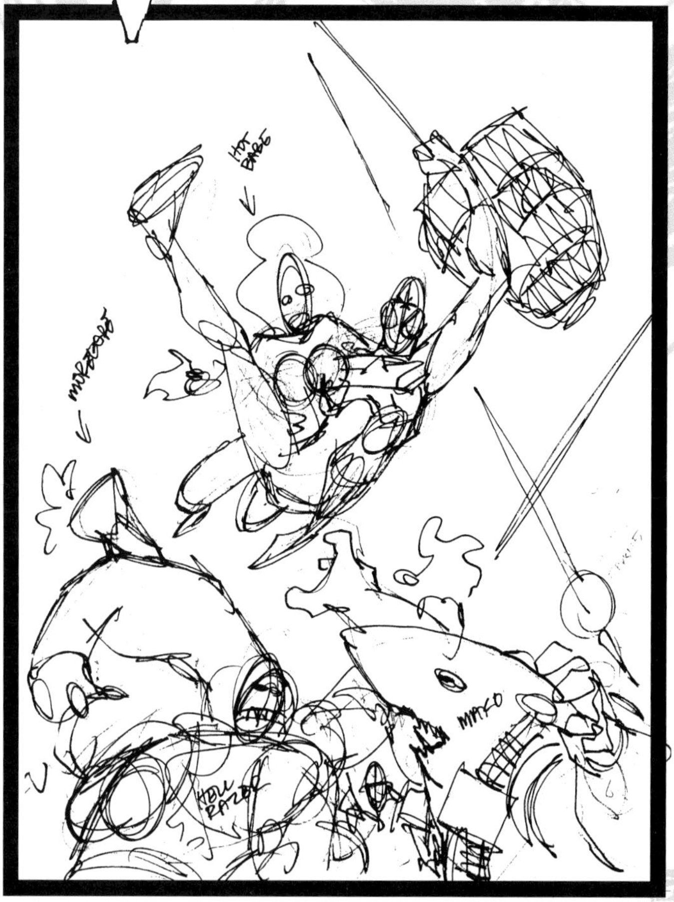

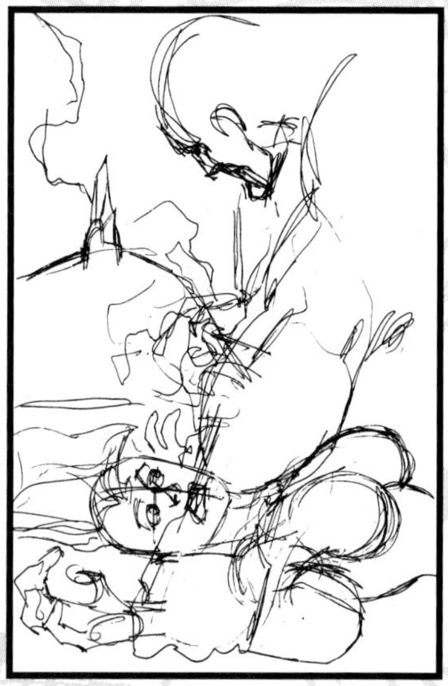

More random crap.

The sketch below was for the cover of Savage Dragon #52 (which wasn't collected in this issue).

I'd done a different cover that didn't feature all the Eternal Youths characters on it, but I wasn't totally happy with it. I ended up ditching it and using this instead.

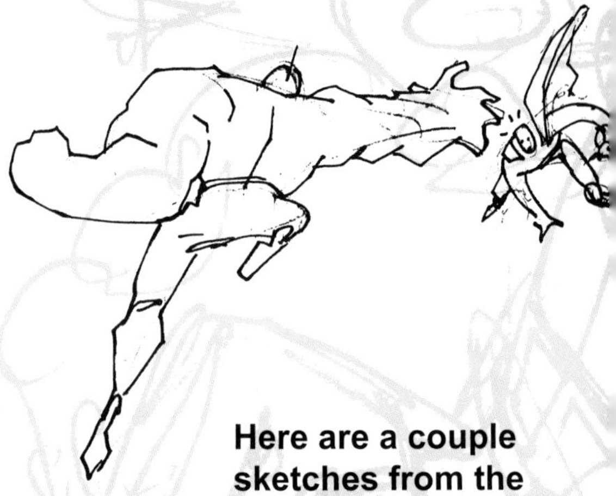

Here are a couple sketches from the Savage Dragon cartoon, Volcanic and Maw.

The cartoon wasn't everything it was cracked up to be but live and learn.

At least the check cleared.

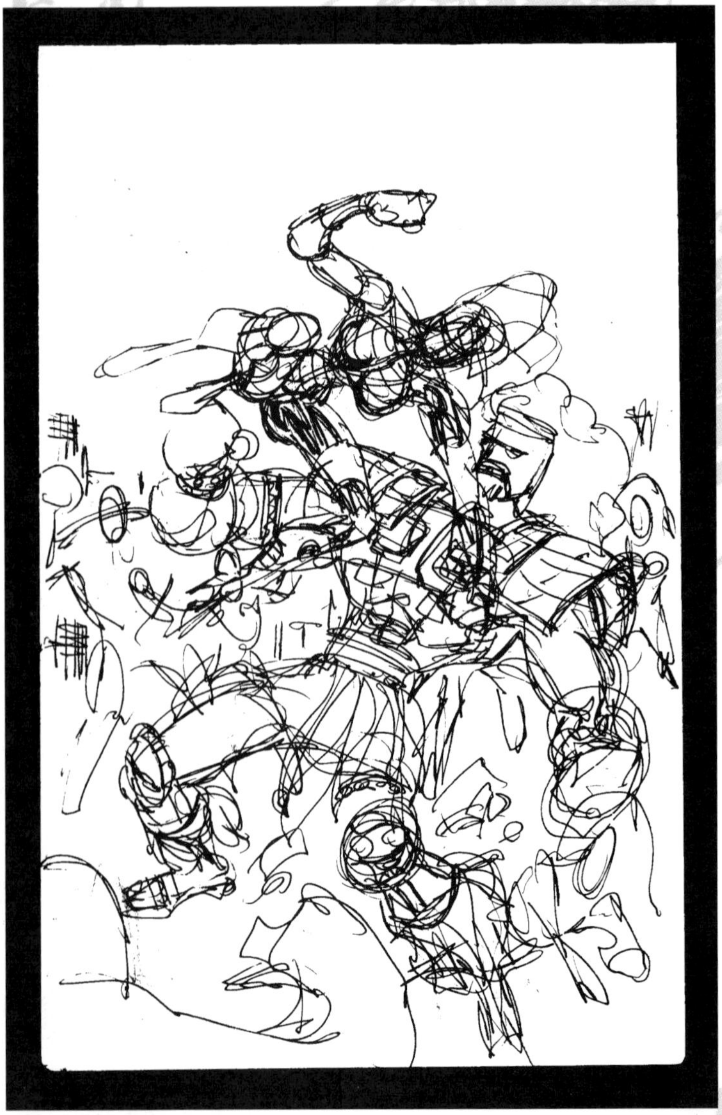

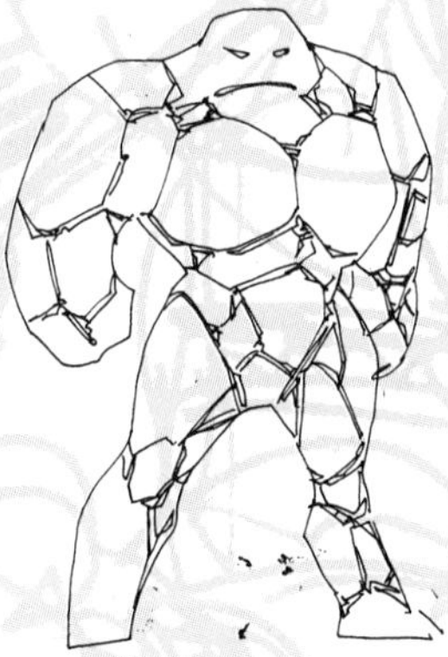

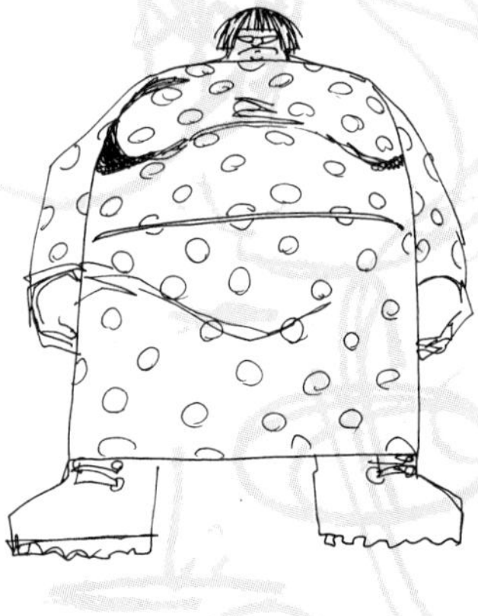

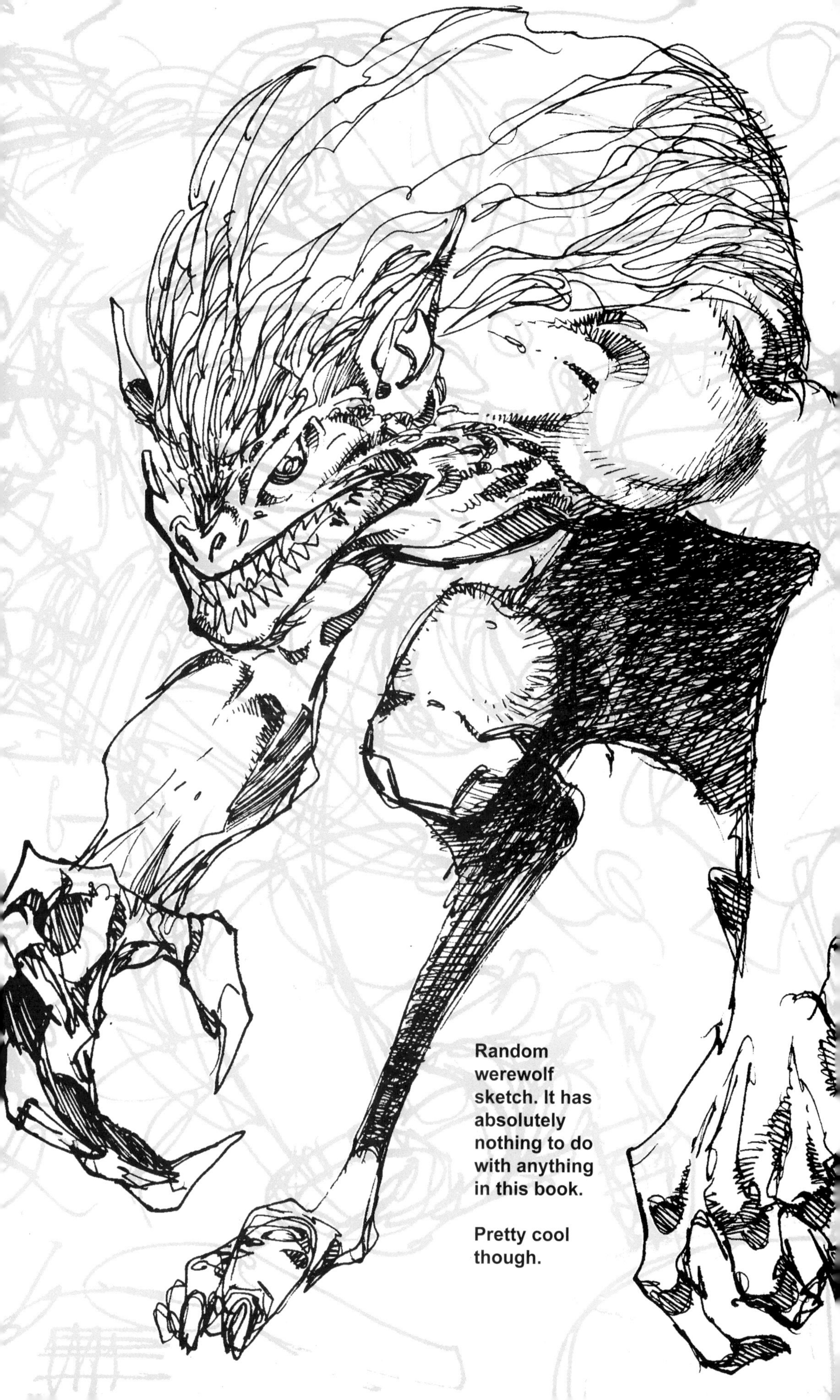

Random werewolf sketch. It has absolutely nothing to do with anything in this book.

Pretty cool though.

Brute Force sketches. Trying to figure these guys out.

Below--a cover sketch for Savage Dragon #55. I'll do cover sketches to figure things out but almost no preliminary drawing for the book.

For this cover I was going for something of a Dark Knight vibe without copying anything directly.

Still, that was the idea.

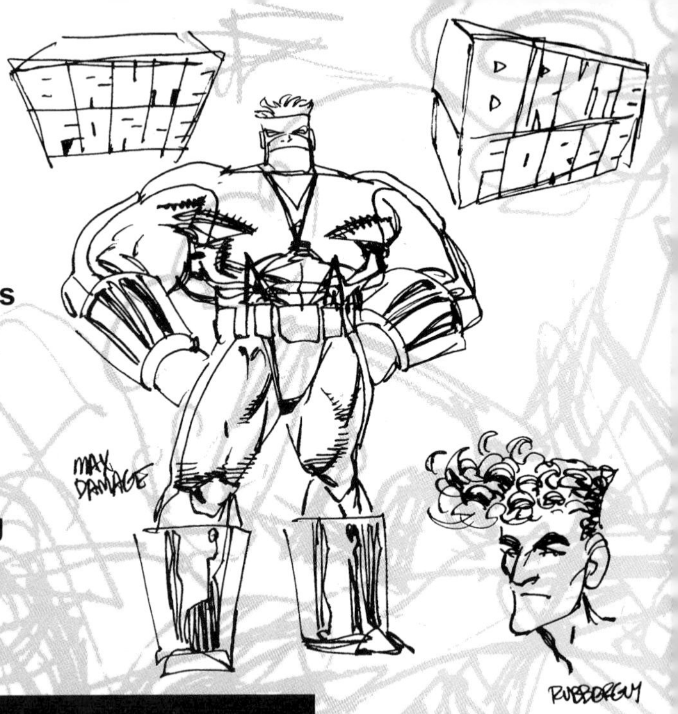
MAX DAMAGE
RUBBERGUY

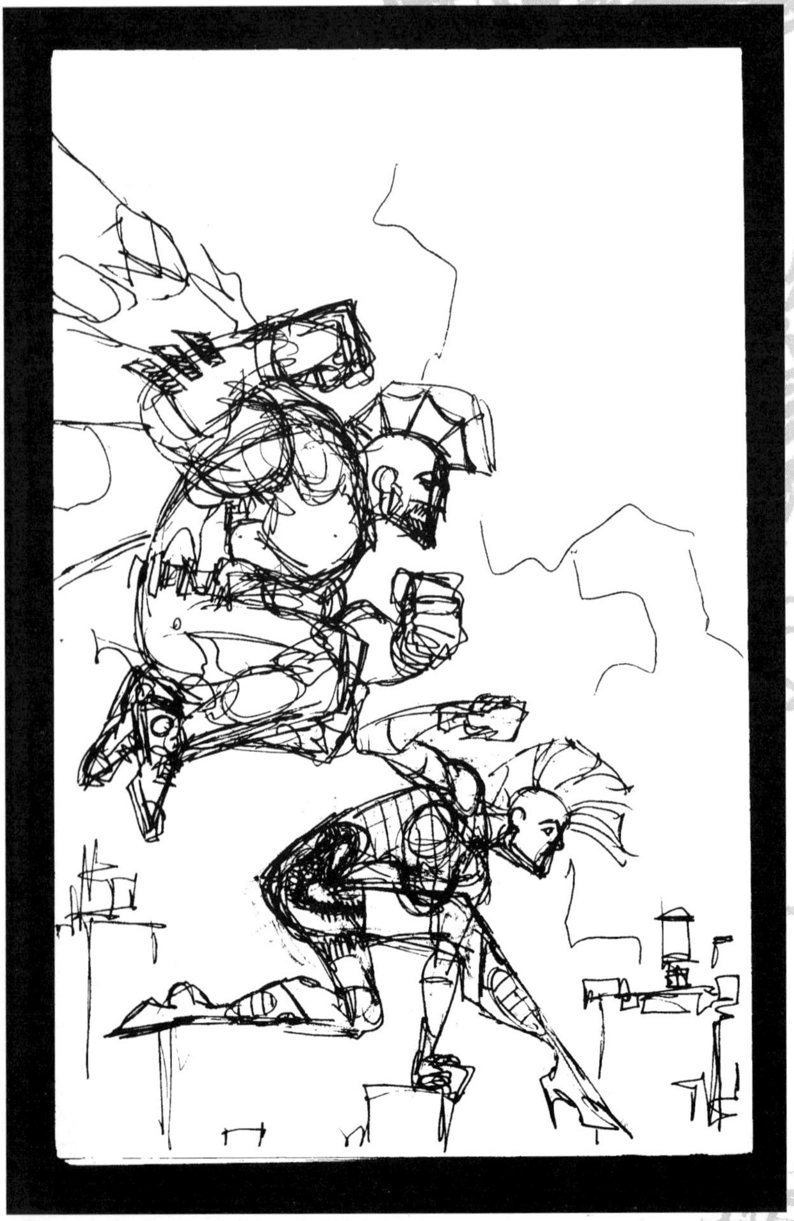

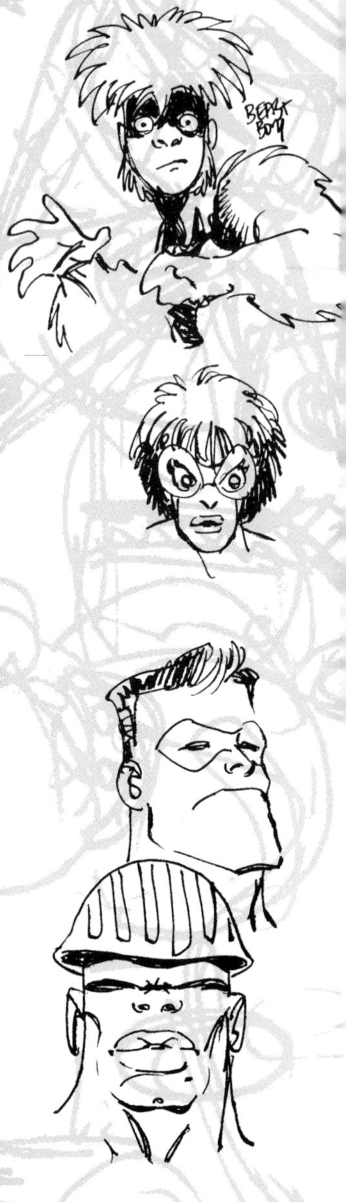

More cover sketches.

At left is the one for #54, at the right was the one for #56. Generally for covers I'm aiming for something pretty straightforward and easy to read.

These were pretty much on the money in that regard. The cover for #54 got that silhouette thing I was going for, nailed. And both had curvy skirts on them.

Kick ass!

Dragon fighting some other green guy from some other company.

At one point I was talking to them about doing a crossover. I lost interest after that book took a turn for the worse. I just didn't have the interest to pursue it. Maybe some day...

image

SAVAGE DRAGON

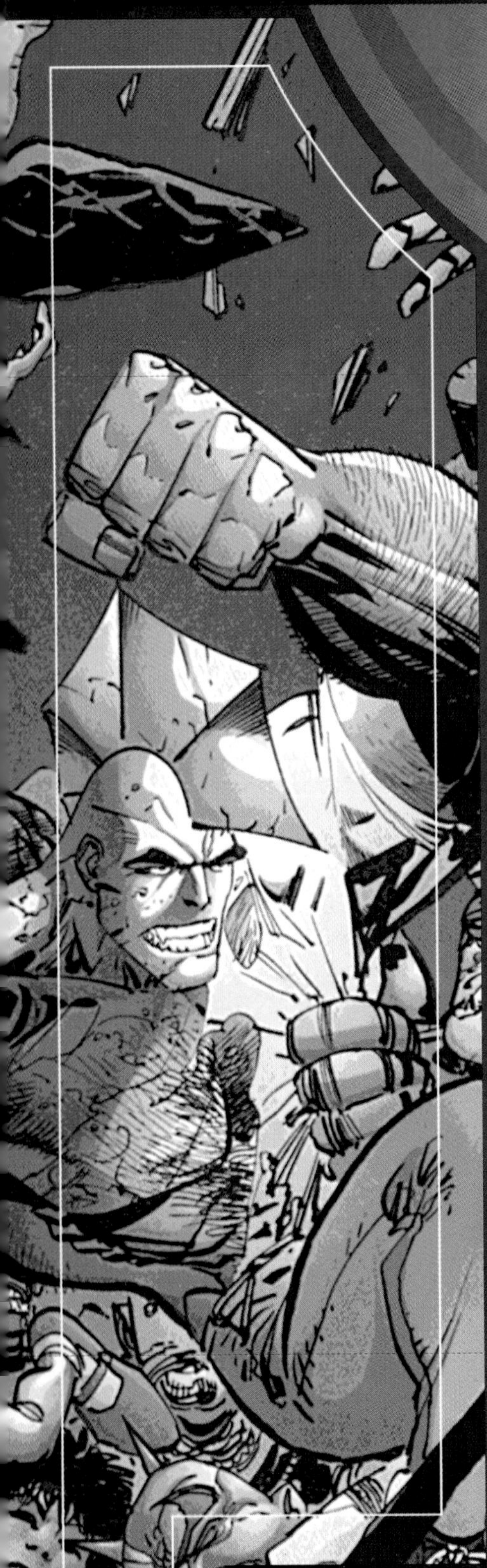

Vol. 1: Baptism of Fire
Collects #1-3 of original Savage Dragon mini-series, and Savage Dragon story from Image Comics #0
ISBN 13: 978-158240-165-2
$14.95

Vol. 2: A Force To Be Reckoned With
Collects #1-6
ISBN 13: 978-1887279-12-3
$14.95

Vol. 3: The Fallen
Collects #7-11
ISBN 13: 978-1887279-83-3
$12.95

Vol. 4: Possessed
Collects #12-16, WildC.A.T.s #14
ISBN 13: 978-158240-031-0
$12.95

Vol. 5: Revenge
Collects #17-21
ISBN 13: 978-158240-101-0
$13.95

Vol. 6: Gang War
Collects #22-26
ISBN 13: 978-1887279-90-1
$19.95

Vol. 7: A Talk With God
Collects #27-33
ISBN 13: 978-1887279-59-8
$17.95

Vol. 8: Terminated
Collects #34-40, #1/2
ISBN 13: 978-158240-336-6
$15.95

Vol. 9: Worlds At War
Collects #41-46
ISBN 13: 978-158240-324-3
$16.95

Vol. 10: Endgame
Collects #47-52
ISBN 13: 978-158240-346-5
$15.95

Vol. 15: This Savage World
Collects #76-81
ISBN 13: 978-158240-261-1
$16.95

ALSO AVAILABLE:

Team-Ups
Collects Vanguard #3-4, Velocity #2, Freak Force #10, Savage Dragon #13A, 25, 30
ISBN 13: 978-158240-047-1
$19.95

Savage Dragon/Hellboy
ISBN 13: 978-158240-238-3
$5.95

TO FIND A COMICS SHOP IN YOUR AREA | 1.888.266.4226

www.imagecomics.com | www.savagedragon.com

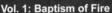